OJIBWA RELIGION AND THE MIDÉWIWIN

Ojibwa

THE UNIVERSITY OF WISCONSIN PRESS

Ruth Landes

Religion and the Midéwiwin

MADISON, MILWAUKEE, AND LONDON, 1968

Published by
The University of Wisconsin Press
Box 1379, Madison, Wisconsin 53701
The University of Wisconsin Press, Ltd.
27-29 Whitfield Street, London, W.1

Printed in the United States of America
By the George Banta Company, Inc., Menasha, Wisconsin

Library of Congress Catalog Card Number 68-19574

For Will and Maggie

PREFACE

SINCE THE CLASSIC REPORT by W. J. Hoffman in 1891, called "The Midéwiwin or 'Grand Medicine Society' of the Ojibwa," the present is the first detailed record of the Ojibwa midéwiwin ritual and organization. The field work behind the present study was done in Ojibwa villages of western Ontario and northwest Minnesota during the summers of 1932 and 1933 and the fall and early winter of 1935; and there was intensive correspondence with a few informants writing me in New York from the field during 1932 to 1936. This volume follows my two early ones—*Ojibwa Sociology* and *The Ojibwa Woman*, published in 1937 and 1938 by Columbia University Press—which describe, respectively, the society of these traditionally hunting bands, and the highly individualized personalities I found.

My great informants for this book, who figure equally in the two earlier ones, were the midé shaman Will Rogers, or Hole-in-the-Sky, of Cass Lake reservation, Minnesota, and Mrs. Maggie Wilson of Manitou Reserve, near Emo, Ontario. I worked separately with each at different periods, except for a brief interval when I brought them together. Both Will and Maggie spoke a competent though simple English, like that of surrounding whites, and we worked in this idiom. I strove to adapt my tongue to their uses. They provided nearly all my considerable Ojibwa-language texts, each analyzing meanings, and so teaching me their language and thought. When I quote them directly in the following pages, it is from their English, with my slight editing, unless Ojibwa is specified.

At the end of the book a Glossary lists the Ojibwa words, including some personal names, used in the text.

Funds for my field studies during 1932–35, for the correspondence with informants, and for my drafts of results were provided by Columbia University's Anthropology Department (out of appropriations from the Rockefeller Foundation) and the University's Council for Research in the Social Sciences. Professors Franz Boas and Ruth Benedict supervised the work, including consultations, that I too pursued, with Dr. (Father) John M. Cooper, Professor of Anthropology at Washington's Catholic University, and with Dr. Truman Michelson, the distinguished linguist at Washington's Bureau of American Ethnology.

I thank the American Philosophical Society for the current assistance of a Phillips grant. Besides, I acknowledge appreciation that this work has been published with the help of a grant from the Social Science Research Council of Canada, using funds provided by the Canada Council.

R. L.

Hamilton, Ontario
November, 1967

CONTENTS

Contents

LIST OF ILLUSTRATIONS

Part I

Ojibwa Religion

Chapter 1

INTRODUCTION

THE OJIBWA INDIANS who figure in these pages belonged to village groups, speakers of an Algonkian language, inhabiting reservation lands in western Ontario and northwest Minnesota during the 1930's. They lived still much as their forebears had a century earlier, except that their hazardous subsistence had worsened from encroachments of white settlers. Hunters and food-gatherers, ever threatened by starvation and disease, they were profoundly religious. They saw all life as a personalized Mystery, voicing this in their tremendous esteem for visionary shamans who succeeded at life's risky activities. They pursued magical formulas, philosophies, and techniques which we outsiders can separate from religion only by our civilization's alien opinions about magic's impersonality. Adept shamans were believed to manipulate the manito Supernaturals as we do electricity.

These Ojibwa, individually, strove to locate the founts of Mystery and contain them for survival, both on Earth, which they called an "island," and in the ghost-phase they conceptualized as following death. The preoccupation appears in all reports, from the first European records of missionary and trade encounters with the tribe until present ones.* A highly institutionalized setting for it in many Ojibwa localities was the Midé (meaning

* Pertinent discussions of religion, magic, folklore, disease treatment, and herbal medicine may be found in Bailey (1937).

3

"mystic") Society, or midéwiwin (meaning, literally, "mystic doings"). The Society functioned to treat with Supernaturals about curing ailments. The curing procedures were, simultaneously, modes of instructing novices and adepts about the midé rites' origins in ancient revelations and about using the curing powers. Part II of this book details the Society's activities, during the 1930's, in Ontario and Minnesota.

ENVIRONMENT

These Indians inhabited the subarctic, farthest margin of the north temperate region, pressing by historic intent upon the eastern edge of the Great Plains, holding woodlands of many lakes, scrubby timber in the Canadian portion, and harsh climate. During long frozen winters, from October's start to March thaws, traditionally they pursued game and fur, their basic economic resource. For them, spring and summer exploded as short interludes punctuating the ice-locked winters.

Their pine country—meager in Ontario, much richer in Minnesota—did not offer great means consistently to Indian or white. Before the days when intensive white settlement disturbed the big game, some numbers of the solitary caribou (a North American reindeer), deer, moose (one of the deer family), and bear frequented the region; by the 1930's, only a few of the animals visited the hinterland, and the caribou were gone entirely. Upon these creatures the Ojibwa had always placed prime reliance, using meat and fat for food, bones for implements, tendons for thread, the large viscera for cooking pots, some glandular parts for medicaments, the skull and shoulder blades for religious ends, the hides for clothing. As the density of the game animals had always been slight, and in the 1930's was at its slightest until then, the Indians scattered widely to insure returns to each man. They hunted singly, each man claiming many square miles for his exclusive domain.*

* In 1958–59, the 229 villagers of Round Lake in northern Ontario exploited approximately 5,000 square miles, averaging a population density of one person for 22 square miles (Rogers, 1966, p. 99).

Need drove the hunters so far apart that ordinarily they did not meet. Each man was alone in his hunting world, shut off not only by his great lands but by the hard stretches of ice and snow, by storms, heavy skies, and very low temperatures. These features color Ojibwa mythology and religion, in the appearances and psychic characteristics of the mystic personages, in their fates, and in their activities. A hunter's human companions were only his wife and immature children.

The Ojibwa have trapped fur animals intensively since the arrival of the early French traders and *voyageurs*. Less territory was needed for this enterprise, and up to five or six families of close bilateral kin would "go together" on adjacent, though separate grounds. A man, with wife and children, would trap on or alongside his father's or father-in-law's grounds, depending on how well they got along together. One trapper, who lived on Manitou Reserve, told me that his domain, bounded by the trees he blazed, covered seven miles southwest, eight miles north, four miles east, and four miles west, in western Ontario. Except for beaver and muskrat, the fur animals were esteemed as secondary to big game and were caught chiefly for the trade. Though all traditional thought, especially the religious interests, focused on the large solitary animals, the returns on fur figured prominently in individual budgets. The Ojibwa conserved the sedentary fur by selective killing and by allowing sites to lie idle for periods varying from a few months to some years.

A man's hunting territory included at least one deep stream, pond, or lake. Usually there were fish in his waters, and the women set nets low in the lake for a winter catch. From the virgin forest (as Red Lake's still was in the 1930's), the Ojibwa got bark and wood for the wigwam, dishes, fire, utensils, traps, canoes, and snowshoes. A man's grounds met all his important economic needs.

SEASONAL ROUND OF TRADITIONAL LIFE

With the thaws of late March, Ojibwa families left their hunting territories for their customary groves of sugar maple trees.

Sugar-making began at first running of the sap. Two or more families worked alongside at the same grove while carefully maintaining separate households. The sugar manufacture was only a pause in the general movement to the summertime villages.

Five to fifteen small families met each year to constitute a village at some body of fresh water where fish, berries, and wood were plentiful. A village remained an aggregate of autonomous households, with no official organization. (The Ojibwa in the 1930's had no political system; modern band chiefs were nominal appointees by the Canadian or United States governments.) Yet the village offered a sociability that contrasted acutely with the winter isolation. Especially in smaller villages, the families were closely related: one entire village consisted of an aged couple and the several households of their married sons and daughters. More distant relatives, those related through marriage as well as blood-reckoning, appeared in larger villages, but also in some small ones. Sometimes there were present also families not known to be related but invited by a household with whom they were friendly. A village locale belonged by custom to the families occupying it regularly; strong ties of sentiment reinforced the custom. "Mine" and "thine" became categories with a certain collective reality: the lake, for example, belonged to each family on it, and also to the village as a whole. The collectivity was felt heightened when one village met another on visits, or when an outsider visited a village. It was tacitly understood that each villager had rights in village territory, though a man did not allow this kind of right even to all members of his family on the winter hunting grounds.

The summering families moved in at slow stages until they were established by June. The summertime activities sprang alive: tanning and cooking, berry-picking, games, visits, story-telling, puberty rites, marriages, dances, adulteries, divorces, war parties, religious performances. The crescendo hit a climax early in August. During visits, games, and ceremonials, the villages mingled and approached some awareness of the broader horizons of a tribe. Then a man was at his farthest remove from the winter's mode of isolation. Traditionally, it was only during the summer gatherings that the midéwiwin was performed.

During the summer the wild rice was maturing, and by later August the households moved off to the aquatic beds. Each family proceeded by itself, choosing its own company and rice bed. By the second or third week of September, ricing time ended, and with it the last of the year's sociability. Each family went to its winter grounds slowly, shooting departing ducks, trapping, catching postseasonal fish. Slowly the families penetrated the hinterland, until by early October they were established in the winter lodges. Temperatures were now falling, there was considerable snow, and by November each family was locked in for winter.

The hunting lodge (usually a birchbark wigwam or canvas and bark tent) was erected at about the center of the game range. It "belonged," in Ojibwa parlance, to the wife, who occupied it with the young children. The woods and the hunt "belonged" to the man, who left the wigwam almost daily for his quarry. He might remain away days or weeks at a time, and return home only for rest.

CHARACTER AND INDIVIDUALISM

Definite traits of personality were fostered within this economic framework, pitched to the men's ways. The hunter felt himself a soul at bay, against cosmic forces personalized as cynical or terrorizing. The North Wind was a trickster manito, splenetic toward warm-blooded man. Ice and snow could be friendly, as when crippling the tender-footed deer; but often they shaped up into cannibalistic skeletons, each called windigo. The family shared the hunter's tenseness. Scarcity of game prohibited invitations to any but the very needy, in general. Then the stipulations were exact: for a trapper, they allowed only short periods of work and regulated the numbers of traps—and even the kind of traps, which had to resemble the owner's. Trespass was punishable by death at sight, with gun and sorcery.

From birth, the boy was told he would be a hunter, and given toy bows and arrows, toy guns and pea-shooters, and encouraged to strike at birds and other small creatures. He heard that life is a battle with the manitos for meat and blanket; and a battle he must fight all alone, desperately, for mere survival. He could not expect support from another human, but must work techniques that wrenched it from a Supernatural revealed in a vision. Ojibwa tradition created its intensest religious expression through this pursuit of a private guardian spirit who revealed (or yielded) himself in "dreams" or visions to a boy or man undergoing ritual fasts and other privations, ritual or not (see Benedict, 1923). In the 1930's, the visionary guardian was still sought and made to manifest himself among the Ojibwa I knew, against the heavy pressures of Christian society and civilization. Over twenty-five years later, Edward S. Rogers recorded the persistence of the guardian-spirit complex in northern Ontario (Rogers, 1962), and the complex survives in all accounts of Canadian Ojibwa bands contemporary with his.

By the age of three the Ojibwa boy should strike birds dead; a few years later he could manage simple traps; soon he was hunting with his father; by twelve or fifteen years, the boy should leave the family lodge for his own hunting grounds. Over the boyhood summers, the elders drove the youngster out to fast in some lonely spot, to receive news from one or more Supernaturals about his future. Actually, at any time of the year, he might lie down on isolated sandy or rocky ground, or upon bare rocks, uncovered; or he might build himself a huge "nest" in a tree (which meant some shelter and cover from branches and leaves) where he remained for the vigil of days, clarifying the desired revelation in his mind. The proper stay supposedly lasted four days without food; eight fasting days was considered remarkable; ten days was manito-like.

The pose of voluntary starvation served physiologically and psychologically to goad the desired vision. Also it was a culturally potent enactment of the ultimate disaster that could befall a hunter at any time, so it bore the aspect of a toying with suicide,

8

of assuming defeat, of bowing to "shame"—all frequent possibilities in traditional Ojibwa life and thought, which here became a ritualized discipline to force the hand of some manito to yield his power. The faster also thirsted, perhaps simply as an extension of hungering and self-abnegation, for the woodlands' endless lakes and lengthy snows yielded water constantly. Humbling his vigorous body and untried mind, the traditional boy, especially at puberty when adulthood must be established, enacted a humbling of spirit and cried softly, "Help me, Supernaturals, against hunger, sickness, poverty, and the Sioux!" When he swooned, the Ojibwa said he was being carried to the sphere of the manitos.

People who received visions turned more away from simple, warm relations with their kind, partly because of the new manito intimacy, partly because visions had to be kept secret to conserve their power. It was no passive relationship but one requiring the boy's lifelong self-discipline. Others would appraise his changing behavior, which grew more confident until eventually he acquired renown in his skills and referred to himself arrogantly as the manito. In ritual acts, he wore the face paints and feathers of his guardian, talked in his voice and idiom, as tradition standardized these, and carried amulets. The great or "evil" shamans were those who had sprung high on secret visions bred of proper fears.*

Elders would stop a boy who wanted to present his experience for clarification, with the traditional caution: "You will forfeit the Dream by talking about it with others. So, do not tell us. Keep it secret even on your deathbed, else the manito will be offended and leave you. Keep returning to him. Fast continually

---

* A shaman is a personage with supernatural attributes (described in Landes, 1937, chap. 5). The shaman had doctoring and other skills acquired by vision alone, or vision and purchase, or purchase only. "Good" or ethical shamans ranked below "bad" ones, the latter ranking as most powerful, the degree depending on their repute for evil. Powerful evil shamans, including midé ones, were feared as sorcerers who hurt and killed until eventually they were destroyed by their own success. "Good" shamans were much less respected.

until the manito is so real, you can practically touch him. This is the most valuable thing you will ever have." So the boy would learn to query indirectly and receive indirect answers, as though pertaining to an imaginary situation or to someone else's experience. And the receiver of the vision would hug his patron to himself, jealous of losing him in free talk, concentrating on the power the manito offered. The closemouthed visionary observed sacred tabus and injunctions which others studied and from which they inferred the nature of his manito. These would be discussed, as they were with me, and undoubtedly they cued future visionaries, and constituted a real communication between each visionary and everyone else.

The ritual fast for a vision, traditionally required for all boys and only for boys (and selectively, later, for men), determined basic differences between male and female personalities. First, it dramatized the Indian's unending dread of starvation, hence his pitiableness; it was this which trapped a manito into giving supernatural power to the faster, henceforth termed endearingly "my grandchild" or "my nephew." Ojibwa tales explained, "The manito came to me because he pitied my state and wanted to comfort me, to cheer me up." Second, the voluntary ritual fast reminded the seeker that hunger is defeat and therefore shameful surrender to sorcery; now he would hope for that gift of power that would defeat other sorcerers who lured off his proper share of game.

In time the visionary introjected the qualities attributed to his manito guardian, who might be a super-deer, or super-moose, or super-bear, or some other. In this mystic identification with the guardian, partly revealed in sacred observances that included tabus, mimetic enactments, and kinship address during public invocations, the visionary saw his winter solitude as the solitude of a woodlands manito animal. Nights he would leave his human shape on his bed to stalk the country in the guardian animal's shape. He might assert that its tiny replica existed within him, as did a man who claimed a tiny moose in his lumbar region and

10

said that he sickened when the replica did. The usual Indian was uneasy with Supernaturals, as is evident in my informant Maggie Wilson's account of her war vision (see Appendix 1); but the one who followed a shaman's career might regard himself eventually to be a manito, as did William Rogers, or Hole-in-the-Sky. Then he would meet with his traditional Ojibwa fate of insanity or death, as Will did. Midé shamans ritually called themselves manitos, individually and collectively.

The lonely stoicism imposed on males from birth included the tabu on overt signs of affection, besides marked avoidance among housemates of opposite sex, especially brother and sister. However, spouses also were restrained in gesture, if not in speech. A similar "respect" existed between parents and children of opposite sex and among siblings of the same sex. When families met during spring sugaring and at the summer village, they did so warily, with a cheery surface that was suspicious of everything and anxiously alert.

Attitudes of suspicion, fear, and potential high respect followed each other in Ojibwa general behavior. All important communications were acknowledged slowly and stonily, with great preliminaries, interspersings, and sequences of tobacco, food, and yard goods. Haste was disrespectful and irresponsible; all matters had to be pondered over and questioned, skeptically or fearfully; nothing was taken for granted or accepted on a permanent basis. Everything had to be negotiated with, from children to Supernaturals; shamans were only the most alarming party. Women served men of the household, storing and cooking the meat they brought, tanning and tailoring the hides. So mother served father, sister served brother. The women worked together in the lodge while the men were gone on their individual trails.

During hunting and trapping, as during all the summer activities, each man resorted to protective "medicines" for himself and his belongings; the "protection" included aggression against rivals and even friends. These habits grew stronger with age, becoming most extreme in the "evil" male shaman. who saw taunts in any-

11

one else's well-being. As a hunter and trapper shot a trespasser on sight, so the evil shaman struck those who offended his self-esteem. A winner at the summer games might be in danger of his life for encroaching on a loser's self-regard. But a man was ashamed also to be outshone by a partner, so partnerships and teams often broke up during the village season, with stealthy knifings and magical duels fulfilled in winter as starvation and death. Yet in winter the housemates, who were the closest kin, played summertime games without hostility.

Sex relations of men with women also acquired aspects of dangerous conflict between the male winner and the loser. Men regarded sexual irregularities as they did poaching or a deadly race. The phrase for flirting is "hunting women," which uses the same verb as "hunting meat." Summer encounters provoked continual adulteries, elopements, and domestic breakups in an atmosphere of male violence and reprisals.

Even children's quarrels triggered combat among the parents and the shamans they enlisted to aid them. The quarrels and ensuing deaths constituted blood feuds that lasted generations. Alone on his winter trails, the brooding father saw his children's vengeful enemy in every game failure; the mother cautioned her children accordingly at the lodge. Tales show that when fewer families returned to the summer village, it was partly because quarrel-intimidated ones stopped at other villages, partly because feuding sets met en route and killed each other.

The Ojibwa have always recognized traditional psychic disorders among themselves, overwhelmingly among the "evil," vision-empowered shamans (Landes, 1938b; Barnouw, 1950; Parker, 1960).* All insanities were termed windigo, after the mythology's

* Parker notes that the illness, which he terms "wiitiko psychosis," is "associated mainly with the Cree and Ojibwa Indians who inhabit Canada's forested northland" (p. 603). He makes a comparison (p. 611) between the guardian spirit's resemblance to a desired game animal and the wiitiko (or windigo) sufferer's cannibalistic-phase blurring of humans into edible beavers. He concludes (p. 621) that the "personality predisposition" to the Ojibwa psychosis "is nurtured and developed by the day-to-day competitive

12

giant cannibalistic skeleton of ice. Windigo disorders were affected powerfully by the men's economic and religious practices and seemed to be the peak and the penalty of male achievements. Only rarely did they occur among women; then it was among those who, for some unusual reason, had followed male practices (Landes, 1938a). The people believed that any mishap and any calamity—starvation, illness, unhappy love, death—must be the work of a rival, usually a fellow-villager, employing sorcery through magic and manitos. Psychically, the windigo disorder involved projection of the sufferer's fears and vindictiveness, besides the experiences or anxious anticipations of starvation. The symptoms brought to my attention ranged from profound melancholy to violence; in the latter phase, the sufferer yearned to kill and eat all human beings around him, and ultimately he wished to kill himself; his manic obsession was with eating beaver meat, which is considered like human meat. Insanities erupted often in the winter, when the despondent hunter saw himself abandoned. If the raving sufferer passed out of control during the village months, his fellows and his family burned him to death; in lucid periods, the windigo shaman warned his family of his recurring cannibalistic need and asked to be killed. Anciently it was custom

---

emphasis and self-reliant isolation imposed by adult institutional life," besides "sorcery and the precarious economic existence of the Ojibwa."

Barnouw found that "In the Rorschach test, the emotional isolation of the Chippewa individual finds expression in a characteristic avoidance of color. Out of a total number of 107 Rorschach records taken at Court Oreilles and Lac du Flambeau by Ernestine Friedl, Robert Ritzenthaler, and myself, 53 records were without any color responses at all. Of the remainder, only nine individuals gave more than two color responses. According to Dr. Bruno Klopfer, so marked a degree of color-avoidance in our own culture would only be found among extreme compulsion neurotics, patients with psychogenic depression states, and catatonics. This does not mean, of course, that the Chippewa can be lumped under one of these clinical manifestations; the Rorschachs of the clinical groups have other distinguishing characteristics which are absent among the Chippewa. . . . Dr. Klopfer believes that the rarity of color responses among the Chippewa implies that the individual is under pressure to become as emotionally independent of his environment as possible, and to expect very little from others" (p. 27).

to cremate a corpse; with windigo men, burning held also the symbolism of melting the ice-skeleton and so destroying its power.

In the summer village, the evil shaman was the most quarrelsome at games, most suspected of rape and adultery, the relative most dreaded and held responsible for misfortunes. Village life roused all the dormant ill feelings of relatives, as they measured obligations and weighed slights. A man's own son might commit him to the Indian police: the shaman Will Rogers, living in the permanent village environment of the reservation, anticipated commitment by his stepson. Elsewhere (Landes, 1937a), I have noted that the traditional Ojibwa was a lawbreaker, especially regarding customs of marriage, incest, and sib. For he brooked no laws that clashed with his whims, as he brooked no rivals in games, no team mates who outshone him, no trespasser on his grounds. Yet he demanded conformity from others: the resistance triggered shamanistic combat. But it seemed to me, judging from many stories over the years, that the individual generally escaped punishment, even in the two most difficult situations of a hunt trespass and of flouting traditional sib requirements about mourning and remarriage. (Similarly, neither my tutor Will Rogers nor I was punished during our months of midéwiwin study, undertaken by our private decisions.) In earlier times, the empty spaces of land favored escape until the crisis ended. Besides, only the immediate family undertook the accounting even of sib demands—and each year the family faced chances of disintegration from death, madness, other disease, or marital breakup. Nonetheless, while violating rules with relative impunity, each Ojibwa knew the rules well. The situation was not one of ignorance but of joy in sabotaging the social game.

Sure retribution followed a shaman's extensive abuse of magic and vision powers, all records and all informants assert. The abuse was revealed in personality traits (the shaman was called "evil," "greedy," "living only to kill"), in outstanding success at all Ojibwa pursuits, and in misfortunes attacking the family, especially illness and death. The latter would occur because the over-

14

used "bad medicine" had returned home to its shaman "owner." Mrs. Wilson told me how her father-in-law, Chief Namepog, challenged his "evil" brother, "Why do you kill your grandchildren? Why don't you stop your work?" Mrs. Wilson described vividly how a woman gave the villagers permission to kill her shaman father, so that they fed him poisoned food at a ceremonial dance where he was an officer, and they kicked him furtively in their dance round, as he lay dying. He may not have expected poison, for the great or evil shamans, unlike normal people, were supposed to use only magical weapons, like "balls of fire" (will-o'-the-wisp), and powers of their guardian spirits.

The pursuit of visions and the acquisition of wealth were intimately related, since neither game nor health could be controlled without supernatural aid. (Aboriginal material wealth consisted of furs and supplies of fresh seasonal and dried foods—pemmican, berries, and rice, supplemented by smoked and frozen fish. During my acquaintance with them, there were no rich Ojibwa.) Achieved by dream power, the wealth was partly shared with the close family, and partly hugged by the owner. No property was owned jointly or by groups, except for village-owned dances, which the Ojibwa actually regarded as held by individual villagers, in severalty; and the individual had complete rights of disposal.

A man had firm economic obligations only to his very young children. Everyone paid for what he or she needed, in services or in kind. Dealings with the supernatural involved barter and sale principles; the offerings of tobacco, goods, foods, and prayers were increased or reduced according to the Indian's calculations of what the expected favors were worth. A doctor would not cure unless his fee was displayed in advance; nor would a manito, as the midéwiwin emphasizes. Property of the deceased, which by dogma should have been dispersed in the community (to send away the attending ghost of the deceased), was actually carefully examined, and desired items were concealed by the mourning family.

The talk I heard seemed to expose a preoccupation with mate-

15

rial possessions, as when deaths were suspected of being caused by greedy kin; and the sib of the deceased conventionally termed the survivor the one "who killed the deceased for his personal advantage." When an Ojibwa possessed some money, as happened occasionally in families of war veterans, he refrained from showing it, but the villagers knew and talked resentfully. It was supposed to be associated with early sickness and death, as was explained to me in the case of a young woman for whom her grandmother ordered a postdeath midéwiwin.

INFORMANTS

Generally, the shamans were the ablest and richest Ojibwa; those I knew were, by our standards, energetic, intellectually keen, and sophisticated. This included my great informant Maggie Wilson, though women's lives were supposed to follow other ways than men's (Landes, 1938a). Shamanism and similar male pursuits among women were episodic, usually called out by necessities such as widowhood.

When I met Mrs. Wilson at the Manitou Reserve near Emo, Ontario, she was in her mid-fifties. When I met Will Rogers at Red Lake reservation (he had come visiting from his own Cass Lake reservation) near Bemidji, Minnesota, he was in his early eighties. Mrs. Wilson was a Christian convert (or perhaps re-convert, since her father had been one). Will Rogers, or Hole-in-the-Sky,* was no Christian but an adherent of belief in vision revelations and the system of supernaturalism that is expounded in the following pages. Mrs. Wilson's Christianity raised no doubts in her mind about the mystic beliefs and practices she

---

* I use both names for Will Rogers, according to the situation. When we dealt with secular matters, I called him Will, as others did. When he acted the shaman by tutoring me, I should have used a kinship term like "Grandfather," and occasionally did. In this book instead, I use his Ojibwa "mystic" name of Pindigegizig, meaning Hole-in-the-Sky. I retain the two names as indicators of the secular or mystic nature of the situations in which they figured. In tribal life, however, the English name would have appeared chiefly in an English-language setting.

shared with Will, for it consisted largely in profiting from the missionaries, as she explained in casual, artless remarks. Will's paganism connoted no anti-Christian sentiments, but only indifference. Both people were wary, brilliant, immensely alert and curious about events. Neither showed the least curiosity about me, but they accepted me with ease and dignity; the enormous difference in our ages seemed not to enter. Yet youth was a category in their world connoting irresponsibility and violence, at least for males. They reckoned a little with my female sex, for Mrs. Wilson intervened mildly now and then between me and her son when he joked rudely, in Ojibwa (knowing no English when around me); and Will remembered the female tabus when making a sweat lodge for me (to cure the grippe) and during portions of the midé narration. On the whole, perhaps, I was less a personality than a "power," in their sense, because I paid them each a dollar a day for long periods during that desperately poor decade; and I yielded myself to their instruction. Mrs. Wilson was always serious and restrained with me, talking and teaching while she did tanning, beadwork, or cooking, but she continually dropped wry, penetrating comments. Will was serious and also humorous, often in the irresistible manner of his Oklahoma comic-philosopher namesake; laymen said his jovial humor "proved" his evilness. I respected them both because they worked superbly despite illness, destitution, and a deep restlessness within. The many subordinate informants paled beside them. Like Kroeber's "geniuses" (Kroeber, 1944), they expressed high points of their culture; to me they seemed immensely civilized. Father Cooper left me gladly indebted for guiding me to Mrs. Wilson; and the Indian Agent at Red Lake did equally for presenting me to Will Rogers.

Mrs. Wilson lived with her husband's Manitou band in their village on the Reserve, neighboring six other Reserve bands. She was worldlier than her fellow villagers, as the daughter of a Cree or Cree-Ojibwa teacher-missionary-trader who had moved among whites. She had been married several times and reared children who in my time had already married and were rearing children; she was also rearing an adopted white boy then aged seven or eight, despite the voiced jealousy of her family. Will Rogers' repute for shamanism rested on the names of his father and uncles besides on his own feats. He had been much married and had been a lumberjack in the former Minnesota Territory, during which period, he boasted, he had been "wanted for murder." Perhaps he meant murder by sorcery, rather than violence. Speaking adequate, unaccented English, he yet thought in Ojibwa forms and habitually "talked sacredly" with Supernaturals, especially with his "twin brother," Thunderbird, who had never entered Will's mother's womb because he had not wished to live on Earth. (Will remembered and described his uterine months.) Will's last wife and adult stepson had put him out of their house when I met him; finally they had him committed to a mental hospital as a nuisance; he wrote me sad letters from there. Other Indians held that Will had been worsted in shamanistic combat with his wife, meaning that she had engaged another sorcerer to do away with him. His life ended in the come-down traditionally expected to befall the Ojibwa sorcerer; in earlier days he could have died of starvation, murder, illness, or even windigo-burning. Death was never easy for the traditional Indian but it was expected to be terrible for the "evil" shaman.

From July to October, 1933, I lodged Will at Red Lake, Minnesota, with Indians who knew his alarming repute and who discovered also distant kinship connections with him. Although they needed the money I paid, they took the old man in because there was no way of refusing without raising their own anxieties about his avenging sorcery. I brought Maggie Wilson and her small white son from Emo, Ontario, to Red Lake during that period, to give her a treat and me some experimental situations, and then I saw real terror break through the old lady's poise. I lodged her with a young Christianized women whose intense conversion gave her no defense against fears of Will's sorcery, so that morning after morning I found the two gibbering nightmare tales about the old man. Yet I would have said that he tried to be kind to them and that their hysteria surprised even him—but they whispered that the badge of his evil power was precisely his traditional front of kindliness. (Later a young midé shaman elsewhere wrote me that my "smiling" expression "frightened off the Indians" because it drew attention to my own shamanism.)

Alignments, qualified by customary links of kin and clan, sprang up in the Indian village around Maggie and around Will, as outsiders with shamans' attributes (for Maggie was a known visionary). These two people were acutely alive to the atmosphere; probably most of the Ojibwa particulars escaped me, so that I was amazed to see Maggie's bearish figure shrink before my very eyes. Will, on the other hand, continued to walk erect as a tree, wrapped in wool underwear beneath his jeans even in tropically hot August ("What keeps out the cold will keep out the heat," he informed me), seldom without his felt hat and his eyeglasses. The general tenseness reached me and I understood that Maggie was only exposing, off-guard, the heightening of a habitual state. This was the atmosphere within which Ojibwa sorcery flourished. Months later I found the same atmosphere among the Kansas Potawatomi, though *they* said they feared Ojibwa shamans more than any others.

Teaching me midéwiwin under conditions required by dogma, Will proposed that we marry to consolidate our shamanistic partnership. He said, "With your brains and my knowledge, we should rule the world." He pursued this seriously, using the courting cross-cousin terms and conduct until I terminated matters by driving him back to Cass Lake, forty miles away. Yet a week later, under the blistering sun, he had trudged back and we resumed uncousinly instruction. Daily we pored over his birchbark scrolls depicting midéwiwin lore. I provided the other necessaries, which were the tobacco that sanctioned talking to and about Supernaturals, Will's daily fee that also sanctioned any instruction, and his food and lodging. And he stinted nothing. At the end he gave me a "powerful" name (of an eagle manito), the promise

19

of guarding me after his reincarnation as a Thunderbird, also his sacred scrolls (old but in perfect condition; see Plate 7 and Figures 1 and 3), little sacks of protective magic or "medicine," his handsome, large redstone peace pipe, and two fine new quilts just earned for serving midé rites at Red Lake.

When we parted under a snowfall at Cass Lake and I let him out of the car, he stood erect by my window, reached for my hand, asked me to return, then removed his glasses to dry his tears. So the Ojibwa begged ritual "pity" of a guardian spirit, seeking "power" after humbling himself physically and mentally, and weeping. He wrote me until his death a few years later. At my present writing, he should be stationed above Niagara Falls in his Thunderbird aspect, as he anticipated.

Chapter 2

COSMOLOGY AND THE VISION

IN THE WORLD-VIEW provided by Ojibwa religion and magic, there is neither stick nor stone that is not animate and charged with potential hostility to men, no circumstance that is accidental or free of personalized intent, not one human creature to be taken for granted. At the same time, all difficulties may be appeasable through governing spirits. So every single male, for whom the honors of Ojibwa life were intended, to the formal exclusion (with unacknowledged exceptions) of females, was obliged to closet himself with world speculations at least once in his life, which was at puberty. One summer in a wood, he was to examine his ambitions and prostrate himself through ritual fasting, thirsting, sleeplessness, fierce concentration on the goal of "seeing and hearing" a well-disposed manito, weeping and blackening his face with charcoal from the fireplace and rubbing ashes on his hair. He recalled all he had heard about "power," in his ears were the pleas of grandparents and parents to "make something" of himself, "to fill [his] emptiness." To the manitos he declared his pitiableness, his utter dependence on spiritual aid, the desperateness of life. Through the miasma of hysterical fear there came to the fortunate seeker—dry-mouthed, empty-bellied, and light-headed —a kindly spirit voice that assured, "My grandson, here is something with which to amuse yourself. . . ."

The Ojibwa I knew in the 1930's repeatedly employed the Eng-

lish word "amuse" as if to cover, not the word's everyday conno-
tations merely, but also their hopes of rescue from wild fear. It
was a bare moment's rescue, reminiscent of our occasional saying
that true pleasure lies in the lifting of pain. Unremittingly,
Ojibwa visions, sorcery, rituals, gossip, and midéwiwin told of
fears: about hunger, sickness, crippling, infidelity, betrayal, ridicule, failure in trapping, games, and war, about weather and poi-
sonings and insanity. The youngest child was taught to fear an
ogre. However, spiritual forces would respond predictably to
rules which tradition knew and some of which midéwiwin expounded in connection with its curing and initiation.

THE MANITOS

In the Ojibwa's overwhelming commitment to the vision pursuit, hope of tangible benefits merged with spiritual concerns.
The tangible appeared as temporal conveniences allowed by the
eternal spirits, or manitos, after the creation of the world. The numerous manitos, of fairly equal rank, appeared as spirit proto-
types of plants, birds, beasts, elemental forces, and life circumstances such as Poverty and Motherhood. They included useful
trees like cedar and birch; certain roots, plants, and berries; hummingbird, woodpecker, arctic owl, golden eagle, baldheaded
eagle (the last three being Thunderbirds), hawk, loon, lynx,
sturgeon, beaver, moose, otter, deer, wolf, black bear, caribou,
turtle; and the sun, moon, thunder, lightning, meteoric stones,
and winds of the cardinal points. The seasons might be personalized as supernatural; so also were extraordinary circumstances
like cannibalism, the heedless self-assurance of elder sister or
brother (represented in the mythic figure of Foolish Woman),
the vulnerableness of the mighty (represented by the mythic hero
Nehnehbush, called also White Rabbit). These Supernaturals
possessed different powers but were esteemed similarly, unlike
the dreaded windigo, the Water Monster, and ghosts. A mirror
and a horse figured as manitos, in dreams reported from Ontario.

Cosmology and mythology dramatized great figures of misfortune as Supernaturals who paradoxically brought great fortune. One such, a potential guardian spirit, was miserable Poverty, who appeared during hunt failures and long starvation to promise richest blessings if offered tobacco and fat. In tales I heard, this figure intervened to defeat vengeful midé shamans: in this context, "midé" was synonymous with highest power, always chiefly of vision origins. For example, a young man rejected a marriage offer made by a girl's midé-shaman father. As the young man had passed summer nights with the girl, to everybody's knowledge, the father became furious. So during the winter he magically caused game and fur to avoid the young hunter. After twenty days of winter starvation and semi-illness, the persecuted hunter came upon a mournful, skeletal figure with vast empty eyesockets, and asked, "Who are you?"

"I am Poverty, miserable Poverty. . . . I am the failure of hunters. Some old woman [mother of the rejected girl] told me to follow you for a month. So if you hold out ten days more, then do as I say, I'll be able to help you."

The hunter doubted his endurance and begged Poverty to quit now. But the terms were fixed. At month's end, the hunter still lived, again met Poverty, and agreed to his conditions.

"I am not really a manito," said the figure, "but I help Indians who remember me [with offerings]. I mourn because they pass by me. I stretch out my hand for tobacco but always find it empty. So I fell away to a skeleton and I shrink into corners. Now it will be different. . . . Offer me tobacco when you start out hunting. When you are successful, leave me some grease. That is all I ask. Tell others to do the same and they will find luck. And I will give you this [hunting] medicine."

So the hunter grew renowned despite the shaman.

Another supernatural figure of misfortune, who bested even midé shamans and brought luck to the intended victims, was called *baguck*—a tiny bird skeleton with a shrill bird call. Among many stories of his origin, some say that in childhood he was starved to death by his parents, for his stubbornness. The Super-

naturals pitied (blessed) him and made him a sort of lesser manito. Another story has him starved nearly to death by his jealous
father-in-law, with the same mystic outcome. As a manito, he en-
riches hunters with great quantities of game, expecting in return
only tobacco and sometimes sweets.

Among the manitos the mighty ones, like the great birds and
beasts, were solitary Characters (a respectful appellation for
them) who met in smoke-filled councils to discuss cosmic affairs.
Such a meeting produced the first midéwiwin. Vast, unremitting
hostilities were pursued by Supernaturals of equal might, like the
scourging feuds of shamans. One was the eternal enmity between
Thunders and Water creatures; another, the bitterness of midé
Lion toward Snake, though Lion was inclined to resent all other
Characters. The most human-appearing Supernatural, Nehnehbush, suffered from an authentic Ojibwa willfulness, which
brought death to people. The more an Ojibwa concerned himself
with the Supernaturals, through revealed and traditional anec-
dotes, the more he found that these resembled him in thought
and act, and the pleasanter he felt about them. The shaman could
feel so intimate that he joked about them, showing them to be
even sillier or weaker than he, as in the silly, lewd trickster accounts of Nehnehbush and in the midé accounts of the Lion.
But this easement, based on reactive abuse, was fleeting; old fears
always reasserted themselves.

Hole-in-the-Sky dictated to me that the great shamans told
how, long ago, before the advent of Indians, before the appearance of the Earth we know, the Supernaturals gathered at "the
center of the world" (meaning, between Earth and Sky) and
made the following declarations. They said that an Indian was to
be created, a man fashioned of brown sand, but only after the
world was cleared of dangerous beasts. (Midéwiwin develops
this origin tale.) Accordingly there was conceived the superhu-
man named Nehnehbush, by the Winds out of the body of
Mother Earth's daughter; at birth he was charged to make Earth
habitable by Indians. Accordingly, he destroyed the ancient mon-

24

sters. He assembled game and fur animals and fish to suit the Indian's hunting prowess. He equipped the Indian with language and society. He created and roistered until the end of the mythical age, when he withdrew to some "island" where he still lives, accessible only rarely to some vision-seeker.

After Nehnehbush completed his work, the manitos declared that they found it to their liking and could withdraw to their own sphere but would always welcome a ritual approach by the Indian. (The listener to the tale would understand that the "approach" should be through offering tobacco, beloved of the Supernaturals. When tobacco was smoked, in large or tiny amounts, or was offered in plug form, it exerted an irresistible pull.) The manitos, being approached ritually, would "reach out," that is, listen attentively to the Indian's recital of his needs.

Bird Supernaturals seemed favored patrons, except for hunt dreams where particular animal patrons, and occasionally fish patrons, were favored. Through curing and war dreams, bird Supernaturals gave of their characteristic talents. Mighty Thunderbird, also called admiringly "the Thunders," was favored for war because it was swift, silent, enduring, and fierce, and also because it influenced sky and weather. Arctic Owl and Golden Eagle were at times called Thunderbirds and assigned Thunder traits. Frequently the Thunders patronized curing, often in association with lesser manitos. Thus, curing by vision had four major subdivisions, each of which was governed by Thunderbird in association with another manito. In hunt dreams, each animal spirit bestowed its strengths and talents and additionally gave the promise of its body, delivering this as the game the hunter killed.

Bird patrons never received the rituals elaborated for animal patrons of the hunt, even when the animals (such as caribou, bear, or beaver) were not personal patrons of individual Indians. Real animals were viewed as "honored servitors" of their manito chief, or spirit, one such spirit apparently representing his earthly kind; and they were viewed also as temporary incarnations of the spirit who sent them to be killed by a favored Indian for his sustenance. Upon killing big or fur game, the Indian observed deferential rituals, wanting the game "essence" to give its manito head a glowing report of the beneficiary's courtesy. The most elaborate ritual was accorded the black bear; this was a local version of a far-flung practice among northern hunting cultures (see Hallowell, 1926). The carcass was saluted in the classic formula of "dear, honored guest"; its heart and tongue ligament were cooked separately; its skull was scraped clean, hung high out of the dogs' reach, painted prettily with red and blue and beribboned with silks of these hues; and tobacco was offered. The hunter invited neighbors to a feast, prepared by his wife and friends who contributed dainties like dried wild rice and dried blueberries.

Moose were treated similarly but less elaborately and perhaps less ardently. Upon killing one, the hunter or a substitute removed the beard and hung it aloft. Sometimes attached to it, but always nearby, was placed tobacco wrapped in a black silk kerchief, or some fine rag.

Regard for fur creatures like beaver was ritualized by keeping dogs far from the meat, strewing the bones carefully in water (their natal element) and ensuring that they drifted cleanly and gratefully to the head beaver spirit with the recommendation to send more to the Indian. The bones were prevented from falling into the fire lest Windigo cause the scorchings to assume his appearance. This particular scapulimancy was read anxiously.

MANITO PATRON AND THE VISIONARY

Further rituals were required of animal visionaries. For example, besides observing the general bear-hunt obligations, a Bear visionary also periodically erected a Bear sweat lodge, to which were invited all, especially men, who dreamed of Bear. A variant of their traditional sweat bathing, it was considered by the Ojibwa to be a "terrible" ordeal. This emphasis was partly honorific, partly realistic. Emulating the manito's giant strength, the visionaries exposed themselves to excesses of steam heat.

26

Where other lodges, observing curing procedures apart from the Bear cult, employed four to sixteen burning stones, a Bear lodge employed eighty and continually reheated them. Where other lodges were only moderately blanketed in, a Bear lodge was swathed in tiers of birchbark and blanket. Where elsewhere the sweat-bathers could poke out their heads briefly from under the walls, a Bear lodge forbade it. Men remained in the Bear lodge much longer than in others, a period that can be calculated from the ratio between the hours spent cooling sixteen stones and the hours spent cooling eighty larger ones. Bear visionaries in the lodge maintained constant rituals; anything less was an admission of inadequacy or of false claims. Each man invoked his protector, mumbled his dream in the ceremonial, rapid, half-intelligible way, and sang the songs revealed to him. There developed a kind of vision-matching. Women were not admitted to a sweat lodge, because of lochial tabus, but the woman visionary stood outside and gave tobacco to an occupant to sing for her.

The visionary erecting the lodge and issuing the invitations sent ceremonial assistants among the villagers on various errands; and they told marvelous stories of doings in the lodge. Chief among these, transmitted down the years, were stories of the transformed appearances of sweat-bathers and of the lodge itself. While reciting and singing, sweaters assumed fierce aspects of bears; the lodge itself came to resemble the cavernous insides of a great bear. All Indians, including visionaries, expressed great fear of the lodge.

This view of the bear manito was amplified by a large cluster of sentiments, expressing some awe and also some love. For the bear was considered quasi-human, in anatomy, erect carriage, cradling of young with the forearms, enjoyment of sweets and liquors, manner of drinking any liquid, shows of intelligence, inclination to moderate conduct despite great physical strength. There were Indians who could not bring themselves to eat bear flesh "because it would be like eating a man," despite the glory of bagging bears, of securing a Bear patron, and of celebrating a Bear feast. However, a Bear visionary was obliged to eat the flesh at the ritual feasts or forfeit the manito's patronage; the logic exactly paralleled that of the Christian rite of consuming wafer and wine. Women Bear visionaries were not as rigidly committed as men; their participation in mystic activities was considered uncalled-for and disregarded by tradition (Landes, 1938a, esp. Part 3), so they could evade the eating mandate. The woman visionary's formula of evasion was to announce that the tiny Bear secreted in her body complained of sickening when she ate bear meat. Maggie Wilson, a Bear visionary (though also a Christian), had the tiny Bear in the back of her neck (she showed it to me). She said that when she ate bear, her neck-creature swelled in size and activity, from distaste.

Other game visionaries seemed characterized by negative injunctions about the patron's meat, especially Ojibwa befriended by the sturgeon manito or by the giant Fish claiming the visionary as spouse. Often associated with misfortune, like all underwater creatures, the fish manito nevertheless conferred prowess in netting big, valuable sturgeon, whitefish, and pike, and power for controlling waters. The price of this vision was a tabu on eating fish, usually one kind of fish but sometimes a blanket tabu on all kinds. Infringements were punished supernaturally, even when involuntary.

A famous tale reported this, about a father and son trapping together. Wandering, they had reached a large lake or river where the father secured a fine fish, prepared it, declared it excellent, and pressed it on his son. The boy refused every urging, and the father demanded explanations. The boy refused to explain. Finally the boy agreed to eat the fish, on condition that his father bring him pailfuls of water to drink. Father complied, boy ate. Lugging pails of water, after some hours the exhausted father fell asleep. Awakening, he found the boy no longer at his side but at the water's edge, his body three-quarters submerged. That portion had turned fishlike; the rest on land was still human until, before the father's eyes, the son's whole body slid into the

28

water as a complete fish. The old man heard his son say, "I told you I could eat fish only if you brought me water constantly. Fish cannot live on dry land. But you would not, and I must leave." Then he added fondly, "But I am not lost. If ever you want me, I am here and will always help." This meant he had become his father's guardian spirit.

War patrons were secured generally by fasting male visionaries who sought them, but surprisingly many women also gained war visions, usually without specific intent (see Landes, 1938a). The Ojibwa told of a woman who defended her husband in a sudden Sioux onslaught by invoking Fog. Fog or mist was closely associated with Thunderbird and Rain, who must have been the woman's dream patrons. Invisible behind her mystic weather-screen, she killed two and scalped one of the enemy, for which the Ojibwa honored her as a male "brave."

One warrior, blessed by Hummingbird, flew among the enemy invisibly, and killed and scalped at ease. The narrator explained that probably the warrior did not really transform himself but mesmerized others so that the enemy saw him as a bird or not at all. A fellow warrior, blessed by Buffalo, possessed immense strength but also immense size so that he was a clear target for the enemy and indeed the only one of his party to be seriously wounded. His companions had tried to dissuade him when they learned of his patron. Mistrust of Buffalo was peculiar to southwest Ontario, for the manito was favored around the Plains region. On another party, a warrior had Bear power and succeeded in creating the illusion of being, or of being with, many people. The bulk and visibility of Bear were not objected to as they were with the unfamiliar Buffalo. The Bear visionary carried a bear claw or a string of claws to which he smoked at intervals and of which he begged aid.

In southeastern Minnesota, an Ojibwa had Fox for patron, becoming endowed with its speed, quiet movement, strength, and cunning. Another had the power of a mirror, which dazzled the enemy with its glancing surface, and invoked Thunder's control

29

over weather. All war visionaries on the path were said to have had the power to transform themselves into semblances of their patrons, or into aspects of their patrons. This was not affirmed of other visionaries, except for sorcerers transforming themselves into bears or "balls of fire" while speeding on evil missions.

Unlike curing patrons, the war patron did not grant powers for protracted indefinite periods but for specific limited occasions only. It told the visionary the exact number of the enemy to be scalped or slain, the duration of the war party, the number of warriors to compose the party, whether or not the beneficiary was to be leader, how many of the party would be killed. To organize a further party, the visionary required a further revelation; there had to be a separate communication for each undertaking. If the usual Supernatural refused aid, it was unlikely that another would bless the vision-seeker.

A similar specificity characterized "naming" visions, where the patron told the dreamer how many persons he could name and thus cure. But naming visions might be granted by more than one patron to the same dreamer.

GOOD AND EVIL VISIONS AND THE MIDÉ ORIGIN TALE

The people distinguished instantly between the great dreams of "power" and common dreams, because of the figures in them and the affect attending them. The combination of dream incidents marked the great vision: a mythic Supernatural who offered blessings and addressed the dreamer by a tender kinship term, in an endearing manner, "so you will know what to do with your life." Should the dreamer respond with reluctance, the Visitor would beseech, and, when pushed, would threaten. That is, the dream conveyed awesome direction and insistence to the novice.

The traditional boy fasting for manly powers was to dream of One approaching him whom he could see, or hear, or both, who acted and spoke kindly, promising power which might be small or great, making the boy his protégé for life under conditions

30

revealed in the first or ensuing dreams. The Ojibwa conceived of the manitos as bound in groupings, so that the protection of any one could imply interest of others. When the traditional faster experienced his fruitful climax, he knew personal success and showed it to his family by changes in his manner and by observing ritual obligations imposed by the dream. His immediate family was impressed and proud, and through their oblique references the facts became known to the village—how they discovered the boy in a swoon, carried him home, and observed him silently to learn his wordless news. The village too felt strengthened with this additional resource and with this confirmation of the Supernaturals' attention to Ojibwa needs. Only later might the promising novice develop an ambitious shaman's excesses, fatal to family and village.

The traditional beneficent vision-complex had an obverse in the evil-working vision. Evil Supernaturals, mentioned earlier, were windigo and underwater creatures, all calamitous for their protégés. The latter manitos included water lions, water serpents, occasionally water bears, mermaids, and mermen; all are mythic figures and may appear in visions. In myths, an often recurring water monster is the Great Fish, whose name is sometimes rendered into English as "whale," sometimes as "shark." Water monsters are the perpetual and recurrently defeated enemies of Sky Supernaturals, especially of Thunderbirds. The battle, eternally resumed, is analogous to the conflict between God and Satan in Christianity.

Water monsters represented a sexually romantic obsession and turned their protégés into celibates, mated only to the manito. The Ojibwa man or woman received visions of the monster, who appeared as an alluring person of opposite sex. Should the visionary have children, they risked being killed by the jealous water spouse. The visionary secured some respite by throwing offerings, in spring, to waters that were thawing and, in fall, to waters that were starting to freeze; the offerings were decorated sticks, tobacco, and lengths of cloth (called "print"). Failing to make sacrifice and to observe the tabu on marriage, the visionary endured a "miserable life," which the *tcisaki,* or divining doctor, could divine, but not even a midéwiwin could cure.

Midé rituals contradicted, by ignoring, Ojibwa tradition's demand for fresh secret visions as the road to survival and distinction. Midé shamans ritually intoned to others the origin tale about the ancient revelation gained by a mythic ancestral Indian called Cutfoot: Four Supernaturals (a "powerful" number) spirited him away as a child (that is, appeared to him in a trance) and taught him midé rites in two sessions of four years each.* The child, who later received the name Cutfoot, narrated the revelation to his family, who transmitted it to descendants and friends. As the original midé vision belonged to a mythological Character who was also a forebear, but not to any private or historic Ojibwa, and was broadcast by leading midé shamans at every teaching and curing session, its exposure did not conflict with the secrecy tabu attached to personal visions; and it could be employed by people who paid for it, as they could employ herbal prescriptions for whose knowledge they paid. However, the unofficial politics of midé notables took on the appearance of duels among shamans with great personal visions. Each one had to assert his views.

Watching Will pray to his own Thunderbird guardian, he standing facing a tree while I was put to one side behind him, listening at other times to Mrs. Wilson narrate for me the "power" dream of her World War I Star Dance, I sensed that to each visionary, his own experience was uniquely worthy and could be subordinated to others only against the deepest protest. Such subordination was expected yet defied in war parties and other group activities, such as village games (see Landes, 1937*b*).

* Corroboration of the vision sanction even for midéwiwin appeared during my research when two additional midé societies of contemporary *dream* origin sprang up among Ojibwa of southern Ontario. In 1933, one was called "sahgimah midéwiwin"; *sahgimah* means "gleaming, attractive" and perhaps implied "superior." Some Ontario Ojibwa said that the new societies were far more potent than the traditional one.

32

IMPLEMENTING VISIONS

The Ojibwa visions about which I learned fell into three classes, according to the promise of each. One class promised success in the hunt, which included trapping and fishing. One offered success on the warpath: that this was still a real concern in the 1930's was evidenced by the fame of Mrs. Wilson's dreams about World War I, told below, in Appendix 1. The third class offered knowledge for curing sickness. The three classes were respected equally; some of the greatest men, and some rare women, acquired all three. Each class was again subdivided according to the methods of fulfillment and according to the time the power was to last. Persons with only one class of dream might "own" it in its several subdivisions. All the Supernaturals of visions also "protected" midéwiwin, according to Will Rogers, in his account of the Minnesota society.

Dream powers and magic powers, the latter taught usually for a price, were used jointly or alternatively for every possible end, and they exchanged psychological values. In hunting, as explained earlier, the great powers came through revelations from, or of, some animal or bird manito. The Thunderbird gave his protégé powers over the weather, usually working in conjunction with the North Wind manito. Invoking them, the favored Indian could raise a wind that formed crust on the February snow, or froze the thawing March waters, or made snow fall thickly, or cleared stormy skies. Simultaneously, the same Indian used a kind of bull-roarer or cedar horn whose noise evoked rushing winds by sympathetic magic. Bull-roarer and horn weather-influencer were widely distributed among northeastern American Indians; individual Ojibwa may have regarded them as vision tokens. Such visionaries also led midéwiwin.

Again, a man may have been "blessed" by one or more fur animals who vouchsafed him a picture of rich trapping returns. The visionary proceeded to concoct a magical brew of herbs, whose good will he invoked with tobacco; he dropped the brew all

33

around his trails to cripple interlopers. He shaped a magic horn when hunting deer, to simulate the mating call. This horn acquired personality as an extension of the parent vision.

Reverent though they were, even feasts for guardian spirits could be regarded as binding magics. These included hunting feasts of various types, notably the feast for the spirit of a slain bear; and also feasts for naming, first fruits, menstrual purification, and general manito feasts. The great feasts attending every midéwiwin must have been viewed similarly. The very evidence, at all feasts, of tobacco, foods, goods, and other wealth connoted "purchase" (hence the possibilities of sorcery), though in the language of visions and midéwiwin this wealth was termed "offerings."

Normally and routinely, all Supernaturals were to be given tobacco and food, whether they were personal guardians, mythological characters mentioned in story-telling, the corps associated with midéwiwin, or those linked with the animals hunted and trapped. If the guardian spirit was Eagle, then tobacco was placed in the neighborhood of an actual eagle's nest, as it was also when an eagle was spied during a hunt, and always when a thunderstorm was brewing, for this was Eagle action. Sacrificial "eatings" for manitos were likely to be given during spring and fall, if the visionary had ample food—meat, fish, dried berries, wild rice. The ritual eating was done regularly only when a man was unhappily "blessed" by the water monsters whose attentions he wished to avert. Neighbors were summoned to such feasts and, with their eating, the food's spiritual aspects were taken by the host's guardian spirit and shared with other such spirits who then became well disposed toward the host, perhaps also toward the village. Ojibwas said that they appreciated invitations to "eatings" because thus they shared in a communion that "gives us life."

The tone was given by the "old man," or shaman, requested to address the Supernaturals. He smoked, pointing his ceremonial pipe of red or black pipestone to the four cardinal directions and to sky and earth, offering the contents of the bowl in a sunwise circuit, beginning in the west of the powerful Thunders, or beginning with the cardinal direction corresponding to the season of the year—north in winter, south in summer, east in spring. He said, "Oh, manitos, see this sacred tobacco and food. They are for you, and in return we request life. Take them kindly, regard us gently." Then he directed the Indians to eat and so participate in the Supernaturals' feasting.

The "eating" became a forcing formula at times, as did the visionary's supplication, and the midé shaman's. A desperate, starving man might be reduced to offering dried willow bark in place of true tobacco and food. The act, being ritual, was a binder on Supernaturals' grace and should be as effective as earnest pleading or a successful man's material generosity. When a bear was bagged, the sacrifice to the manito Bear was elaborated into the Bear Feast mentioned earlier, the Ojibwa version of a far-flung subarctic rite (see Hallowell, 1926). But sacrifices to the respective animal manitos were offered also, for thanks and binders, when the Ojibwa caught moose, beaver, sturgeon, or a very large supply of any other meat (including caribou in the days when it was present), or fish. Since Bear was regarded, still in the 1930's, as more humanlike than any other nonhuman form, greetings to him were embroidered to that effect, both by hunt visionaries and by shamans in the midé rites. Thus, he was not addressed simply as "manito" but hailed and invited as "honored guest." Special foods were offered to suit his known appetites and humanlike inclinations. "Manito, here is tobacco for you, and berries and sweets that you like! All that you wish! And here, a bottle of whisky to show our respect! We thank you for the fine bear you have sent this man, and ask that you favor him again. That is what we want."

SEEKERS WHO FAILED

Some Ojibwa men never secured dreams, remaining "empty, fearful, and cowardly" for life, the complete opposite of those who secured rich dreams and in arrogance later abused them, to the eventual destruction of personal and family happiness. Some who failed to secure vision would, like Paul Radin's Winnebago named Crashing Thunder, pretend the contrary, even overreaching themselves by boasting (Radin, 1926). To boast of visions was tabu; to boast falsely brought the manitos' revenge. Such tales were told me in Ontario and Minnesota, chiefly about young men who were scorned for their irreverence and want of discipline, but equally or more for lying. The Ojibwa demanded blunt honesty; the vilest sorcery was preceded by some public announcement, which, however, served also as taunt and boast. There was a notion, not inconsistent with other ideas, that favored visionaries were exceptional, and that possibly some were human incarnations of their Supernaturals. Will Rogers boasted so, in quiet tones; it backed his formidable position as a midé shaman, and he was never accused of falsehood. Rather, his standing was acknowledged by the terror he inspired.

Will told me of a young man who boasted falsely and paid with his life. He and his cousin had gone hunting cranes on the northeastern prairie. The cousin worried, and the young man exclaimed loudly, "Oh, *I* can get the birds! I have no reason to fear them." This implied that the Crane was his guardian. The cousin, himself a manito protégé, was appalled. He said, "I do not know the reason for your statement. If you have none, it is terrible to speak thus. If you have reason, it is also dreadful. I hope you will not be hurt." The other insisted, "I can handle the cranes. I'm not afraid." His cousin galloped on. Soon a flock of cranes appeared. They allowed the reverent cousin to kill some of them but they ganged up on the boastful one, gashing his horse with knife-sharp bills until the bloody entrails dragged over the prairie. The horse collapsed, the cranes jumped the young man and tore him to shreds before his cousin could save him. The dying man confessed, "Tell them at home it was all my fault. I had no right to speak that way. They had never talked [in a vision] to me. I lied. Go home—tell them you could not help it."

Another young man nearly met the same fate but escaped. One

36

Plate 1. An Ojibwa family of the 1930's, at Red Lake, Minnesota. Photograph by Ruth Landes, 1934.

Plate 2. The Minnesota Ojibwa shaman Will Rogers, or Pindigegizig (Hole-in-the-Sky). Photograph by Ruth Landes, 1934.

Plate 3. Mrs. Maggie Wilson, a Cree-Ojibwa visionary at Emo, Ontario. Photograph by Ruth Landes, 1933.

Plate 4. The son and daughter of Mrs. Maggie Wilson. Leonard Wilson is helping his sister Janet adjust the eagle feather completing the regalia for her role in Mrs. Wilson's mystic Star Dance. Photograph by Ruth Landes, 1933.

winter, he and his cousin were trapping, working apart days but spending nights together. One evening he asked his cousin, "Of what are you not afraid?"—meaning, What manito protects you? The cousin answered, "I'm not afraid of a lynx [whose fierceness the Indians respect]. And you?" "Oh, I'm not afraid of a ghost." While both risked punishment in naming the Supernaturals as guardians, one sinned further in claiming a guardian—the Lynx—falsely. Subsequently, trapping led them to pass a night apart. The one claiming Lynx had slept several hours when he was awakened by a hot breath. He saw a lynx crouched above him, passing its extended tongue, rough as a file, over his naked body. Back and forth went the tongue, roughing the body until the skin bled; the man lay in terror, sickened by the beast's fetid breath. On and on the tongue went through the night until it was "coming daylight," when the animal left the man nearly dead.

Meantime the cousin too had been awakened, by a ghost who grasped his arms and wrestled. Silently the two fought all night until light glimmered. Then the ghost pleaded, "Please let me go. I must be home before day comes or I am lost. Please let go." The man would not, and at daylight he saw he had conquered. His opponent was just a rotten log! The Indian had conquered because he did "own" the manito, but he had been attacked for speaking lightly of it. Now he searched out his cousin and found him near death. "So you lied?" he said weeping. "So Lynx was not your Power?" But he nursed his cousin back to health, laboriously.

The workings of what we call conscience are obvious in these tales told by midé Will Rogers—conscience reinforced by the dogma that manito "pity" stays only with the youth who is modest and reflective, who seeks more and more visions, in order "to learn" and to secure mystic protection, until by his early middle age the "power" has matured. Hence, the mighty shamans are "old" and always termed so in deepest respect and fear. To say "old man" was synonymous with saying "great shaman of midéwiwin," in Minnesota and Ontario during the 1930's.

VISION EMBLEMS

A visionary, and also a midé shaman, kept mementos of the manito bond. Thus, a Thunderbird protégé sought for and kept a small stone, preferably of meteoritic origin, or distinguished by some other quality such as its odd or lovely shape or its smooth surface. Mementos might be manmade, such as a tiny cane showing revelation of long life, a tiny set of bow and arrows revealing a hunting gift, a hand drum or a larger one painted according to mystic directions. Other binders were contained in styles of face-painting, in special sacrifices like the dry-goods sunk in lakes as offerings to Water Monsters in spring and fall, in highly charged rituals like a periodic sweat bath (taken over by Ojibwa midéwi-win, for its shamans who were Bear visionaries), or in food tabus. It seemed that an Indian came to use the mystic stone or face-painting somewhat as impersonally as a tool: when he carried it on him the whole vision worked.

Neighboring tribes cultivated visions similar to the Ojibwa's (see Benedict, 1923) but often externalized them in artifacts serving as amulets and as sizable bundles which were also portable altars. One such "dream" could serve generations, possibly centuries, through its materialization; the original experience of dreaming then became a sacred tale explaining the origin and powers of the bundle. Except for midé equipment such as the hide "shooting" bags, so-called *migis* shells, and mnemonic scrolls of birchbark, the Ojibwa had no hereditary bundles that were dangerously powerful in themselves, though individuals did carry the sorts of externalizations listed above.

Consistently with the Ojibwa's established secretiveness and individualism, it was within his very body that he developed and hid tokens of a great dream experience. There Maggie Wilson kept her Bear manito, identified by her sucking-doctor (see Chapter 3 for a discussion of sucking-doctors). When Maggie fell ill and called in the curer, he noticed a lump in her neck and sucked the Bear out: it looked like a tiny black worm. He re-

38

placed it and she was well. The doctor explained that she was a Bear protégé (unwittingly, until then) and had sickened the manito in her by violating a food tabu, probably.

The great shaman, Chief George, claimed that a couple of Bears inhabited his back, one on each side of his spine in the lumbar region over an area of two square inches. The spot was so famous that I heard about it from others at Manitou. George had fallen ill after a drinking spree, the lumbar region quavered, and the doctor discovered that the Bears were suffering. He cured George with an herbal prescription and a session in the Bear sweat lodge, for George was a Bear visionary.

Another man was treated for severe back pains. The doctor extracted iron from the region through the sucking-bone, took the iron away, and returned to blow the iron back into the patient's neck through his tube. He explained that this patient held Iron, a sky or water manito symbol, as others held Bear or Moose in their bodies. But the iron wasted, and if it had gone completely the patient would have died.

One man had a thrilling area along the back of his head. A shaman interpreted this to be the habitat of a miniature bird Supernatural, as Birds lodge in the upper body. The spot's behavior could anticipate a storm by three days.

An old woman acquired her mystic warning-spot not by vision but through eating the flesh of a Sioux. Hole-in-the-Sky wrote me:

> She came to eat this because she was starving. Some returned braves near her had dried Sioux meat, though she did not understand this. One of them told her, "Here is meat for you."
> She warmed it on a spit and ate. When she finished, he told her it was Sioux meat and asked, "What did it taste like?"
> She said, "Like bear meat."
> "No!" he said. "It was a piece of a Sioux!"
> She said, "It tasted good anyway."
> Ever after, the woman sensed when a Sioux skulked around.

Hole-in-the-Sky explained carefully that a sensitive spot which thrills often, unexpectedly, and in an isolated way must be linked with a vision. As the manito safeguards his visionary, so the spot thrills warnings of ill health, evil weather, or other conditions hostile to the carrier. Hence it was called the "warning spot." Hole had one such on his back but could not tell until after the event if the delicate thrill boded good or evil. He believed everyone had such a spot somewhere but that most people ignored its thrill. He knew a man with such a spot in the sole of his foot, another with one in the palm of his hand. Hole had one near his middle that operated at times. He explained:

When I was a boy of six, I was always dreaming about snakes, that wherever I went I was being covered by them. One summer when I was about nine, Someone [in vision] told me to strip and sit under an oak. I was just foolish enough to do that. [This phrasing was a comic mannerism of Hole's.] I sat there with a cloth around my middle. Two [garter] snakes came near, then more, and more, and pretty soon they were crawling all over me—you couldn't see my skin. After a while, they left except for two around the front of my middle, who stayed with their heads nearly meeting.

I heard a Voice say [in vision], "You will have this till you die."

So these are my two manitos [in the body]. When they get sick, I get sick. . . . I have another manito between my shoulder blades— a little yellow Bird.

Though a healthy spot protects its host against disease, sometimes it fails or is overcome, as Hole experienced. He related:

Do you see this lump at the top of my spine? It came from doctoring by sucking. Four others and I were doctoring a little boy and I got something out of him. My manito should have killed it, but this that I drew up [in 1902] was too strong. It lodged in me, I guess, and the lump got bigger and bigger. I was sick! I was desperate. So I had my sister-in-law [with whom lewd joking is mandatory] step over me [so exposing him to the lethal force of menstrual and lochial blood]. This is something the manitos do not like [for they are vulnerable]. It is bad for a woman to step over anyone except her young children. I was so sick I could barely drag myself to my sister-in-law, Mrs. Fisher.

I told her, "I want you to doctor me."

She kind of laughed and said she didn't know how.

"Step over me," I said, and I threw myself flat on the floor.

40

Well, she wouldn't.

I said, "The responsibility is mine. I'm telling you to do it. It's all right if it kills me."

So she did it—and I got well. I suppose her action killed what I had drawn up from the boy, because that lump stopped growing.

Chapter 3

SHAMANS, CURING, AND SORCERY

THE OJIBWA REGARDED all religion and magic as "medicine" or as "power," expressed through visions and purchased formulas and exercised responsibly or hostilely toward society. Calling all their mystic practices "medicine" in English but noting their sources in visions and acquired formulas, they ranked them by their apparent effectiveness, and always found that highest effectiveness was visionary. It seems that the towering prestige of the midé shamans rested mainly on their private vision achievements; seen thus, the Midé Society was the academy of shamans.

The midé origin tale, like the general reasoning about visions, says that the midéwiwin brings the blessing of "life" for Indians —a blessing that resolves conflict between Good and Evil among the fates, or among the manitos, or between the hero Nehnehbush and his brother, according to the different versions. All traditional Ojibwa lived with an acute awareness of this conflict, expecting Evil to triumph but ever optimistic about Good. This gave their ethos an ironical, sophisticated aspect, free of despair. It bespoke a Gallic-like concern with elegance of conduct, so that *what* one did was less important than *how* one did it, up to a point.

Public midé teachings stressed neighborliness, forbearance, concern for the sick, respect for all, paternalism (shown in kinship usages between the principal officers of the rite and the pa-

tient), honesty, and homage to patron manitos (expressed notably in handsome goods and honors for the shamans and in concentration on the rites). Yet the midé patient and onlookers
knew that they must watch every step, and still be vulnerable
even during the rites to the covert evil of the leading shamans—
manifested as a shaman's transforming himself into the death-fore-
boding "ball of fire," night owl or hooting owl, bear, or dog, and
whisking himself to a lodge or grounds to spy on events. The evil
shaman's victim, usually harassed by hunger or exhaustion, and
observing the signs, might go insane, convinced of a horrible
death. Shamans knew everyone in the village, but their patients
were peculiarly theirs, for the curers ritually gave patients life,
though covertly they might also bring death.

Midé patient and onlookers were convinced that a death-deal-
ing shaman gloatingly cut out the tongue of the corpse, to use in
love and other bad medicine, and to keep a tally of victims. (I
found this extraordinary concept among the contemporary Prairie
Potawatomi also.) When the victim was a visionary or able to
hire a shaman to exercise power on his behalf, great duels ensued
that employed magic and visions at a distance, besides poison
and knives upon actual summer meetings, accompanied by public
accusations, all preserved in tales narrated constantly by men and
women. Such epics were not inspired by "good" shamans, but
their example kept alive the enunciated *principle* of "good-
ness."

SHAMANISTIC POWER

The elevated "old" midé shaman was taken to be the most evil
of shamans, an attribute consistent with the logic of vision power,
the more readily so since all great midé figures happened also to
be great visionaries, in the 1930's. The traditional shaman of evil
power believed that nothing he desired should be withheld.
When he smoked requests to his guardian, he used the collective
term, implying that the aid of *all* Supernaturals was to be gained.
He came to use his pleading and physical abasement like formal

conjurings; results convinced him that his spirit guardian was now his creature.

As will be shown in Part II, all midé shamans became merged with the Supernaturals and addressed one another as "manito." The vision and midé shamans in rituals spoke of their kindliness to fellow Indians but traditionally were expected rather to be enemies of the people and to be felled eventually by supernatural retribution. Unlike the true Supernaturals, such a shaman entered the last stage of his "power" as his sorcery hunted down the normal Indian maniacally—because a girl was desirable, a boy was gay, friends chatted privately, a patient chose another curer, another shaman was honored, or for no reason beyond the habit of hunting down others. The shaman became a killer in opposition to the dogma that the midé manito, like most guardian spirits, brought "life." The doctrine of the midéwiwin was hope and cheer, but the individual shaman heeded also indoctrinated fear and limitless aggression. Kind words were ritual in relations with the manito, yet the Ojibwa vision-beneficiary was alert to best him.

The Ojibwa took it for granted that midé shamans, as a college of ranked midé officials, transmitting lore for pay as they had acquired it, were otherwise all private visionaries, who never abandoned their particular non-midé revelations even when pooling their purchased midé powers. Actually, a local Society, as Will commented, would incorporate a member's dream-revelation about midéwiwin, although this violated the Society's dogma and tradition that revelations subsequent to Cutfoot's had no place. Will never said so bluntly in our way, since it was obvious to his Ojibwa logic. The procedure appeared hardly different from the way a war leader in former times put up with a follower's vision irregularities, such as power-dreaming of a large animal like a buffalo instead of a hummingbird tiny enough to elude the enemy Dakota's eye. In the following pages, I let the issue stand in Will's manner, which offers comments on others' departures from his own standards. During the months that he taught me, he betrayed a proprietary attitude toward midéwiwin, as he would toward his guardian spirit. Both might have been equally "his." Such might well have been the true conviction of every seasoned midé shaman. This would help explain why other midé shamans let Will teach me without interference, and why midé shamans were "known" to fight and kill each other magically, as did the free-lance vision-blessed shamans.

On later stays at Minnesota Santee Dakota and Kansas Prairie Potawatomi reservations, I was told that the Ojibwa midé (the word is used both as noun and as adjective; e.g., a ritual officer is a *midé*) was the most fearsome sorcerer known; the Ojibwa simply agreed. How did the reputation get established?—for the Ojibwa war-tellers would never agree that their forebears were the ruthless aggressors against the Dakotas which the latter and history alike picture. They saw themselves as innocents on the defensive when pursuing the Dakotas. However, shamans were special personalities and the "evil" ones sought ever higher peaks of cruel attack that might have exceeded the peaks of Santee and Potawatomi sorcerers, in these other tribes' eyes.

No matter how arrogant his behavior towards others, however, the shaman vision-beneficiary always observed the *forms* of self-abnegation and pleading when approaching manitos—fasting and praying with tobacco to pry favors from them. But the mood of personal supplication deteriorated to the formal minimum. The Indians waited to see their great shamans start referring to themselves as Supernaturals. Mrs. Wilson never wearied of telling, in shock and scorn, how people endured this from Chief George of the Little Fork band, a man with every Ojibwa power, who terrorized with his self-appellation of manito. If we equate Ojibwa "terrorize" with our notion of "respect," and equate Ojibwa "evil" with our notions of "unscrupulous" and also "highly skilled," we may bridge the meanings. Chief George was taken very seriously for accomplishments that presumably lay open to other Ojibwa men who might care to confront Supernaturals but who did not; this included his exalted midé status, which had to threaten evil by its very superiority. The threat was taken up by rival shamans as a challenge of comparable mights, but ordinary Indians simply

45

cringed under abuses that finally caused the village to turn upon the shaman-tormentor after he had been rendered feeble by sickness or, it was said, by vengeful poisoning. Perhaps restrained by Canadian law, they had not reached this point with George.

The Ojibwa view was not hopeless, however. The people invoked old stories that showed great shamans to be good always— exercising power only to cure sickness or to lure game in amounts needed by the household or to kill for proper revenge. But in contemporary life of the 1930's, such good shamans encountered mistrust of their very virtue, and they were little respected.

Some young shamans would not restrain themselves and suffered accordingly. During my stay at Manitou Reserve, an Indian named Billy M'Ginnis was said to be one such. Mrs. Wilson gave me details. His shamanistic maternal uncle had trained him from childhood to assist in curing; by the time Billy reached twenty, he had his own curing visions. At thirty, he was an established "doctor," though some fifteen years ahead of time. Shortly after, his fate changed. Wife, children, and brother fell seriously ill in rapid succession. He used every resource of vision and herbal knowledge, to no avail. These near ones died. All attributed this to manito punishment of his "greedy" precocity. And Billy agreed. He threw away his manito paraphernalia, of medicine tools and sacks, and abjured his erstwhile guardian spirits, to remain "empty." It was a kind of suicide, which struck both Indians and me. Mrs. Wilson told of a similar occurrence with a shaman named Red Cloud, who restrained himself after failing to cure his wife, infants, and brother. Another story told how a Manitou shaman named Soldier was met one morning by his daughter who screamed, "You have killed my son by your manito life! Now I will hand you to the Mounties!" And she did.

Women experienced vicissitudes with Supernaturals, but less systematically and disastrously than did men. This may be interpreted in cultural terms, since the Ojibwa regarded shamanism as a male activity, preëminently. Mrs. Wilson and others of Manitou told and wrote me innumerable tales of the sort; Mrs. Wilson herself had a series of vision-dreams that became celebrated (see

46

Appendixes 1 and 2). One tale that illuminates women's uncertainties about adopting shamanism, which kept all but rare exceptions from reaching midé heights, was the following, told at Manitou. A freshly nubile girl fasted four days upon her menstrual onset, as was often suggested to girls, and began a vision of long, healthy life: she was approached by a dream-figure with white hair. Abruptly she gave up the quest. She explained that she felt too sick, hungry, and scared. Though ever after she avoided pursuing revelations, she did pay for learning magical prescriptions and midé lore.

CURING BY VISION

Shamans' skills or professional activities were called "powers," "medicine," and "doctoring" by the Ojibwa in English (see Landes, 1937a, pp. 111–44). The heavy emphasis on illness and its cures explains the last two terms. It is not farfetched to understand that war parties too were considered "cures" for the blood-revenge duty and lust advanced to justify them, that weather control and hunt skills were "cures" for hunger, that "love medicine" cured emotional yearnings, besides all the "powers" that "cured" every other need, from recovering lost articles to healing diseases. The greatest skills, by traditional esteem, were supernatural gifts transmitted in visions by supernatural patrons, as for hunting, war, curing, and *tcisaki* divining (which centered on the mystically shaking tent that concealed the diviner). Other great skills were said to be learned through visions amplified by purchased instruction, such as midwifery, and notably tcisaki again, despite the concurrent dogma of its sole source in visions; and other skills were acquired only by purchased instruction, such as midéwiwin curing and minor healing specialties of herb-brewing (*mashgigiwaboge*), tattooing (*azhassowe*), and vomiting (*shigagoweïwe*). Laymen and great doctors alike could use purchased herbs and magics.

Curing by vision, in each of its four major categories (to be described), invoked Thunderbird (or Thunders), associated with another manito. In the vision about "curing by sucking" (*nanan-*

dawi iwe winini) Thunderbird's associate was Woodpecker, for his ability to scratch out hidden things; his pecking became the doctor's "sucking," which extracted the cause of the disease, conceptualized as a foreign body "sent" by a sorcerer. Sometimes Thunder's associate was Lightning, though natural lightning was considered a function of Thunder's activity. Some shamans said also that Snake was the doctor's lesser patron, because its jagged progress resembled lightning's "snaky" appearance. Yet the Ojibwa feared and hated snakes as strongly as they admired and loved Thunder and Bear, and they considered Snake to be Thunder's traditional enemy. One person was reported to have had Bear as a sucking patron.

Tcisaki was a second curing vision, which stressed stunt divining, solely by men.* In these cases, again, disease (or loss, as of some person or article) was said to be caused by a sorcerer; the doctor divined the evildoer's identity, summoned his soul into the divining tent or lodge, and admonished it or even killed it. Thunder figured here as a kind of remote overlord. Real activity was assigned to Snapping Turtle, who was perhaps ceremonial attendant for Thunder. Turtle's duty was to summon lesser Supernaturals into the divining lodge to hear the doctor's request and act upon it. These lesser associates varied from one locality to another. In northwest Minnesota they were chiefly birds or birdlike, and included big swallows, the raven, and the horned owl. Bear also appeared upon occasion. Thus, in western Ontario, the diviner employed Eagle and Thunderbird, Turtle, Woodpecker, three kinds of Owl, Jackfish, and sometimes Bear.†

---

* A careful examination of Ojibwa divining appears in Hallowell, 1942.

† In manuscript notes left by Dr. William Jones before 1930 to the Bureau of American Ethnology, which I consulted in the 1930's through the courtesy of Dr. Truman Michelson, other divining Supernaturals are recorded. Their provenience is not indicated, but Dr. Michelson conjectured that they belonged to Minnesota's Bois Fort Ojibwa. They include Bear, North Wind, Horse, and Buffalo. The last two were lacking in Emo, Ontario, whose bands also told me that they preferred Bird patrons for their swiftness in locating guilty parties.

Each of the diviner's manitos had a special voice. The Indians who thronged outside the closed divining tent or tents to hear the performance going on inside strained to recognize each voice and understand its talk. At Red Lake, they said that Eagle possessed a "deep, kind voice"; Turtle, a thin, shrill one; Owl, a harsh one. At Emo, they said similarly that Bear's voice was deep, Turtle's small and shrill, Night Owl's like a parrot's, while two other little night owls had cackling small voices. Woodpecker's voice was higher than Turtle's, Jackfish's had a nasal shrill, Eagle's was gentle, and Thunderbird's was full.

A third curing technique was to give a ritual name to a sufferer, at any age, the name being a new mystic identity carrying a new power to live. The namesake became identical with the visionary namer and automatically received protection from the latter's guardian spirit. This spirit was often Thunderbird, and sometimes a kind of eagle that ranked just below Thunder. But almost any other major Supernatural—such as Bear, Moose, Lynx, Sun, occasionally Moon—might bestow the naming power. One person dreamed of a mirror and related it to Sky Supernaturals because it gleamed like an eagle's eye or like lightning and it suggested the sun. It also carried the white man's power. Sometimes trees appeared in visions, especially Cedar, bearing the ancient title of "Grandmother."

Supernatural patrons always addressed the dreamer momentously by a close kinship term, commanding, "Do as I do. . . . Look, learn, amuse yourself, and your life will be pleasant. If not, you and your family will die." The ritual namer also spoke so.

The fourth major vision-curing technique was by undergoing the Sun Dance torture, according to Red Lake and Emo informants, who esteemed the Dance as a great curing rite, though they did not practice it on home grounds. They said it originated about 1900 from visions of a tribesman in Manitoba, and it spread to Buffalo Point, near the Ontario border. There had been Sun Dances within the recent memory of my informants but not at the times of my visits. Numerous Ojibwa from Ontario and Minnesota had formerly attended a Sun Dance at Buffalo Point, I was told; they took with them presents for the visionary's Thunderbird patron. The tribesmen, gathered from far and near, grouped in hundreds as a broad circle around a center pole of poplar. The pole was stripped to the very top, where a remaining tuft of branches represented the ritually phrased nest of Thunders. Each Indian seeking "power" surrounded himself with a comparable nest of branches and stood in it the prescribed number of days, shifting from one foot to another in Indian dance rhythm, straining his entranced gaze up to the nest of the Dance patron. At commands from the Dance-giver, who was a Thunder protégé and the doctor for all assembled, each participant chanted praise and invocation and altered the rhythm of his feet.

A subsidiary patron of this Manitoba rite was Loon. Each faster held in his mouth a whistle made of the loon's leg bone and blew it constantly, producing a chicklike peep. As the loon is a water creature, the whistle was to alleviate thirst.

Some zealots had themselves suspended from the pole by thongs passed through two gashes in the breast. When the thongs ripped through the flesh, after constant dancelike movements in the air, the sufferer was cured of sickness and blessed by Thunders in other ways too. Women tortured themselves fasting and thirsting but did not tread air.

As the avowed purpose of midéwiwin was curing illness, it challenged the domain of the vision doctors. But there was no real trespass, for midé shamans and visionary doctors were one and the same. The patient always summoned a visionary doctor first; only when the latter failed in his vision capacity or himself advised midé treatment, did the Midé Society start to operate. The Indians' explanation of the sequence was that vision doctors demanded smaller fees. Midé cure was always the last resort and, in strange emphasis of this, it "cured" even a patient who had died and it sped the ghost to its destination.

In the 1930's I heard much at Manitou about the curings of an orphaned girl named Gleaming Thunderbird, which illustrated

50

the practices. Mrs. Wilson and my other informants dwelt on the sad case, which had dragged on for years; everyone took sides over symptoms and treatments, weighing personalities and techniques of the doctors called in. At about the age of twelve, the girl had her first menses, but periods were exceedingly irregular, interrupted for months at a time. Her grandmother, old Mrs. Blackbird, housed her, made her rest, gave her teas and poultices. When nothing helped, they called in a blood-letter (called *patchishga'owe* or *patchishgaïge*, meaning one who employs a pointed tool; he may also be called *pasgigweïge*, meaning one who lets blood), named Jack Horton. Mrs. Wilson said that his vision empowered him to cure stoppage and inflammation. He cut the girl on the thigh twice, whereupon flow came. Later she sickened with a hacking cough. Her grandmother summoned Billy M'Ginnis to cure by sucking out the cause of the cough. Billy was "too young to doctor" but he was the only one at Manitou with the specialty.

The Ojibwa believed that disease came from intrusion into the body of a foreign substance due to supernatural punishment of a slighted tabu; sometimes a sorcerer might send it, sometimes no reason was given, or the victim offered a reason, or outsiders did, and contradictory reasons were advanced at times. In this case, Billy extracted several threadlike white worms with tiny black heads, according to Mrs. Wilson, sucking them out and spitting them into a white saucer holding a little water in which they wriggled. He doctored this way during four successive days, singing and beating his hand drum, swallowing the leg bone of the bird representing his guardian spirit, regurgitating it repeatedly and simulating unspeakable agonies, applying it to the patient's chest and sucking out through it a few worms daily.

Some months later, the girl fell sick with tuberculosis. Billy's sucking could not help. People surmised the girl was suffering from "the work" of a sorcerer, because she was desirable, secluded years at a Catholic school, and was now guarded jealously by her grandparents. Perhaps "some old man" wanted her, or a young one had engaged a shaman to work revenge for him on the aloof family. This would need divining. So Billy and the Blackbirds agreed to call in a tcisaki.

The diviner sent forth his spirit turtle and other helpful spirits and discovered that the people's surmises were mistaken. The actual reason he gave, according to Mrs. Wilson, was the anger of midé Supernaturals at the girl's ritual conversion to Christianity. The sole cure was to put the girl through midé rites; this was arranged. The Blackbirds approached midé shamans of their own choice, neglecting the diviner, who was also a midé shaman. When midéwiwin failed to cure the girl, the diviner's family felt avenged. Nor did the girl respond to white Canadian medicine. A second midéwiwin was held without effecting cure, so a third was arranged for. Before it could take place, the girl was dead. But the third rite had to proceed, for midé manitos had been solicited, led to expect tobacco and food, and had promised aid; midé officers had been engaged. This rite now became a Ghost midéwiwin for strengthening the deceased girl's soul on its journey to the midé land where it would sing and dance as an initiate of the Society.

CURING BY MIDÉWIWIN

The Ontario and Minnesota midéwiwin of the 1930's was structured as eight successive grades of curing—the first four called Earth grades and the second four called Sky grades—the "power" rising with the grade. Each candidate had to begin with the first, at the first curing. "Renewal of life" increased with ascending grades, as larger numbers of Supernaturals were enlisted to pledge gifts of health; fees also increased markedly with each grade. According to Mrs. Wilson and Chief Namepog at Manitou, the first four or five grades were considered desirable but the last three or four grades were considered dangerous because they taught sorcery. Namepog and others were very clear about the dangers of excessive power and ambition; so was tradition in picturing shamans' mental disorders (see Landes, 1937a, pp. 133–36; 1938b). It seemed that relatively few people underwent more

than three grades of midéwiwin, for costs were heavy, supposedly rising geometrically with the grade; at the last grades,
fears of automatic penalties for bad-medicine practice were
joined to anxieties over heavy fees. Only the very ill or substitutes
for dying or dead kinsmen went through the seventh and eighth
grades. People implied that personal visions could be resorted to.

The curative and ethical aspects of midéwiwin powers appeared inseparable. The nature of heightened powers and esoteric cures meant inevitably that the evil attending the more potent second set of four grades, especially the last three grades,
should succeed the good of the weaker earlier grades. The Indians' reasoning here duplicated that applied to dream powers,
stating that both midéwiwin and personal vision were revealed
with cautions about being used carefully for the Indians' good—
actually to become abused by overreachers. In the visionary's tie
with his patron, the Indian's behavior was expected to undergo
progressive changes toward impersonal exploitation of his powers,
slighting their origins in the personalized patronage of the manito.

In Ontario of the 1930's, and earlier in Minnesota, the hunting
life limited midé convocations to the summer village. At the
other seasons, a sufferer depended on his immediate resources of
guardian spirit, herbal prescriptions, and powers of other visionaries and herbalists in the household. These powers were continually invoked anyway for trapping, hunting, and physical well-
being. But there were efforts to accommodate midé rites provi-
sionally to the lone winter conditions, as midé shamans described
to me in the 1930's. To help a sick child, for example, the man of
the family apportioned ritual between himself and his wife,
usually the sole adults around. A first-grade curing required ten
midé officers or manitos, all the roles to be met by the man and
wife, the heaviest part falling to the man. A second-grade curing
needed sixteen manitos; a third-grade, twenty, and so on, according to Cass Lake's reckoning. Red Lake demanded greater numbers, such as thirty-two at third grade.

Only three or four shamans had prime importance throughout

the rite. As reported in more detail in Chapter 6, they were (1) the *gitchi webid*, or "chief person," (2) one or more assistant chiefs, the number depending on the grade, (3) the *naganid*, or Bowman, who was leader of the lesser manitos represented by midé officers, and (4) the *wedaged*, or Steersman, who was the end man in the body of lesser manitos. Frequently the chief sha-man, who was the one approached by the prospective patient, ap-pointed the others for the full summer rite. In the truncated emergency family arrangements of winter, the head of the house-hold named those whom he would choose to officiate at full rites. The naming invoked the presences and thus the midé Superna-turals they represented.

In the homily that validated this proceeding, a traditional story was recited about the enduring spirituality of everything, overrid-ing the brief aspects of materiality; the version that follows was known to only a few old shamans in 1934:

Once an old Indian decided to talk with his guardian spirit and so collected offerings for him and went around inviting neighbors to listen to his sacred talk. [For this "benefited" listeners, now in a communion.] When his guests entered his lodge, he filled their pipes with tobacco [those at such a mystic talk became earth representatives of the Supernaturals, for the time], smoked to his manito, and began to talk [or chant a prayer]. At the end, he discovered that his offerings [to exchange with the Supernaturals for their good will] had disappeared! [They had been "accepted."] The manito said [to his fellows, seeing the amazement of the Indians], "This will not do!" The others agreed that things must be altered for the Indian thusly: Let everything used by the Indian have a perpetual spiritual aspect and also a material one that remains with the Indian, so that he sees it. Let the Indian take care of the earthly part of things, and the manitos of the spirit part. Thus will it be arranged on Earth for the Indian. So it happened. Thus we believe.

After this recitation, the man of the winter family-proceeding executed the strenuous business of narrating, singing, drumming, and dancing the parts assigned to the three or four main officers, while his wife performed the silent business of the lesser manitos. As at a full rite, the ample goods and fees had to be displayed before sunrise to the midé Supernaturals, and again during the day to their named Indian surrogates. So the child improved. But his health was affected by the alacrity with which his father paid the debt in summer, at the village, to the officers named in the winter rite. The father must hand over the goods displayed originally, even with an increase, or risk reprisals.

Midé shamans told of a primeval Ojibwa who performed midéwiwin so and restored his child to health:

Long ago there was an Indian. In autumn he moved around by himself, with his wife and child. The child fell sick and the man did not know what to do. Troubled, he consulted his wife but she could not answer. So the man said, "It would be better to put him through midéwiwin." The wife said yes. So they put the child through and it became well. The man hoarded the offerings they had used and, immediately upon returning to the village in spring, he delivered them to the ones he had named. And the child improved nicely.

Midé theory never specified kinds of illnesses or symptoms, unlike curings by special visions. It offered a cure-all that gave "life," on all planes. Thus when parents mourned extremely for a dead child, or when one mourned bitterly over a dead spouse, midé rites were arranged "to strengthen" the mourner, because "it gives him joy."

Midéwiwin promised initiates long life and happiness, the latter concept seeming intrusive in Ojibwa thinking. Could the idea have come from the Christian missionaries haunting every reservation? The most that other Ojibwa mysteries promised, through visions, was power, sometimes phrased as "amusement." Besides, there was a hoary conviction that the duration and character of a man's life were fixed by Supernaturals before each man's birth. Will Rogers assured me that the decree of fate was irrevocable and that midé curing merely gave the patient ease of mind. However, Will was a bold thinker.

The midé shaman guided his patient to express the basic attitudes driven into all Ojibwa males pursuing a power vision: already humbled physically and mentally by disease or sorrow (as the young vision-seeker was by fasting and thirsting), the midé patient was told to supplicate, "Oh, midé manitos! We beg life of you!" He showed his sincerity and respect with many fine gifts—formerly, of furs; in the 1930's exclusively, of prints, blankets, prime hides, cooked and fresh fruits and cereals, and tobacco. Tobacco was indispensable in opening all Ojibwa negotiations, even a serious conversation.

The midé Supernaturals had to respond, by implication overriding fateful decrees of the patient's birth hour. Lacking means for a full ceremony, the patient provided for monthly feasts with the officers he had selected, so that they could plead on his behalf: "Oh, midé manitos! See this food and tobacco! My nephew offers it to you! He means that you should give him life. There will be a midéwiwin when he has gathered sufficient means." The feasts were held at about each new moon until the patient had assembled sufficient for the full ceremony. No midé rite was possible without the offerings, even if the patient must beg them from neighbors, since with them he "traded" for the Supernaturals' pity and his own life.

Along with a man's purchase of midé lore and status, a history of his notable visions seemed necessary for fame in the 1930's Midé Society, though this was never stated. However, observation and discussion of shamans' procedures made it plain. A midé curer sought his guardian spirit's advice for any crisis of the moment or the future, to cure his own sickness or a relative's. The only really necessary condition of admission to the Society—that is, of gaining a curing—was ample wealth to offer the curers; Hoffman (1891, p. 164) emphasizes this when commenting on the exorbitance of the fee. Yet a prospective patient or initiate was frequently directed in the 1930's to apply by a vision. Anyone with the price was taught to be a midé curer, whether sick or not; yet there remained also the unspoken recommendation of visionary power. A rough modern analogy exists in the requirements of both therapeutic and didactic analyses for training a psychoanalyst by highest standards. Anyone may request psychoanalytic therapy as a patient, but the practitioners must demonstrate further abilities. Hoffman (1891, pp. 151–52) viewed all initiates as doctors, however.

In the 1930's at Manitou and Red Lake, people knew that candidates for midé curing could offer one of the four established justifications, besides the indispensable wealth, although these may have been cultural idioms rather than midé dogma. To summarize, they were the dream advice, the advice of the tcisaki, substitution for a deceased applicant (as Hoffman, 1891, p. 161, also mentions) and "to strengthen the spirit" of one mourning a deceased child. Perhaps the extreme poverty of the 1930's favored the emphasis on midé payments. Elsewhere I itemize considerable fees that were paid then at Manitou, such as old Mrs. Blackbird's distribution of goods among her second-grade midé shamans to the amount of fifty dollars; and Mrs. Charlie Namepog's distribution among the second-grade midé shamans curing her son of "five yards of print and a lot of store rice, two new quilts, five or six pieces of quilting, a pair of flannelette blankets costing two and a quarter dollars, a man's new shirt, a common tin pail, tobacco . . . in great quantities . . . , brown sugar, and raisins" (Landes, 1937a, p. 127), besides huge amounts of cooked and canned foods for days and nights of ritual feasting. People had to ask even remote kinsmen for aid, as when Mrs. Namepog called upon Mrs. Wilson, her brother-in-law's wife; and they asked unrelated people also.

SORCERY

Most people were ailing at some time and desperately anxious over this handicap in their marginal economy, so they were vulnerable to midé shamans threatening sorcery (from "twisted mouth" to starvation) against those not hiring them. Gossip and tales document this, as well as resentment of all shamans (Landes, 1937a, 1938a, 1938b). One summer at Manitou, midé shamans terrorized Mrs. Wilson with threats when they suspected that she, a Christian, was telling me about the Society and getting paid—for *they* wanted the fees. She felt no guilt, however, but hoped they would not "give me a twisted mouth or make me crazy so I would not know when I moved my bowels or made water. Edith Bones got a twisted mouth like that."

The availability of purchasable magic—like various madness-inducing love medicines or spells for hunting, midwifery, war, and friendship—implied and encouraged the practice of all the sorcery imaginable. Magics were apart from the personalized manito sanctions, but shamans like Will Rogers explained to me that magical formulas or practices were revealed anciently to several Indians who then taught them to their descendants. In the 1930's, they were still taught either gratis or for pay. Because Mrs. Wilson got a love prescription gratis from her adopted mother, she gave it to me as a gift. Apart from the ready frank instruction and sale of magics, the practice carried no absolute difference from behavior addressed to the guardian spirit. For example, the depersonalized approach of magic also entered visionary procedures, and the personalization of vision concepts arose during magic-making.

Mrs. Wilson knew from close experience that the highest ranks of midé shamans learned and used sorcery, and she documented this for me; Will Rogers never stated this bluntly but it was implied in his remarks and in the fears of him shown at Red Lake. Mrs. Wilson said that she and her husband were once approached by an old, drunken midé couple who offered to teach them "bad medicine" in exchange for "a pile of goods." The couple assured them, "Whatever harm you wish to do to a person can be done with this bad medicine." Nothing like this was ever declared publicly. Incidentally, the Wilsons refused because they did not want the mortal boomerang of windigo insanity and death that follows use of sorcery. Chief Namepog, Mrs. Wilson's father-in-law, was the only one of four brothers known not to practice sorcery; he continually warned his family against the midé practitioners and other sorcerers.

Sorcery was the mighty sanction behind midéwiwin. It was a necessary aspect of the rite's prestige, consistent with the Ojibwa's absolute conviction that a man's power lies in ability to do evil, knowingly. All midé officers were understood to be familiar with ways of sorcery and were expected to practice these in varying degrees, and all other shamans were regarded in the same light. It was said that at the higher rite grades, from fifth or sixth on, patients were taught sorcery. Visionaries bought formulas and tools of sorcery, outside midéwiwin; an ambitious layman with no known "powers" could also buy them. (I was offered specific magics, in the 1930's.) But if the layman's capacities became marked or extensive, midé men were likely to coerce him into their Society, to control him.

A sorcerer was the Ojibwa ideal strong man, defining and holding at bay the terrible forces of existence, manito and human. His skills were inseparable from his alarming personality, seen in the manifestations described as jealous, greedy, bullying, and extremely ambitious. In dogma, the sorcerer was a creature of Powers that made him thus (such as windigo, described earlier); in practice, he was continually rebuked by kinsmen for his ruthlessness and was pleaded with to change. He could forfeit the grip of his Powers by "throwing away" their symbols, which also held their essences, as was reported of several Manitou individuals who thus rendered themselves "empty." Traditionally also, he brought upon himself the punishment of being burned alive by agreed kinsmen, or by villagers whose leaders were the kinsmen (see Chapter 1; to act without the kinsmen invited blood and shamanistic feuds). Occasional elder women sometimes evolved into feared shamans.

The shaman's evil powers were conceptualized as a Frankenstein devil that returned to its "owner," the sorcerer, upon completing an assignment and so wreaked evil in the sorcerer's family by the noxiousness of its mere presence. Some shamans attempted to nullify the returned evil through spraying countermedicines around the dwelling. In the 1930's, I was told that herbal formulas were employed heavily in the practice of and protection against midé sorcery. As children died constantly and their numbers included grandchildren of old men who were stamped by ugly dispositions and cravings for wealth, everyone recognized that the deaths proved how sorcery could boomerang. The countersprayings appeared of little avail. Yet the shaman who avoided practicing sorcery was also mistrusted. People pondered aloud in the 1930's, "What is wrong with him? He knows all the secrets. He lacks the courage. Does he want to keep his grandchildren from dying?"

Hole-in-the-Sky, noted sorcerer and son of a sorcerer, told me he was always advised to eschew evil: "My father said I could learn if I wished but that I should never *use* it, for then it would never bother me. He meant, if I never sent evil medicine out, it would never become active, and return to trouble the house. So he never taught me to *compound* a prescription—he just handed me one ready-made and said what it was for. [Hole did the same with me.] Of course, he gave me a great deal, enough to last years. Maybe my father didn't really know any more, because *his* father may not have told him how the medicine was made, putting off telling him until finally he died. . . . No one should know bad medicine, it should be off the earth. People die off fast enough anyway."

The mother of Red Lake's Esther Iceman, the latter a fervid youthful Christian convert, refused to teach Esther the evil methods. She explained, "I'll tell you only if the time should come when you need to know for your protection." In those years, Esther did not want to know.

Midé sorcerers were said to drop herbal and other "poisons" into a victim's food, causing ailments that ranged from partial paralysis to death. Hoffman (1891) mentions the possible use of strychnine. At Ponemah village in the 1930's, informants said shamans used a poisonous local spider, also frogs and worms, besides human excrement, nail parings, single human hairs, porcupine quills, and midé shells. These fastened in the victim's flesh, they said, traveled within the body, and festered. Doing as directed by the "owner," they were removed best by the one who "sent" them, extracted through the bone of the sucking-doctor.

The sorcerer was understood in the 1930's to disarm a victim emotionally before feeding him poison. He did so through a trusted intimate of the victim. This intermediary could not refuse, on pain of being victimized himself. So it was believed that one's own friend was a prime agent of one's destruction.

Specific signs warned of sorcery. These included a sound of whistling at night, a dog's howling within earshot of the lodge, the sound of a night owl hooting, the sight of the owl or of a "ball of fire" (will-o'-the-wisp, or marsh gas) drifting towards the lodge, the sight of a particular rodent "with twisted legs" lying dead in the path. The omens occurred singly or in combinations. They were viewed as transformations of the sorcerer pursuing a victim.

Seen in winter on the isolated trapping grounds, they promised failure with the fur, starvation, perhaps insanity, and death. If the victim was also a shaman, he was believed to come to grips with the aggressor, both transformed into semblances of their respective guardian spirits. The combat ended in one or both deaths, reported in many long-remembered tales. Some feuds were pursued by succeeding generations of the families, identified for me in the 1930's.

When the omens appeared in summer among the village families, they foreboded illness, rape, winter starvation. The victim might challenge publicly the suspected shaman, and then the struggle came into the open, with knife duels added to the covert tools of sorcery. The suspicious victim might employ a diviner to lure the persecutor's soul into his divining tent for scolding and perhaps killing. Hole-in-the-Sky's father did accordingly, after being engaged for years in battling a shaman of a neighboring village. This duel had been unable to get further than a draw, for the men's powers were matched. Then, one summer, Hole's father sent his army of guardian spirits after the other's soul, had them bring it to him in his conjuring lodge, and there he killed it. The attentive villagers, squatting outside the lodge, heard the din of the fray. Some days later, they received confirmation in news that the other "old man" had died in the woods.

Besides the sexual submissions forced by "love medicine," the commonest injuries inflicted by sorcery were said to be paralysis of various body parts. The notorious "twisted mouth" supposedly was visited upon women who gossiped unduly or who laughed too readily. This looked like a partial paralysis of the facial nerves (Bell's palsy?), causing one side of the mouth to droop slackly while the other was pinched up noticeably. It never resulted merely from frostbite, the Indians said. Active boys were inflicted with severe paralysis of the legs. A Canadian physician near Manitou Reserve told me of a boy stricken this way for seven years, from no known cause other than sorcery; finally the boy was relieved by baking treatments. Hoffman (1891) mentions a similar occurrence. Trappers used sorcery, in the form of a "medicine" that they sprinkled around, to cripple the legs of poachers. Other victims were rendered incontinent of urine or feces, with associated loss of local sensation. Mental disorders were understood to result from sorcery. The insanities described in myths, old tales, and current gossip were extreme (see Landes, 1938a, 1938b; Parker, 1960).

One summer day at Ponemah village, I drove to Esther Iceman's little house, where Maggie Wilson was staying for a while. I found the two of them, the handsome younger one fresh from her mission school, the canny careworn older one uncertainly cast between her worlds, both rattling and bestirring themselves in some hysteria. They turned upon me, for I bore responsibility. They dreaded Hole-in-the-Sky, they declared—Esther shrilly, Maggie restrainedly. Naïvely astounded, I asked why, for I rated him a good, clever old man.

"No!" retorted Esther, "he's wicked, a sinner, he kills! He's a bad medicine-man! That's why he's midé! I know! I led the same dirty life [his daughter] does even yet! He gave a dance in his house and he made a man so crazy, he rolled in his own dirt! We're afraid when he comes here. He may hurt us because he's jealous of us—when you visit us and when you leave us money. You must send him away or we'll go away, yes, I'll go back to

62

the mission with my little boy, or you must stop visiting, because surely he'll kill us."

I interpolated firmly that he had kind ways and a good heart.

"That's how the bad ones do! They don't want to show what's in their hearts. They use a 'friendship' medicine, to get advantage! They pretend to be without, and beg all you have! We heard a night owl last night." Her voice rose hysterically. "*He* sent it! Please, don't tell what we say . . . we don't want twisted mouth. Oh, oh, you must be good to him or he'll work love medicine, or paralyze you. Don't take a thing to eat or drink from him, it'll hold poison. He might even get *us* to pass on [bad] medicine, because you trust us. You aren't safe from the midé people. Everwind sent twisted mouth to his own daughter-in-law because she left her man when she found him with another woman. All these women here know about [Everwind]. He sickened a woman because she wouldn't give him her canoe; he growled, 'You! Your vagina is no good!' [She was living adulterously.] He made a man impotent. And turned another man into a bear . . . people hate to become animals because their own kin drive them out to live forever with animals. He had a boy freeze to death, because he threw lip at him.'

Esther returned to the subject of Hole. "Oh, that old man has done enough, even if he didn't do all they say. His daughter Ruth told me about his medicines, when she got drunk. He keeps his midé sacks by the door in an iron bucket, covered. That bucket holds in the medicine and protects it from damp and dirt. He's got the whole thing covered with cedar boughs, to protect the house from the bad medicine. He has medicine to protect *him* from the midé sacks when he handles them! It's a 'preventer' he drops in the fire to smoke his body, clothes—the whole house. The boughs warn off younger women [because menstrual blood enfeebles men and medicine], and the medicine would hurt a pregnant woman. Ruth said, sometimes he used a whole bear hide for his medicine! She said he travels at night around the Indians' camps *looking* like a bear because he wears the hide

63

[containing] the medicines. She knows! And late at night he gets to look like a fireball, people saw him like that from a distance. We hear about these devils! He's out of his senses from his medicine, when he starts a journey. Then is the time to catch him and ask him what he's about because then, before he has time to realize, he names the person he means to hurt. A young man stops an old one like that, sometimes, and then he has the old one. And the old devil tries to buy him off by offering to teach him the medicine. A foolish young man agrees, and his family suffers [from deaths by sorcery's boomerang]. If he's wise, he buries the medicine. That's how the old one gets revenge: the young one's family must die if he doesn't know the talks and songs perfectly! That old man might do the same to you!"

I asked what happened if the bear-man got past his challenger.

"Well," said Esther, "he's sure to get by if he has sacrificed eight dogs and tobacco. When he gets to the [victim's] tent, the dogs around there can't bark, they fall asleep, like everybody inside. So, the old midé enters and touches his victim, who dies . . . he must die in four, six, eight, ten days, whatever that old man wants. We're telling you, that's how these old men are. And some old women, too."

At the time I thought that Hole was most courteous and conciliatory to the women, never glancing full at them, bringing gifts of food and calico, preparing firewood. In our urban society, his ways would have been admired for their quiet poise, efficiency, and propriety. In Esther's cabin, he joined the denunciations of sorcerers, by assenting, not by elaborating, though he did assure us that he himself never used poison. And, trembling, Esther invited him to join us at dinner, where we ate out of the same dishes. No one ever sickened, it seemed to me. But Maggie remained tense even as she departed for home.

Informants said that sorcerers boasted of collecting tongues of their dead victims, as trophies. Everyone had heard of others who had "seen" the tongues after a sorcerer's death, when they raided his deserted house. (A few years later, a Kansas Potawatomi midé shaman, just past thirty years of age, told and wrote me repeatedly of his own tongue-collecting raids, at homes and burying grounds. I never understood what he meant to say, suspecting fantasy, though fantasy was "real" in that life.) The sorcerer was believed to disguise himself or transform himself into a bear the night of the victim's burial, traveling then to the grave where he slit out the fresh-dead tongue. Relatives of a deceased would keep watch over a new grave. Though it was never so stated, probably a vital connection was seen between the tongue and the soul starting on the journey to the afterworld.

The Ojibwa horror of love medicine suggested to me a horror like that they attached to the tongue-abduction. Both were sneak assaults on human will. Love medicine was considered the ugliest sorcery and the explanation of rape; romantic sex was prized, seen as a "hunt" and a game, by men especially. There were several love-medicine prescriptions, transferred with or without cost, depending on the relations of the parties. W. J. Hoffman speaks of love medicines, in his 1891 report. Like any sorcery, including the herbal, love formulas were revealed anciently in visions and were subsequently transmitted verbally.

In old and contemporary tales, the victim falls into a hypnotic relationship with the sorcerer, showing abnormal or overwhelming lust. The victim, male or female, trails the medicine-wielder or "owner" and makes shocking sexual displays and demands in public. Women, reportedly, would throw their skirts over their heads, exposing themselves (though white communities told similar tales of some of their own women), regardless of age. An afflicted man attacked the woman sorcerer sexually at any opportunity, pursuing her constantly. Those who conquered thus were defeated in the end, however. For the victim underwent complete decay, informants said. If the sorcerer then deserted, it appeared that the victim could never be cured. Shamans' feuds might result, as kinsmen sought revenge on behalf of the victim.

To compound a prescription for love medicine, an Ojibwa would make two tiny dolls, male and female, of wood. Before cutting the wood, he approached the tree, offering tobacco which he smoked or deposited in the ground or on a branch. He begged the tree spirit to regard him kindly and keep off discomforts like frogs or snakes, and he thanked this spirit for the uses he planned. Further, the dolls needed red face-paint. Anciently and historically this would have been made of clay or vegetable dye; and the dye-spirit would have been approached with tobacco and pleading prayers. In the 1930's, a red powder was purchased at the Hudson's Bay stores and incensed with tobacco fumes. Next, the dolls were tied together with native hemp. The women had made this, probably with no special thought of the application to magic, and had observed the requirement of offering tobacco to the growing weed. Next the prepared dolls were wrapped in a small piece of buckskin and the power-wish was muttered over them: that even as the dolls were bound together within this hide, so should the reluctant girl or man in question desire to be clasped to the body of the magician, under his blanket. The magician carried this fetish somewhere on his body, often in the armpit; he stole a hair from the head of the desired one and wrapped it in the little bundle where it too got soaked in his sweat; he rubbed the bundle on his hands along with a love powder (prepared with the same invocations to spirits) and passed his hands over some part of the desired one's body, via the doll—and the victim was secured.

Though it was considered most evil to coerce love or anything else intimate by prescriptions, even the vision might serve for coercion, despite the tenet that vision power was highly beneficent. This evil vision came chiefly from underwater creatures and the windigo spirit; it rode the dreamer. Mrs. Wilson said that sometimes a person was unaware of having been so "blessed" until the diviner discovered that his client's misfortunes were sent by the manito who had been ignored. Will Rogers decided against using his love magic on a reluctant girl and invoked instead his love vision of two charming female guardian spirits; they had declared themselves his spouses and "protectors" in love ventures. He smoked to these spirit women, reminded them of the pact, and they brought him the girl. "They had to." The virtue of the dream, he explained to me, was that it stirred spontaneous desire in the girl, whereas the magic would have forced her. But Will reinforced this subtle move by employing also a certain attraction-prescription whose magic was ampler than the sex sphere and less violent. Bystanders like Mrs. Wilson could not disentangle anything Will did from his midé personality.

Part II

The Midéwiwin

Chapter 4

ORGANIZATION OF THE MIDÉ SOCIETY

A PUZZLING QUESTION about the Midé Society is why it took root at all among these individualistic Ojibwa bands whose traditional ways ignored a political system and supported only loose, short-lived organizations, chiefly for summer games, dances, and war parties, which ended with each occasion. The puzzle feeds on the secrecy that curtained off knowledge of the midéwiwin. When Will Rogers lifted this secrecy for me, it became evident that the traditional rampant individualism actually operated here too. First evidence was Will's personal decision to teach me, without need of consulting his colleagues, or fear of reprisals, and without any interference. My Indian acquaintances nervously retailed the hostile sentiments of Will's midé equals, who saw us studying daily in an empty meadow, using sacred birchbark scrolls, but the midé men pursued matters no further. One old shaman, named Everwind, even contributed mystic tales. Clearly, Will had the right to teach, because of his status as a leading midé of the region, strengthened by his fearsome sorcerer's reputation. And I had the right to Will's instruction because I paid the required fees.

Just as the outsider exposed to casual encounters with a Maggie Wilson or a Will Rogers could never imagine the potency of personality and of shamanistic consequence in an Ojibwa community, so outsiders could not imagine the great energies and ten-

71

sions behind a midé rite, binding its shamans, patients, and witnesses with fierce interests. The long record of American and Canadian governmental neglect and abuse in tribal dealings shows this. While I spent a few short months being tutored by Will in the midé texts and rites that follow, the Indians spent their lives in the heavy shadows cast by midé and other shamanistic personages.

As shown in previous pages, no Ojibwa was a midé shaman solely. This societal aspect was only one of several other aspects composing his complex shaman's whole, and his midé stature actually rested on his private, prior visionary accomplishments. It seems as if a man's midé repute were a public formality acknowledging his sorcerer's power, dangerous from its unique openness, unstable from its group or guild midé ties that were seen as mutual challenges and covert duels. For the standard Ojibwa was trained to solitary mysticism, creative and impassioned. But the Midé Society introduced a collective formal approach to the Supernaturals, employing supposedly traditional tales of origin, hoary songs, and formulas, and it officially ignored private revelations. The excitement of every midé ceremony, for the Ojibwa, was in tracing shamans' and patients' manipulations of the polar values rather than in the official outcome of curing. So much ritual activity was demanded of the patient during the protracted day and night ceremonies that the goal of cure seemed a bare formula at best, for justifying the tremendous sorcerers' performance.

MAIN EVENTS OF THE CEREMONY

A midéwiwin curing lasted through seven or eight daytime or nighttime sessions of closed rites, besides one final day devoted to a public ceremony. Each day the officers recited a fraction of the origin tale about midé functions and organization; this was also an invocation of midé Supernaturals. More was told at higher grades, where fees were higher and officers more numerous, than at lower grades, and the patient was entitled to more midé work and transfer of power. Theoretically, the patient could not skip

72

grades, for he had to be inoculated by the grade-succession to the increments of power discharged into him; nor did he repeat grades. The power emanated from the whole performance and from the sacred shells, the tinier the more powerful, supposedly "shot" into the patient at the end by officers; each shell, called a *migis,* carried a charge of "life." The migis was discharged from the furry hide of a small animal, like otter (see Plate 8), whose spirit master was a midé patron. Each midé initiate and officer personally owned such a mystic hide, called *wayan,* and a number of shells.

The "extracting" and "regurgitating" of shells from the patient's body, by various mannerisms described subsequently, signaled the cure, whereupon midé initiates of all ranks began a dancing round of "shooting" migis shells into one another, to demonstrate their relative powers. Among the Ojibwa, shifting pairs continued shooting one another and singing midé songs or chants of power for hours until the chief midé officer pronounced the ceremony over.

Subsequent to my stay among the Ojibwa, I visited the Prairie Potawatomi of Kansas, who were close cultural and linguistic kinsmen of the Ojibwa, and heard from a young midé shaman about the sorcery contained in the shooting, especially when performed by Oklahoma Sauk. He related, with intense admiration, that Sauk midés would shoot in deadly duelings of power, where dancers fell "dead" in free-for-all dance duels, and the one up longest was considered strongest and victorious. This may well have been only his Potawatomi view. He admired both Ojibwa and Sauk midé powers but did not fail to conclude that he had stayed on his feet until the end, when visiting an Oklahoma Sauk midéwiwin. However, my impression of Emo and Red Lake midé dueling was that it expressed formal fellowship, showing the newly "shot" one that all were colleagues in that he too could now resist the shell, could shoot and be shot, and yet dance and sing. This seems consistent with the Ojibwa's avoidance of open attacks and preference for secretive ones.

The public ceremony, with its endlessly expressed good intentions, could be penetrated by evil doing, tacitly; this was described and anticipated fearfully in classic tales, village gossip, and private conjectures. Even Will Rogers, following a Red Lake midéwiwin at Ponemah village where he was a principal officer, told me how the chief midé officer or an assistant might decide that he had not been feed sufficiently (fees, which were goods always, had to be displayed in advance "for the sun to see") and so curtail the curative "talking." This meant condemning the patient to further suffering. The fact, known instantly to the village, caused sorcery exchanges between families of the patient and the hostile officer. Shamans, resembling ambulance-chasing lawyers among ourselves, would urge the patient's family to hire their services.

Again, the formal, comradely public dueling with migis shells could provide occasion for allegedly vicious assault. This could happen when one party to a dispute was a midé initiate and the other party was not; or when one had reached a higher midé degree of initiation than the other. Mrs. Wilson told me of an occasion involving her daughter Janet at fourteen years of age; a Christian convert, she attended an Emo public rite as an onlooker. Her "sister" cousin (father's brother's daughter), Helen Namepog, was a third-grade midé member participating in the general duel. Helen bore grudges against Janet and during the final dance flung her mink-hide at Janet, so shooting a defenseless person. The family held that Helen had tried to "kill" her cousin. (Janet showed no ill effects, though her mother, telling me the story twelve or more years later, still carried resentment.)

Villagers told me about a local white man who strode drunk into the midé lodge mimicking the shrill staccato singing. The chief officer gravely lifted his wayan and, from a far corner, aimed it and shot. The white man collapsed, writhing in agony with an injured leg and foot. The chief midé let him lie a while, then went to him and declared loudly, "You make fun of us! Do we go to your churches to ridicule? You are drunk, you come here to mock. We are talking sacredly, all the manitos are present, working for the sick one's life, yet you mock. You said you did not believe our power. Now you see: with this migis I stopped you! You should not get well but I will cure you—for it is the purpose of midéwiwin to do good." They carried him into a sweat lodge, worked over him painstakingly, and restored him.

Other happenings appeared to lack such excellent provocation for reprisal with the migis, but gossip reported furtive "shooting" at the comradely formal dance, with terrible effects. Fear of this possibility led mothers to warn children against playing or laughing near a ceremony or near a midé initiate.

The general outlines of midé practices were common knowledge because of the repeated public ceremonies, the many patients who had been midé-cured, and the many who filled the officials' ranks. Certainly information spread through the strong habits of boasting and of gossiping. Much of my information, whose reliability was checked from several others sources, came from Mrs. Wilson, who had never herself been midéwi (subjected to midé ritual) but was connected with midé people through marriage, kinship, and other acquaintance.

But midé shamans tried fiercely to guard details of their secrets. I saw the state of nerves they roused in Mrs. Wilson the summer they suspected she was discussing the Society with me; however, all kinds of shamans intimidated laymen. Midé secrets included two important classes. One was the knowledge taught its doctors, which cured its patients, a matter of open pride. The other was sorcery, practiced surreptitiously for evil gain (see Chapter 3), never acknowledged except in anger or drunkenness. Higher-grade members, like Will Rogers, said that the sorcery was not midé therapy but was learned concurrently with the advanced initiation, and paid for. Was it rooted in the confidential bond between the shaman and the seasoned learner who paid heavily—a pact of brotherhood sealed in evil? Villagers thought so. Of all midé people, it was chiefly the headmen who were suspected of sorcery, which critics said they wielded to get recruits for midéwiwin, earning riches and prestige.

So Red Lake and Emo Ojibwa felt that the very talents to whom they turned for greatest aid were precisely the ones they had to mistrust. But there were none whom they respected equally, and there was no social procedure for controlling sorcerers who had achieved their power legitimately. The principal retributions were through reactive sorcery—"about six months or a year after bad medicine is sent out, it returns to the one that owns it and kills people in the family"—or magic combat with other shamans.

MEMBERSHIP IN THE SOCIETY

The categories of midé membership were (1) patients cured of disease in this life through the Life midéwiwin or treated after death in the Ghost midéwiwin which was the Life's shadow counterpart, (2) ritual officers, and (3) curing shamans or midé doctors. Substitutes represented their dying or dead kinsmen in Life and Ghost rites and themselves benefited from the grade-rite. Similarly, the winter emergency midéwiwin made a midé doctor of the family curer, after he paid the midé officers who had been invoked *in absentia*. Membership in the categories overlapped, but the concepts of functions were distinctly separated. Curing shamans also conducted funerals, apparently always gratis; as the next world was a "midé world," only top midé shamans were to conduct. Among the Canadian Ojibwa I knew in the 1930's, the three funeral priests were also the most prominent of the "bad" shamans—Chief George of Manitou Reserve's Little Fork band, and Gebegabau and Naugumig of the Reserve's Manitou band. Close kin of the deceased were not expected to conduct funerals, because "they are too sad." For a fee, curing shamans assisted with midé formulas at difficult childbirth, their role partly justified by the idea that a birth meant return of the soul of one who had died.

Individuals who had undergone midé curings or "grades of life" (always for ample payment) were classed as patient-members of the Midé Society but not automatically as officers or as curing shamans. An officer received, and usually paid for, special training by helping conduct curing rites. He paid in goods or services, or both, the services alone being usual for close relatives of midé leaders. Most officers were lower-grade patient-initiates, too; but an important officer, occasionally, might never have been midé-cured. One woman was put through all eight grades, at Emo, but this alone did not qualify her as an officer.

In each village assembled at Emo and Red Lake, several men and women would have obtained instruction as midé officers, though women generally were restricted to lesser positions. However, a Little Fork woman, named White Goose, was described as a head midé. In the 1930's five Manitou Reserve women had ceremonial offices. Some offices required the sweat-bath ritual, where direct participation of (usually premenopause) women was forbidden; a woman midé officer could offer a male colleague tobacco and request him to sweat-bathe for her. Close kin often received midé instruction gratis (except for services) or at lower rates; and it was assumed that a midé shaman's family would gain materially from his midé business of curing and officiating at rites. Genealogies documented this. Chief Namepog of Emo begged his (Christian) son, Maggie Wilson's husband, to learn midé skills. The father of Maggie's stepfather (Bunyan) taught his sister and brother's son, gratis, to be the *naganid* officer. Chief George taught his wife and daughters gratis. He himself had learned gratis from his father, and father's two brothers, each a headman of midéwiwin. Chief George's mother, sister, father's brother's wife and two sons, father-in-law, and other near (blood) and affinal kin held high and low midé posts for which they had been prepared by gratis instruction from family relatives. On the other hand, old Bombay (father of a son-in-law of Maggie) had to pay his father-in-law, and Chief George had to pay his collateral "father's brother."

Whether individuals paid kin instructors or not, my numerous genealogical listings from several Ontario and Minnesota localities show that midé activities, of ritual officers and of doctors, ran in bilateral family lines and included both sexes. Chief George paid his "father's brother," named Tebwewadang, probably because he sought him out at Nett Lake, Minnesota, for his renown and because the kinship was largely honorific. (Such kinships were not difficult to establish among these Ojibwa, if only through the gens "brotherhood.") A sophisticated midé doctor occasionally visited other localities to study their lore. This resembled our pursuit of scholarly and professional interests; it enhanced the learner's prestige and his right to command highest fees. Hole-in-the-Sky told me he visited five or six different reservations for this purpose, and he understood my own research in this light. A midé shaman visiting another locality was always snapped up, for colleagues wished to hear his views, and paid for the opportunity.

PRELIMINARIES TO THE MIDÉ CEREMONY

The applicant for a curing chose doctors from among those available locally, though sometimes an eminent midé from elsewhere was invited. Often the applicant selected only the chief officer for his midé curing, and then the latter chose his staff of officers; but the applicant might choose more of the chiefs or even all officers. Selection by both patient and head midé was influenced by immediate factors of summertime neighborhood, personal esteem, and kinship.

An applicant approached kinsmen first, expecting them to charge less. Older multiskilled visionary midé shamans, such as Chief George, Gebegabau, or Naugumig, had the monopoly. They were armed with their terrifying reputations, as Hole-in-the-Sky told me frankly. Why not? This was what the people expected and understood and it was the way supernatural powers functioned. The shamans' creed might have been formulated as "Beware of a humble man," but they did not believe their boasts and threats to be other than genuine. Shamans, in or out of midéwiwin, wanted wealth and constant recognition; they feuded desperately over these. Nepotism was expected, though Chief

78

George was said to be hated for overdoing it by "always" appointing his wife, daughters, son-in-law, and unrelated toadies. Villagers wanted rotation of lesser midé officers, "so everyone will have a chance to get goods," in Mrs. Wilson's words. She thought that her father-in-law, Chief Namepog, rotated fairly among his close kin (brother, daughter, brother's son, deceased cross-cousin's wife and daughter) and unrelated friends (brother's son's unrelated sibmate, and others). But close kin of *equal* midé station did not always work together, as was true of the blood brothers Namepog and Gebegabau, both headmen who always acted separately, perhaps because one refused to subordinate himself to the other. Chief George's alleged undue favoritism and terrorizing were so resented that, gossip said, after his death his family was ignored for midé posts; but other evidence (from canvassing rolls of nominees to posts) contradicted this.

Gossip also accused Chief George of dictating the quantity and quality of his fees. By contrast, complainers invoked a golden age and supposed that formerly midé shamans had been more scrupulous. "The midé doctor will never refuse you if you go to him with cooking . . . fill his pipe . . . tell him, 'I want to be midéwi because I am so lonesome.' Naugumig won't do anything unless you start right off with twenty-five dollars worth of goods." Twenty-five dollars was quite a fortune in the early 1930's. These complaints held a large kernel of admiration, however; for only the strong, with "powers," dared to exploit. The whole situation is echoed when our contemporary legislatures attempt to control excessive price levels maintained by large consumer-goods retailers. Certain Canadian supermarket officials stated at Ottawa hearings of the joint Senate-Commons investigating committee in 1966 that they pegged their profit margins high for lack of competition (Toronto *Globe and Mail,* 21 October 1966). Ojibwa shamans were accused of doing the same, in the early 1930's, by others than close kin.

Application for midéwiwin was always prompted or sanctioned by a personal vision; Hoffman (1891, p. 163) and Skinner

79

(1911, p. 154) commented on this. During the 1930's in Ontario, a woman suffered from miscarriages, stillbirths, and her infants' deaths until her husband dreamed that she needed midé curing while she was pregnant. Yet the next infant died, too. The man dreamed again that the midéwiwin was to be held early in the pregnancy; and the child born following the second midéwiwin lived. Mrs. Albert Cochran (daughter of Chief George) dreamed that "the manito wanted her husband to midéwi, or he would not live to see next fall"; and Mrs. Charlie Namepog dreamed that a midé manito told her to heal her crippled son by "putting him through." "But he didn't live. They hadn't put him through soon enough," as Mrs. Wilson explained. In a similar case, a boy had a broken leg that continued sore until his mother dreamed that he required midé curing. Her Christian husband objected but she, the wife and mother, proceeded to fulfill her dream. The boy did not improve, so people gossiped that his mother had not dreamed but had been coerced by her father, a noted midé shaman.

A bereaved parent sometimes received a vision from the deceased urging a Ghost midéwiwin, at which someone substituted for the deceased "to strengthen his soul"; this was not a power vision. Visions often took the form of interviews with the manito or the deceased relative, but sometimes the vision recommending the Ghost rite took the aspect of a midé ceremony with the dreamer or a relative as the patient. Midé shamans respected the dream injunctions to midéwi. But where her own interests dictated, as in her scorn of Chief George's family, Mrs. Wilson asserted that such visions were manufactured to justify midé manipulations. Thus, she didn't "believe Mrs. Cochran had the dream, she's such a liar"; and she quoted in support an alleged remark of Mrs. Cochran's mother-in-law, "That woman must think she has goods to give away." Though many had such visions in the 1930's still, they appeared less as a midé injunction than as a traditionally indispensable mode of earnest thought, or idiomatic expression.

Of the officials at the public curing ceremony, only the headman, alone or with another, was responsible for the preparatory instruction or private curing of the patient. The instructor or doctor was paid for the private service apart from the public one, as Hoffman (1891, p. 164) observed also in the last century. When a man serviced close relatives, it was likely that another headman would conduct the public ceremony. Thus, Namepog instructed his daughter, but the public rite was conducted by his three brothers and a cousin. Chief George was said to have violated such niceties. Whether he actually did so or not, clearly the violation was conceivable and also rated substandard. Even when a headman required no payment for privately instructing or curing a relative, his office at the public rite (whose incumbent might be another) had to be feed; every other officer also was paid individually for services at the public rite.

MIDÉ PARAPHERNALIA

Midé practices and the underlying, culturally profound devotion to the supernatural have stimulated little in visual arts and crafts. Manitos are shown crudely in the midé rituals: manito Earth is represented by sand, Stones by a stone, Trees by a pole, Birds by a crude carving in wood. Primary colors represent various concepts in midéwiwin but are used more elaborately in secular matters. Beadwork decorates clothing and may also decorate medicine sacks of shamans (see Plate 8). The most pleasing religious forms are the midéwiwin's birchbark scrolls and their pictographs (see Plates 6, 7, and Figures 1, 3); yet these are crude. Tangible arts are minimal in Ojibwa devotions. The tradition cultivated, however, poetic forms, ideas, and words that move like mighty characters in folklore, origin tales, invocations, philosophy, and daily story-telling.

The material equipment of a midé person could have two sources. Some was acquired during instruction and some was bequeathed. The equipment included the birchbark records, the wayan or midé medicine bag, migis shells, midé doll, mystic rattle, and mystic drum. Birchbarks, wayan, shells, and doll were

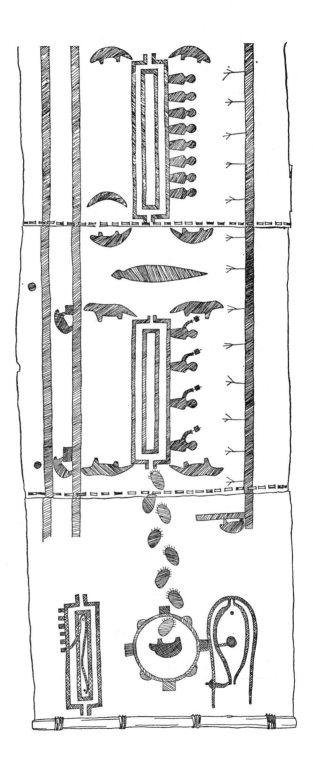

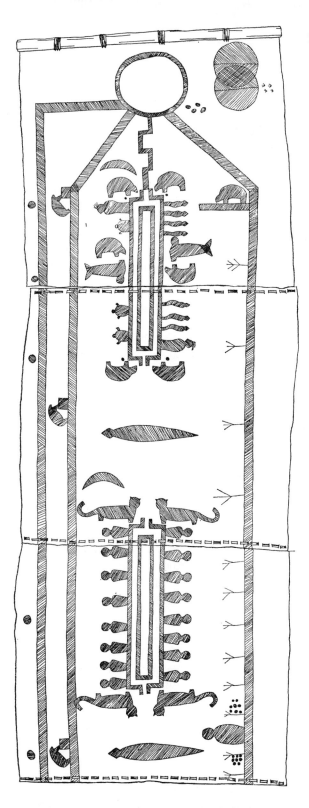

Figure 1 (*facing pages*). An artist's tracing of the scroll made by Will Rogers to record the Life midéwiwin. Courtesy of the Milwaukee Public Museum. The original scroll measures 16½ × 85 inches.

changed and elaborated with advancing grades. Rattle and drum were appurtenances of special offices. All paraphernalia was owned individually: lending was for brief, specific periods, such as an evening rite honored by a distinguished midé outsider who had forgotten his equipment.

Sometimes midé people had their paraphernalia burned after death. This was mentioned by Alanson Skinner in 1911 (p. 168). In the 1930's I heard of several instances, at Ontario and Minnesota locations: Dave Medicine requested his wife and brother to do this for him in Ontario; at Redgut Bay, the birchbarks of Ten Feathers (Medassoguneb) had been burned because the old shaman had no family to bequeath them to.

Some people abandoned mystic possessions, secreting them in clean bush, as I discovered also among the Kansas Prairie Potawatomi. Like others mentioned earlier, in Chapter 3, a great Ojibwa midé shaman at Bowstring Lake, Minnesota, in the 1930's, threw his paraphernalia in the bush and forswore midéwiwin because all of his family had died following his use of sorcery learned from midé colleagues. The case of Billy M'Ginnis, also mentioned earlier, was similar. Will Rogers presented me with the handsome birchbarks from which he taught me Life and Ghost midéwiwin, especially as recorded in texts of the following pages. I kept these over thirty years before entrusting them to the Milwaukee Public Museum. And his vigorous spirit seemed to live in them. In giving them to me for safekeeping, he must have confronted the ending of his career and his existence on earth, though he never used the words. His acts were eloquent enough. His cheery words expressed rather expectations of his Thunderbird manito life after death. The only despair he conveyed to me was in final letters complaining that his wife had abandoned him to a federal institution. Over twenty years later, a Potawatomi midé shaman, then in his vigorous fifties, wrote me despairingly that, though he had a fine family, he felt himself "the last Indian" and must go; he died shortly, in the state of mind that seemed to dominate traditional shamans who abandoned their great paraphernalia.

84

TEACHING MIDÉ LORE

During midé rites, the declamations of narrative were often interrupted by songs; the words of some of these are given in Chapter 6. Though some people knew the personal authorship of particular songs, it was dogma that all songs had been revealed in the original vision and bequeathed, for subsequent visions were not supposed to have been introduced. Yet Hole told me how he combined tradition with innnovation and spoke of a noted shaman, then deceased, who had received midé visions just thirty years before containing songs that he brought, as manito-instructed, into the rites. In her study of Chippewa music, Frances Densmore (1913, p. 34) affirms the point: "The songs most nearly related in origin are the Mide, the dream, and the war songs, as many songs said to have been 'composed in dreams' were used in the ceremonies and practices of the Mide and also on the warpath. The songs classified as 'dream songs' were given as such by the singers." This stylistic discontinuity between practice and certain conventional assertions may not have seemed as important to the tribe as it does to the foreign scholar, or it may not have seemed even a discontinuity. Possibly the dogma of original revelation was an idiom, like our own about the Bible, stressing mystery and anonymous authorship, the only copyright for a preliterate society.

While dogmatizing that nothing individual or modern was added to the original midé tradition, shamans lamented the steady loss of tradition. They said it resulted from midé shamans' rivalries and it harmed midéwiwin. A midé leader, it was known, hated to surrender his learning and skills to pupil or patient, for these were his "power" and "life." His reasoning was the same as a visionary's, though according to dogma, midé lore was open for purchase, like certain herbal lore outside the Society. The vision pursuit, cultivated by solitary individuals, chiefly boys and men, imposed on each the tabu of absolute verbal secrecy, even at the point of death. It clashed, in midé surroundings, with the injunction both to teach midé lore and to study with the

85

masters of midé power. Terrible conflicts resulted in shamans' minds; a midé's logic was trapped in the conviction that by sharing lore or power, he betrayed his life, or was tricked into betraying it.

A midé shaman's complete knowledge of Society rites in the Life and Ghost departments was recorded with mnemonic figures and pictographs, as curvilinear and angular outlines, on birchbark scrolls. Under his teachers' directions, finally on his own authority, the great shaman scratched these on the fleshy inner surface of the outer bark peeled from the tree in spring by his wife or himself. Each pictograph represented a small idea-complex, barely standardized. The script of any individual was peculiarly his own and no one else could fully read it. Meanings of one man's scripts must be interpreted to a reader—there is no general key, the meaning of each element being limited to that composition. The symbols were intended to veil meanings from other than the one shaman. I understood all this under Hole's instruction, hearing him decipher one of his patternings as a man, another as Bear, a third as announcing death, and so on.

Ojibwa hunters and travelers left pictographic notices along their trails for members of the party. These were usually single figures, like a gens eponym, connoting a "Kilroy was here" and moving on; the eponym pictograph, hung upside down, was also a grave-marker. However, the midé shaman was the only one with enough news for extensive recording, and he felt driven to restrain its dissemination.

Hole suffered consequences when studying midé lore with a Leech Lake kinsman. This shaman, in the usual way, dawdled years, teaching desultorily from his scrolls until he died. But he had left the Ghost rites untaught to Hole, though he bequeathed its scroll, useless without the dead sorcerer's interpretations. Hole even felt that an untaught scroll could not belong to the supposed heir, for its mystic contents threatened danger when handled without knowledge.

Like the solitary visionary's invocations, the midé shaman's declamations in the Society lodge were impromptu, though observing the need to present portions of the origin tale, admonitions, and recommendations. Details of an officer's "sacred talking" varied from one occasion to another. All speeches had to include minimum salutations to human and spirit listeners and also protestations of the speaker's humbleness—but no more. Stress was laid on sincerity, a man having to present himself as honest and forthright before midé patrons or suffer retribution. Speakers have taken midé occasions to announce their (midé) revelations, as when introducing songs; some have threatened retributive illness; dead forebears were said to have introduced divination to learn outcomes of midé therapy. Hole presented his interpretations of the midé afterworld, as told later. He also commented that midéwiwin had elaborated itself extraordinarily, since first revealed to the ancestral Cutfoot, through revelations announced by "Great Ones" in the midé lodge. He thought some shamans foisted dream contributions excessively but could not be halted. He conceded that the rites had changed externally, in form, but not in essentials.

As the visionary mumbled the dream invocation with deliberate unintelligibility, so many midé shamans chanted low and rapidly. Hole complained strongly to me about this trick of Everwind, who had invited him to join a midé rite at Ponemah: "That's wrong! He should speak out! so that everybody [in the lodge] can benefit." And as the vision shaman abbreviated vengefully his therapeutic invocation when the patient's advance displays of the fee did not satisfy, so the displeased midé shaman abbreviated his chants.

THE GHOST MIDÉWIWIN

Midé theory described the after-death world as an enlarged society of Earth-initiated midé persons. There, Indians who had never been midéwi were without place. Hence their Earth-survivors might resort on their behalf to a Ghost midéwiwin (see Chapter 8). The passage from life was considered tricky, beset with personified evils intent on murdering the wandering soul. Hence, midé instruction and specific recommendations to the personified evils were required for a soul's safe conduct and arrival, finally to be welcomed by the hereafter's host and hostess, who were midé Supernaturals. Safe passage was managed in the sacred talk given over the grave of the deceased by a chief midé officer, whom the mourning family solicited. My Emo list of funerals one year showed that of six midé funerals, four were conducted by two men chosen solely, it seemed, for their shamans' reputations (Landes, 1937a, p. 135). Midé ceremonials were only additions, however, to gentile and kinship obligations always attending the deceased and his closely related survivors. The latter colored all of daily life, especially for the first one or two years following a death. As with the vision pursuit, the Ojibwa had no being apart from them (Landes, 1937a, chaps. 2, 3).

Though the Life midéwiwin was graded, the Ghost midéwiwin lacked grading of its own, in Hole's version. As a ceremony for a promised but now deceased patient, it attended only the patient's "shadow" and was a shadow counterpart of the appropriate Life grade. In the 1930's, it was the same rite that would have been conducted for the living patient. Now the deceased was represented by a kinsman or kinswoman; the lodge was faced north and south instead of Life's east and west, and some lodge furnishings were rearranged symbolically. Speeches in the Ghost lodge described the after-life. The details derived from common knowledge and from visions. Hole-in-the-Sky mentioned his own revelations of the hereafter, where he "visited" and spoke with Supernaturals; he amplified in Ghost lodge speeches. Each period seemed to know of men who "died" briefly and were transported to the new realm of experience; this was also phrased as receiving visions consistent with midé views. Hole asserted that his views were genuine because revealed, whereas others' knowledge was bought, and suffered errors in the oral transmission.

Chapter 5

MIDÉ ORIGIN TALES

SOME ORIGIN TALES were known to all Ojibwa. A number, which included esoteric versions of the common tales, were classed as secret property of the Midé Society; their general intent was to depict midéwiwin as a treasury of wisdom. Creation stories about the first Indian were familiar in unlike versions that coexisted even in the same villages at Manitou and Red Lake locations. Some appeared more Judaeo-Christianized than others, some contained more detail. The chief differences seemed linked to the status of the midé story-teller, when one narrator was a learned shaman and another a simple Society member. A relevant sanction threatened danger from casual narration in secular surroundings by a layman; it was one with the danger in chattering lightly of manitos. As man's creation was involved with his death, that is, with the establishment of human death, it tempted Fate to discuss these idly. Man's creation led to midéwiwin; the death-telling belonged to the Ghost rites.

CREATION OF MAN

Several tales were told me voluntarily by Ojibwa with whom I was already acquainted. One narrator was Everwind, the high midé shaman at Red Lake's Ponemah village—a respected man of seventy or more. When the matter first arose, he produced a scanty tale, stripped drastically, as he might do in the lowest

grade of the midéwiwin. Weeks later he offered much amplifica-
tion, explaining, "There are many things I'm not supposed to talk
about [secularly] but I will tell you anyway." Hole-in-the-Sky
must have prevailed on him, in a diplomatic sharing of the wealth
(since I paid informants); surely also, Everwind could not resist
vying with him. He narrated the first version in Ojibwa as Hole
translated:

First a woman was born and then a man was born. When the
woman was put down in this world, the Maker sent four men to do
the work necessary for making a world. They provided two of everything, as male and female. Two men worked on the Earth and two
on the Sky. The woman wondered how she would multiply. So the
Great Spirit allowed the woman a man, knowing her wishes. Thus
Indians originated. The man and wife had four children. One child
died; so death began among the Indians. The dead was a fourth son
and he was caused to die by a trick of Nehnehbush. This may have
happened when the Indians lived at the Gulf of Mexico along the
Mississippi, before the people dispersed and different languages
evolved.

The Great Spirit made this world, then he made a human being,
then he made two animals of a species, then he made two fowls. The
two animals and two fowls were manitos serving the Great Spirit,
who empowered them to work on Earth and to make new subordinates.
All manitos having to do with the Indian were created by these four
manitos. When the fowls had finished their work of making more
subordinates for the Great Spirit, they reported accordingly. The
two animals did likewise.

After this report, the Great Spirit met with the subordinate Spirits
in the very center of the world, and the first Indian was invited also
to the assembly. At his creation, the Indian's body had been enameled
with a plate, like a finger nail. At the meeting, the first Indian was told
that sickness could not penetrate his enamel, so he was capable of
perpetual life. All other things were established in the assembly that
the human would follow forever: the Dream was given. It was established that when a manito desired to offer a human a dream, he
would need the consent of all Spirits. Before an Indian came to life,
his dream must be discussed by all Spirits in council where, as at the
first assembly, each man's length of life would be determined and
also the cause of his personal death.

This was how the Great Spirit created the first Indian. He picked up dirt and shut his hand. Feeling something move in his hand, he opened it and saw a human being. The Great Spirit placed the human on Earth saying, "Now take four breaths." When the human did this, he established air, the breathing element. Told to breathe four times more, he did and established the heavens, another breathing element, so creating air for Earth and above. This first Indian, made from earth, was destined for Earth, and if ever he died, he must be buried in earth because he had been made from it.

The fowl Spirits gave the first Indian seeds of many kinds to raise gardens. Also he was given a bow and arrow, though told by the Spirit, "You cannot use the bow and arrow as you will these seeds. Bow and arrow kill animals occasionally but the seeds I give you will provide better living. And I give you a tool for remembering: it is writing. Use it, it can never be erased, it will last generations."

And the human was told that, spring and fall, he must sacrifice to the Characters [as the manitos were termed when figuring in their tales]. Sacrifices would protect his life. After this, the Characters left the Indian.

At the assembly, the Indian had noticed that the Characters were two of a kind, of animal, bird, and fish. And she [the female gender appeared in Hole's English but cannot appear in Ojibwa] wondered why she was all by herself—for the first Indian was a woman. All the Characters read her thoughts. The Indian requested that the animal [of Earth] or fowl [of Sky] Spirit make her an Indian companion. A Spirit was named to meet this wish. As the woman slept, he moved around her to see if he could detach a part of her body from which to shape another Indian. Finally he removed the woman's lower rib. So on wakening, the woman found herself lying with another person, made like herself. That is why a woman has fewer ribs, on both sides, than a man.

The grant of her wish reduced the powers first given her. For when the man wakened and looked about, he saw animals, killed one with the bow and arrow, and they ate it. When this meat was gone, he killed again. Afterwards he hunted regularly, to keep them in stock. They preserved meat by drying. The man would not stop hunting and did not care for the seeds given them. He would use only bow and arrow.

The fowl Spirits, who had given the seeds, noticed they were not being used. So they asked the humans their intentions. The man replied he did not need seeds, having sufficient food otherwise. A Character declared, "Then I will take back the seeds. Since you do not use writing either, I will take that back. Instead I put memory in your head. Had you chosen seeds, your living would be easier and better. Your preference for hunting causes you much sweat, a hard life."

Thus the Indian forfeited the chance of such a life as the white man enjoys today. The Indian considers the white man manito because of his achievements.

But the fate and nature of the first Indian were not yet complete. God had set a date for a second assembly of his Spirits, where all of Earth's dead and living humans were to appear, and they would discuss and renew what had been determined at the first assembly.

Nehnehbush wondered how the system would work. He waited until the first humans had four children when he journeyed all over Earth to discover its size. Thus he concluded that if Indians lived perpetually, the continent could not float them all, for the population's weight would sink it. So he determined to destroy the principles established by the first assembly. But how to do this? He sought out a particular Character who felt slighted by not having received an invitation to this assembly. Reaching the location of this Character, Nehnehbush found him gone and went over the world in search, weeping from fatigue as he traveled. [Tears are the prime tool for wresting Supernaturals' pity, in Ojibwa thought.] Towards the rising sun, he met a Character who helped, speaking but invisible, asking why he wept. Nehnehbush said, "I seek the one who was neglected at the Spirits' council." The Character directed him towards the other's tracks, explaining that, unaided, "You won't be able to find him."

So Nehnehbush reached the place where the Character had halted and pondered over what kinship to claim. Deciding, he greeted him, "Why did you come here, elder brother?" The other replied, "I came to live in poverty the rest of my days, here," pointing to the ground where he sat, bare of plants. "I was left out of the first assembly which told the Indian to make sacrifices [of food and tobacco to the Spirits]. So I never will receive anything, I will be without food and tobacco during all time to come."

Nehnehbush said, "My elder brother, can you break the laws they established for the human?" "No." "Please do! Break them." "Nehnehbush, I may not." Nehnehbush persisted. The Character resisted, "No, I cannot. What you desire is evil for man." Nehnehbush prostrated himself on the ground and wept before his "brother," then rose to coax his brother more, promising that if he broke the laws, Indians would offer him sacrifices in memory of their departed dead and that "I will make you as beautiful as possible."

So the Character responded, "Now, Nehnehbush [indicating cold-ness by ignoring the reciprocal kinship term], it is foolish to ask this. It brings great injustice to the Indian. Yet it is not hard for me to do and I *will* do it."

Then Nehnehbush began to ornament his brother. He took silver and made scales, in between which he placed gold scales. "Well, my elder brother, you can move." So today Indians consider this Char-acter to be the foremost one because he violated all laws established by all other Characters. [This suits Ojibwa thoughts about shamans' duels.] He is called "the great black stone," *Mishi magade wabig*.

Nehnehbush left his brother. A great traveler, he could not remain fixed.

Because Nehnehbush told his brother to move, the latter did so, and all he did was reflected on the heavens [from the glittering scales]. The Character moved towards the rising sun and at one place sur-faced on Earth where he observed the first humans. He submerged to move closer to them. He surfaced again at a rapids to observe the humans, submerged, surfaced at Lake Superior, the "great water," *Gitchi gummi*, where a peninsula jutted out, holding a small lake. At this lake, the Character surfaced and saw Indians close by on the sandy beach. A child, playing there, saw the Character and ran. The Character plucked off a scale and offered it to the child, urging it to come. The child did so. But as he grasped the scale, the enamel cover-ing his own body all fell off, leaving just remnants at finger and toe ends—the nails. Nehnehbush was traveling afar then but, at hearing the Indians' cries, he knew that his "brother" was violating the other Spirits' laws.

So he returned in search of his "brother" and found him with an Indian. Nehnehbush spoke, "Elder brother, you have done a grievous thing," and asked him to correct it. [Ojibwa listeners laugh at this "foolish" contradiction of the Trickster.] His brother replied, "Nehneh-bush, it is you, not I, who do this great injustice to the Indian! You must be very careful. You must discover how the Indian is to overcome this misery, caused by your own folly and wrongdoing." When Nehnehbush had first contemplated violating the manito laws, he had planned not final death but a temporary condition, like fainting. Now matters had gone too far at his brother's hands.

Thus was the Indian created in his present nature. From this wrong-doing was established a land for the dead. This is all I have to say.

Hole listened attentively to Everwind, as he did to all from whom he felt he could learn, and he translated carefully, restrict-

93

ing himself to this chore, never attempting interpretation or comment in Everwind's presence. The courtesy was impressive. It seemed that Everwind understood enough English to follow and approve of Hole's version. As the length of the second version suggests, he warmed to his subject. Perhaps he felt that I was prepared to receive it, in view of Hole's instruction. He must have felt certain that he was not giving out anything novel to Hole, for he would have kept this "secret" and demanded pay. Actually, it was thin material compared with the versions Hole gave me, which appear subsequently.

An elderly lay midé initiate at Ponemah offered me his recollection of the tale as he had heard it in midé lodges, and Hole translated:

After God created the universe, he picked up dirt and made the first Indian. He picked up more dirt in the other hand and made a woman. So he made two humans [Indians]. From these two, the people multiplied. The man was given a bow and arrow to kill game for a living. That was the only thing God gave the Indian with which to make a living.

The poverty of this version is arresting, though as an outline it adheres well to Everwind's. The reason for the poverty is conjectural, due perhaps to a layman's ignorance, or indifference, fear of tampering with mysteries proper to shamans, or an aged man's individual peculiarities.

Hole-in-the-Sky had been a chief midé shaman for years at Minnesota's Cass Lake settlements, besides those at Leech Lake and environs. His tales dispensed entirely with Christian terms and allusions, such as God. His divine agents were always the great bird and animal Supernaturals. But his incidents and plots were essentially the same as those told by others.

He told how anciently a Snake approached the first, spirit midé lodge as it was undergoing construction:

[Snake] wrapped himself clear around the wigwam—one side was shaded by this. The guardian Tiger [or Lion] asked, "Why is this? It seems you do not plan to direct the Indian rightly." [This reflects traditional mistrust of Snake, who therefore is merged with Christianity's devil.] Snake took a handful of dirt and opened his hand to show an Indian was there. It was black. Tiger slapped his hand, knocked out the dirt, and said they were not to leave the matter so. Tiger grabbed a handful of sand, opened his hand, and there was an Indian, glistening like glass. "So will we treat the Indian" [that is, light and handsome, not dark and ugly].

Hole knew about the enameled human but was uncertain about the circumstances that caused him first to gain and then to lose his enamel. He was certain only of Tiger's creations from sand: first an Indian man in the right hand, then an Indian woman in the left hand.

ORIGIN OF MIDÉWIWIN

The great "mystery" of midéwiwin was a long tale about the origin and development of the rites. These and the Society's organization were presented as dramatizations of first events revealed to the primordial Indian Cutfoot in an eight-years' series of visions. At succeeding initiations, the patient or novice was told or "given" increments of the inherited revelation. The Ojibwa termed a totality of "dreams" about one theme, such as curing or war, a single vision, the separate dreams of the series being related items or installments doled out or taught by the Spirit patron. A shaman's recital of the hoary origin tale through installments was the required form, carried over from the vision pattern. The difference between the two situations was great, since the midé initiate placed his faith in the oral tradition and the visionary placed his in the direct hallucinatory experience. But one faith was never challenged in terms of the other, as Christianity and native religion were not challenged in one another's terms.

Manitos of the origin visions and tales were represented by the shamans presiding at a midéwiwin. These officers spoke of one another as "manito," as did the commonalty when in the lodge, with the qualification that these were midé manito. Some "Supernaturals," appointed by the four chief officers of a midé un-

dertaking, remained silent throughout, background to the declaimed tale, dancing, sitting, and feinting at shooting a shell occasionally, as directed.

At a ceremony, the officers used kinship address, real or fictive,
as the true, original Supernaturals were said to have done. Hence,
the midé officer, like a vision patron, called also the patient by a
kinship term, real or fictive. This was not required for other curing relationships by visionary doctors or herbal curers.

For the first midé grade where the cure was simplest and the
fees smallest, the origin tale was only sketched out (as in Everwind's first version, above). The tale had to be embroidered (like
Everwind's second version) for higher grades, with their more
elaborate curings and fees. Hole said the fullest version was told
at fourth grade, last of the "good" ones, certainly at Cass Lake
where he had long been chief midé officer. This would have
held, too, for eighth grade, as the second set of four grades
should repeat the first four, except that the latter's locale was
mythic Earth and the former's locale was mythic Sky.

For many weeks I studied the origin tale with Hole, transcribing text from his speeches and the pictographs of his scroll, working out the allusions, separating it from other midé ritual and
other "sacred talks." When finally systematized, it seemed slight,
much dramatized in the telling and by other ritual enactments,
and much repeated. Also, repetitions appeared contradictory, but
this may well be the illusion of outside (research) standards. On
the other hand, consistency and order cannot be expected from
an old oral tradition nor in a community that tabus open questioning and criticism.

Narration of the midé origin tale always opened with a statement that the Earth-Supernatural, called The Shell-Covered
One, or simply Shell, brooded over the olden Indian's unhappy
plight and sought a remedy. For the Indian was vulnerable to
disease and death, since losing his enamel-armor and receiving
Nehnehbush's gift of mortality. Anguished, Shell cast about for
aid over the four layers of Earth, until he noticed the Great Spirit

96

above. Hopefully he sent his servitor Bear to him, requesting a consultation. This took place and Shell offered a plan of providing Indians with health and long life through midéwiwin. Great Spirit assented, saying he too had nursed the plan. They summoned the Spirits to council and all assented "because it was for the Indian's benefit." Shell's servitor Bear was directed to organize midéwiwin. In Ojibwa idiom, he was given the midé "pack of life" to deposit at various stations. His path was described in detail, from Earth's bowels to the water's surface, from the east near Niagara to the west at different stops near the prairies. During the journey or at its close, in some versions, the midé rite was revealed to Cutfoot and later he taught it to the Indians. The tale did not mention ritual songs, speeches, and divinatory tests (the last particularly being considered modern accretions) for they did not appear in the great ancestral vision. One specific accretion was explained—the establishment of the second set of four grades, called Sky midéwiwin.

Sky ceremonies arose, not from a vision, but because a patient continued ill through all Earth grades of therapy. Shamans would not abandon him. One argued that four additional grades of power were available because Sky Supernaturals had supported heartily the ancient meeting summoned by Shell and Great Spirit —now was the time to provoke their pity. The patient was cured and Sky rites were established, modeled upon those of Earth, patronized however by Above creatures, Shell being replaced by Great Spirit and Bear by Eagle.

As Hole taught me, the leader of midé rites opened thus:

I will try to say a little. I salute that place [where the patient sits], I salute our Grandmother [cedar bough] with her head [boughs] spread on the floor [towards the fire]. Two [or whatever number conforms to the patient's present grade rite] branches [of cedar] he [the patient] brought from which to draw life [as cedar is a midé manito]. Now this white beach sand [in the ritual it carries an esoteric designation] I salute. Two [or whatever number corresponds with the grade] bars of sand he brought to rest his life on. Now I salute the middle [the depth] of Earth where he [Bear servitor] left the midé

97

manito to take care [of midéwiwin]. The Indian salutes when he requests. So now I salute the bottom layer of Earth [where Shell is] . . . I salute the Person-Covered-with-Shell!

Here started the origin tale proper:

Shell began to ponder at learning that the Indian's life had been curtailed, for this altered the original arrangement. Shell manito thought long and steadily. Then he decided [upon midéwiwin]. [But he doubted] "I guess I cannot do it." So he searched for a manito of equal power [to aid him] and saw none. Then up above he looked. Up there [the fourth, top layer of Sky] he saw a midé manito [midé is the indispensable respect-prefix in this context] sitting. He called him down [both were of equal power]; he came; Shell spoke, "Well, here is why I called you. It is too bad this has befallen our Indian, after his life was to last forever. I want you to aid me in a plan to pass my manito strength on to the Indian."

[The Great Spirit answered] "Ho! Thank you for your plan for the Indian. Actually you are just ahead of me, for I was intending a similar thing, practically the same but a little different. This will be good for the Indian. Call all the manitos of Earth; tell them of this that we plan. And I, too, will tell those up there with me."

So Shell called our Grandfather [kinship term for Bear, in the midéwiwin], "There now, go and look for the midé manitos." And he started for the daylight place [east]. He went there. Then to where the land turns blue [south] he went. Then to the land whence comes the strong wind [west] he went. Then to where the land turns white, whence comes the cold air [north] he went. Then he returned to whence his master had sent him.

And now they [the invited manitos] entered. Then he [Shell] spoke, "I'll tell you why I asked you to come here. They [Supernaturals] had planned his [the Indian's] life to be eternal [but this was destroyed]. [We ask you] to help us [Shell and Great Spirit]. I want to give the Indian my manito power [literally, "doings" or midéwiwin]. Help us!"

"Oh, thank you! You will benefit the Indian. We will help." When the midé manitos rose, they were sixteen in number. They approved of midéwiwin.

He [Shell] told our Grandfather [Bear] he was to handle that [gift of midéwiwin] himself and bring it to the Indian. Bear reared himself [with his pack of midé rites]. He turned around [clockwise] once [the number conforms with the degree of the patient], and he was black. He found near him a midé [cedar] tree. He pushed the midé

98

tree up [to the second Earth layer]. There he turned red. He reached up one layer of Earth pushing the tree through, and made a hole where he built a manito wigwam. There he placed two manitos. [He said to them] "And now you must reach out and satisfy [the Indian], giving him anything he requests." He made another run, shoved the tree up to the next layer, and he was yellow. Again he made a hole, and there too, he built a manito wigwam. He placed [three, because this is the third layer of Earth] midé manitos there: "From here you will reach out to give the Indian what he desires." So again he pushed the tree up. Again he reached up to Earth, and made a hole in it [the topmost and fourth layer], and stayed there [looking around] four days [midé years] with his head sticking out of the ground. At this place he turned white. He stayed there trying to decide where to travel to find the Indian. His head out, he looked to the daylight land, and went over.

From there he came down the hill [as eastern country is supposed to be steeper than western] and to the great midé water by which we are surrounded. [This refers to Lake Superior.] Then he did not know what to do. "I cannot get across with this pack I carry to my Indian. How will I manage?" He touched the water with outstretched fingers of his right hand, but could accomplish nothing [by way of controlling the water]; he could not see that it made any difference [in calming the waves]. Then with the other side [fingers of the left hand] he touched the water again, and the waves went still as ice, quieting the midé waters. He stepped on top of the ocean and did not even bend the water.

Hole also gave another version of the paragraph above:

He went to the daylight land. From there he traveled downhill. On his way he heard something behind him. He stopped and looked back. He saw somebody on his trail, and was afraid. Arriving close, this looked like an Indian, but was not—it was a manito. He realized the manito was planning to aid him, walking along with him a little way. When they came in sight of the great midé water, the manito took his own trail. [Hole-in-the-Sky interpolated, whispering that this Being was the Moon, always called only "our colleague."] Our Grandfather reached the water. The wind was blowing so that the ocean was white. Our Grandfather said to himself, "What am I to do? I cannot get across with this pack." He saw a big point jutting from the mainland. He was certain there was another shore to this ocean, went to the point to look across but could see nothing. He returned to where he had first seen the ocean and examined the other direction. He noticed

99

a point there, too, went to it and looked about but could see no sign of land on the other side of the water. He said to himself, "What will I do?" It was too rough to swim across, so he decided to travel on the ocean bottom.

The first version continues:

"Well, then," he said, "I guess I'll go under [the waters] to find him [the Indian]. I'll walk between the top and bottom of the waters. I'll creep up on him from there." Walking along, it seemed daylight. "I believe I will look for Indians." So he reached the top and looking across he discerned dark streaks, like clouds. He said to himself, "I don't want anything to bother me" [willing away the possible disturbance]. The ocean was smooth as glass and he started swimming on the surface instead of going to the bottom. Finally he reached land. "I see close by a rocky island." He reached it and went up. Arising, he sounded like rattling icicles and these were manito shells. Again he started out and soon descried some blackness on his course, which he saw was land. He rushed for it, to try himself against it, struck it, and the land burst open. Earth rumbled, and Sky also. Thunder sounded.

He found himself on top of a mountain and stayed a while. A small lake had formed in a crack on the mountain top. He brought the water down with him and made a river. We call that now the French [or Montreal?] river [*monia zibing*].

He left his [midé] pack on the sunny side of the river and placed a manito in charge. He intended to trace the chain of [Great?] lakes. Returning, he took up the pack and started for the west end of Lake Superior.

At Birch Point, he set them [guardian spirits of this local midé lodge], saying: "From here you will hand the Indian whatever he requests." Again he went off. At Open Beach he established a midé manito: "And now from here you will satisfy the Indian's needs when he so requests." Once again he left. At Flag[weed] Bay, he set up midé manitos: "Now from here you, too, will hand the Indian whatever he requests." And again he started off. He went to Yellow Hammer Beach, made a small lake there, and set down four midé manitos [an unusually large number, indicating a sort of headquarters, Hole thought], saying: "At this place you must take care of the Indians." He went down to Narrow Bar on the lake, and outside its door stood his midé servitor: "When an Indian offers [tobacco, food, furs, in exchange for blessings], you take all and hand it inside [the midé wigwam to the guardian spirits]."

Again he went off. At Narrow Bough Point [Fond du Lac?] he set down a midé manito on each side: "And you, too, from here you will hand the Indian whatever he requests."

He rose on his hind feet and looked west, saw no Indians, and knew his work was over. But later, Indians went west and carried [the tale of] Bear's travel to Red Lake—but that is not how the old tale [vision] went.

All that accomplished, the midé manito [Bear] commenced [new activities]. He rose with the midé rattler: at the middle of Earth he sounded it. But not hearing, many midé manitos did not respond. "He [the Indian, for whom this was being tested] cannot use that," he [Shell] said to him [Bear]. "Well, I have been thinking about it [a noise-maker the Indian could use in midéwiwin to draw the attention of the manitos] and I will get it. Go now for a manito [to aid us]."

He [Bear] left. When he returned [Shell asked], "Did you find him?" "I saw an old man, very old, almost of an age to die." "That will be the one. Go call him."

Bear left. "I am calling you! That One sitting there [Shell] is who calls you!"

Then he [the oldster] came and he [Shell] spoke to him: "Will you not go and help the Indian with a voice?" [The oldster answered] "Thank you. So that is what you want me to do. I will do it."

So he went to the center of Earth. The manitos talked low to one another: "I don't believe the Indian can handle this easily." [The old man turned himself into a drum for midé use. The manito guardians supposed that if the entire man turned into a drum, the result would be far too cumbersome for Indian strength.] Then he [the old man] flew to pieces [by whirling clockwise a number of times, the number being that of the patient's grade]. Our Grandfather [Bear] then took one piece.

Well, now, our colleague [term exchanged among midé members and officers and among guardian spirits of midéwiwin] with short arms [the Otter; another epithet is "our colleague who travels everywhere and rapidly"] was in the land whence daylight comes. And he thought, "Well, I will see what they are doing for the Indian." Running along, he reached the doorway of the manito wigwam and ran right in as fast as possible, circling [clockwise] the midé way. Twice [or the number corresponding to the midé grade of the patient] he circled, dropped over [the drum, leaving his hide as a cover], and left.

Old Loon was in the south. He thought, "I will go see what they have in mind for the Indian." He reached the entrance to the manito

101

lodge, ran in as fast as possible, circling like a midé. He circled twice [or the number that corresponds with the grade of the patient], stretched his head over [the drum], and there appeared a drumstick [of his legs]. Then a manito visitor [Snake] entered, circled the midé way, and wound himself about the bottom rim [of the drum]. Another entered and curled around the top rim.

Hole interpolated, in low tones respectful of the midé guardians, and in English for my benefit only, "They were fixing up the midéwiwin, setting it just like a table for a meal, so the Indian could use it when he was ready." This interpolation occurred during an early stage of transcribing the text of the origin tale, when we were working in the Ojibwa language. The tale continues:

Bear stood on his hind legs and said, "Thus will our Grandfather [the drum] look. Thus will the Indian do forever."

Another manito [Snake] visitor came there [the midé lodge] to see it too. He wrapped himself all around the lodge, and one side of his body cast shade on it [the shade exposed his evil purpose]. The old [and big] Lion [or Tiger] spoke to him. "Why this? I doubt you will do the Indian any good. You are not intending rightly." Lion slapped his hand and knocked dirt out of it, which he saw was to be an Indian. He said, "You will not use the Indian that way!" Then he [Lion] grasped a handful of sand and opened his fist to show an Indian, glistening. "This is what we will do with the Indian. . . . It is better for you [Snake] to stay out yonder [outside the lodge], no closer than within echoing distance of a child's voice. You can take offerings of tobacco from there and sometimes there you may be of aid, perhaps to a child who dies. This is how you may be able to help the Indian." Then the manito sat down.

The midé lodge was crowded with manitos [who agreed], "Thus will the Indian do on Earth. This will the Indian use. This is what the manitos give the Indian. [Henceforth] the Indian himself will carry on what they [the Spirits] are giving him. Thus will he live on Earth, if he is to live long. All the manitos will aid him. This is the power we give the Indian. This is how he must do on Earth, and we will not avert our heads [ears] when he petitions but will aid him with all his needs. Nowhere else will we bend our heads [give prior attention]."

This was given to the ancient Indian, and they showed him how, made certain to show him aright, saying he must explain clearly to

102

future Indians. "The Indian himself must cherish what the manitos teach him, for he must go on alone with it!" All the manito people were satisfied and said, "Thanks, that we will attend to."

The Great Spirit advised him [Shell]: "Tell us when you are ready [to bring midéwiwin from its birthplace in the bowels of Earth]. You [and Bear] be the first ones to lift it out. We will come at the last." They commenced to move it. Earth made a great rumbling. As they came through successive layers to the top layer of Earth, the rumbling grew louder. Then they came out. At that time also he up above [Great Spirit], the midé manito, and other manitos commenced to move it [the midé ceremony]. The noise came down the layers of midé Sky. At the last layer of Sky they paused, then met at the midpoint between Earth and Sky and there was a terrible noise for a long time, indeed, a great noise. Thus it was when midéwiwin assembled from Earth and Sky.

Narration of the midé origin tale seemed essentially the same in each of the eight grades, and midé leaders agreed that only esoterica were added in advanced grades. I tested this minutely with Hole-in-the-Sky, who gave me all the texts for the first, second, and fourth grades. I found the differences to be slight embroideries on the tale; they seemed the variations to be expected in repeated oral accounts of the same theme. Besides, the elaborations seemed exchangeable, equally at home in the second grade as in the fourth or fifth. Possibly the real purpose was to extend higher grade talks for power increments which inhered in repetition.

The following version of Bear's travels with the midé "bundle of life" was told at the first grade, Hole said, whereas the preceding version could be told at any other Earth grade. This first-grade version is certainly more condensed.

Our Grandfather [Bear] was engaged to take these [midé] beliefs to the Indian. So he started off. He built a manito lodge, and set the manitos down in their proper positions: "From here you will reach out to give the Indians what they need." [This was the lodge on Earth's bottom layer, where Shell stayed and where guardian spirits of midéwiwin had had their council.] He reached up, grabbed a layer of Earth, tore a hole through it, and built a manito lodge. He placed the manitos there. [And so on as above, through the third layer. Then he tore a hole through the fourth layer, "on which we sit."] He lay there with his head sticking out. He lay four days [midé years], unable to decide upon a plan of travel. [Then he went east, as told before, reaching the great body of water]. Then he walked out onto the water. After traveling a bit, he saw something and went up to it. It was a big white [sea-]shell. He climbed onto it, and manito shells of every size stuck all over him. Then he went to the country where he found the Frenchman's river. There he rested, stationed a manito, and proceeded straight to Narrow Bough Point. Here he reared, looking west for Indians but found none. "Then here will be where the Indian will talk [plead] about his needs."

One elaboration concerned making the drum out of the oldster's convolutions. It was presented at any grade, apparently, but as it sidetracks the original theme, it was likely to be confined to higher grades, or in lower grades was confined to preferred patients—like close relatives, or people giving large fees.

Now he turns [a number up to four, varying with the grade]. Then at the site in the middle of Earth he crawled out [in his first large drum-appearance]. The Spirits talked low: "I'd guess the Indian will not be able to handle it easily." Then he spun around [to make the drum small, upon manito advice; the number of times corresponds with the grade]. Then one [drum] sliver our Grandfather [Bear] took. Then far, far above [from the bottom layer of Earth to the top, fourth layer of Sky] he [the drum man] stretched himself, so that he reached the Sky. Halfway up the Sky he spread four limbs [now the sliver had turned into a tree, Grandmother Cedar]. To the ends of the Sky he spread his four limbs. Four [or any lesser number corresponding to the grade] holes did our Grandfather [Bear] make [through the drum] and said, "Here is where the Indian will state his wants." Four [or any lesser number] times, he [the drum] stretched his legs [now, roots] to the ends of Earth: "From here [i.e., universally] they will attend to the Indian's wants."

The following elaboration was also placed optionally. Like other elaborations, and even essential points, it might disappear through "carelessness." As Hole became engrossed teaching these midé materials, recollections flooded him, till at times he was at a loss as to whether they represented elaborations proper only to more thorough and leisured therapies of the advanced grades, or whether they were essentials belonging to a conscientious conduct of the lower grades. Clearly a man's mood dictated much of his ritual conduct. It was considered good for officers to be slightly intoxicated at a ceremony, for then a man was pleasantest, likely to be large hearted and acquiescent, least "shy," least "afraid" to talk fully of and to the Supernaturals. The next excerpt refers to the time when Shell and Great Spirit asked the other Supernaturals to aid the midé enterprise. The Supernaturals chose a spokesman, called the "Leading One," or "Bowman," who answered:

"We will help with all our powers. All of us agree. Thank you, we say to you. And now I speak for myself about this that you wish to give the Indian. Do not be afraid to go ahead with it. You are benefiting the Indian. We [all Supernaturals] will guard carefully what you say [for] it will carry the Indian through [his troubles]. All are grateful for the guidance you give the Indian. You show that you think he is pitiful [deservingly]. That is why I answer you."

The next elaboration belongs in Sky grades, from the fifth through the eighth. It shows that the Earth guardians, Shell and the servitor Bear, are matched in Sky territory by the Sky guardians, Great Spirit and his servitor Eagle.

When the manito [Great Spirit] commenced [patronizing midéwiwin], he told his servitor [Eagle] what to do, being the employer [for midéwiwin]. "All right, I do as you say." "Now, when that seated One [Shell] is ready, you come and tell us." Soon [Eagle] told him. "Then, go watch and wait till you see them come out on top [of Earth]. When they arrive there, you blow this bugle [fife]. And you wait for us there [at the Sky opening through which things below could be seen]. That is all. Then we all meet at the halfway place [between Above and Below worlds]."

The next elaboration seemed peculiar to Red Lake, for its account continued Bear's journey west of Lake Superior to Red Lake. Hole's long experience at Cass Lake (south of Red Lake), Leech Lake (east of Red Lake), and Devil's Lake in northeast North Dakota, led him to find Red Lake's extension improper because untraditional, probably sanctioned by a recent dream.

He had heard it told at a secret midé session by the officer representing Great Spirit.

Then he [Bear] went. And here at [snapping-]Turtle River, he built a dwelling place for the midé manito [used collectively]. He departed for Turtle River Lake and established a midé manito. He went to High Bank Portage [between Redby village and the Turtle River] and established a midé manito. At the outlet of Redby River he established another midé manito: "Here is where I give ear to the Indian's requests. I will lean out, looking and listening."

This elaboration carries the Supernatural's route north and somewhat west. Sky-manito, an Ojibwa midé leader who came to Red Lake from Gull Lake about one hundred years before (1835?), was said to have introduced the elaboration, reasoning that it was proper to hold the ceremony anywhere on the globe, for a curing needed Supernaturals established locally, as in the origin tale. He reasoned that midéwiwin was established locally by ritual saying-so, since a favorable outcome to "pitiable" requests was guaranteed in Cutfoot's vision, and in the concept of Spirit patronage. Because the patient comes under local patronage, it was reasoned further that the origin tale need not narrate all Bear's travels when the patient was located at an early station on Bear's route. "One has no business to carry a person's life beyond the place where he lives." But a "person's life" should be carried up to his dwelling-place, even if this was British Columbia, watching only that the travel be on a water route.

Before the patient underwent the final dramatic public ceremony of curing, he underwent private sessions lasting several nights and a couple of days. In these sessions, the patient was taught to make the ancient dream-narrative his own "power," which attached to him midé patronage, as anciently promised to the Indians through Cutfoot. Birchbark scrolls of the midé leader (doctor or teacher) were produced, tobacco was offered to them, they were unrolled over the fire, to ease their stiffness, spread out and weighted down on the floor. The shaman pointed out figures scratched on the scrolls, explaining the scheme (see Figure 2).

106

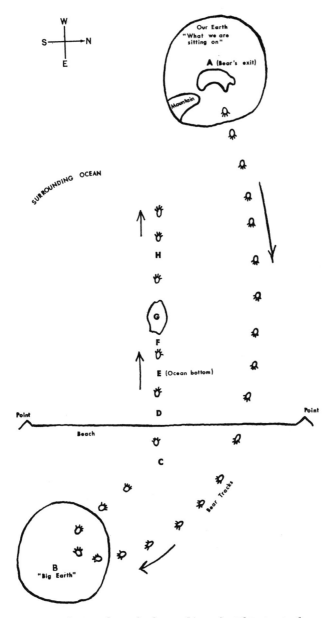

Figure 2. Bear's travels with the midé pack. This is similar to the rough diagrams often scratched on the ground during the secret teaching of the midé origin myth.

Here [at *A*] is where Bear emerged from Earth's center. Then he went down under the water and came out here [at *B*] at a place called "Big Earth." This is somewhere in the east, where he saw the daylight [eastern quarter of the] world. He reared up [at *C*] and went down to the ocean [at *D*]. There he looked north. He saw whitecaps and didn't dare cross. He saw the Point, looked out from it, but discerned nothing. He went to the south Point, saw nothing, and returned to here [*D*] at the ocean. He touched the water with his right hand, but noticed no effect [on the water's behavior]. He tried his left hand, but it too made no difference. The Great Lion [an evil mighty water monster] happened to be ashore in the south. Bear asked him, "Will you help me? I can't get across." [Lion, characteristically jealous and touchy, was especially so with Bear, resenting his appointment as the Supernaturals' emissary.] "Oh, you do want help! You, so brave and strong!" He touched the water with one hand and [for he was the great water spirit] it became calm and smooth as glass. Bear said, "Thank you!" He made four steps, and the water did not bend. He thought, "I will go under," and walked along the ocean bottom [towards *E*]. After a distance, it looked light so he rose [at *F*] and saw that it was calm. He saw [*G*] and took it for a rocky island. Close up, he saw it was manito migis [the mystic shell]. He climbed out on it and rolled about and finally stood up. It sounded then as though icicles were [clinking] on him. [At *H*] he continued west, swimming atop the ocean.

And so on, until Bear reached the last traditional station, at Fond du Lac, and cured an Indian. A working diagram similar to Figure 2 was sometimes traced on the ground with a stick.

One esoteric incident of the midé tale was told usually at certain private occasions and advanced sessions. Its absence does not affect the sense of midé ritual, and its presence rather complicates it, for it serves two different interests. One is the love of personal combat, the other is the ethical triumph of good over evil. The two interests can be extracted in the present little tale by changing the personal combat into ethical issues.

When our Grandfather emerged from Earth's center [this exit was Lake Superior], he saw Someone [evil, hence a Snake] chasing him [for the life "pack" he was carrying]. He [Bear] strung up his bow and aimed it. Thereupon he [Snake] fell down to the bottom of Earth. "It must be that I do wrong [to be worsted in the power combat]. The Indian will not remember me [with ritual offerings of tobacco and goods]. It is best for me to aid our Grandfather." So he went to Bear and said he would help.

There was no firm limit to the number of elaborations about the midé tale. Hole and others, like Everwind's circle, revealed that imaginative men liked to speculate on ethical, philosophic, therapeutic, and even novelistic implications hidden in the tale. High midé officers stayed up late debating these matters, talking with unusual freedom and disregarding jealousies under the influences of quiet nights, ample tobacco, and fellow scholars. Hole would walk miles to talk midéwiwin with his colleague, Everwind. His interest never flagged during months of long studydays with me. A conscientious man, as Hole's conduct demonstrated, pondered elaborations serving the higher grades and better-paying patients, for elaborations carried increments of power.

Generally, elaborations were eulogistic. Thus, Bear was put to cover more distances, overcome more obstacles and enemies, establish more midé localities with Spirit patrons. Bear always solved the difficulties while guarding the precious midé "pack" for the Indians. (By stretching the imagination to our own literature using a similar device, one infers an emotional stirring in the Ojibwa teller and listener that could not reach the anthropologist outsider.) Elaborations included enriching touches such as Bear's posture at emerging from Earth or Water, his color which changed symbolically upon emerging from Earth-layers, and snatches of ritually-courteous dialogue.

The origin tale winds up with a Bear-and-Cutfoot elaboration that I heard in several versions.* This stressed that midéwiwin was revealed to the olden forebear and that it has always worked for therapy:

Soon I will tell a story to the one [the present patient] reaching for manito aid. Now then, hear what I say about happenings at the time they planned to make the Indian a midé. An olden Indian had two children. One fell ill. In the morning [the younger child, Cutfoot]

* Bear is not mentioned specifically here, but, being synonymous with midéwiwin, he was present by implication in every origin tale.

went out and did not return until night. After a while, he saw his father crying. He went up to him and asked, "What is the matter, Father? Why do you cry?" "You are foolish, my son. Your elder brother will not live." "Then it will happen?" "Yes, it will happen to your elder brother."

Again in the morning the child went off and did not return until night. Again he found his father weeping and went up to him, "What is the matter now, father? What are you wailing about?" "You are silly, my son." "Then it will happen?" "Yes, indeed, it is to happen to your elder brother." "I could save that one [his brother]." "You are foolish to say that."

But later he pondered on what his son had said. He [the father] went and asked him, "How would you save him?" "He should be treated in the midé way." "Well, what is that? Never have I heard of it!"

He showed his father what to do. Then indeed, the man hastened and got ready. The boy sat down and commenced [the ritual revealed to him]. After a while some person [manito who looked human] came in. He [the father] could not recollect having seen him before. Still another person entered, whom also he did not know. And still another, and yet another. Never had he seen these four people.

The first arrival walked forward a bit, and motioned as though throwing something [shooting the sacred shell]. The [sick] boy stirred. Another went forward and motioned as though throwing something. [Now the sick boy almost rose up.] Still another went forward and motioned as if throwing. [The patient] sat up. And another went forward, motioned a throw, and the boy jumped to his feet [healthy], and stood there.

This account of the midé curing-by-revelation, has a lengthier version focusing on acquisition of the vision.

A certain Indian was the only one to be taught Earth midéwiwin by a manito. [The manito] was Shell, and he sent for [Cutfoot]. The Indian, then six or seven years old, was playing on the beach with his elder brother. At night the little boy did not return to the lodge, so the folks asked the elder brother. They sought him on the beach and in the brush but could not find him, could not see his tracks. They even went to a distant Indian camp for him. They sought him many days, then came to believe that probably he was drowned, and they dragged the lake. Four years the old folks remained at the same place. One afternoon they saw someone walking down the beach who, when he reached their trail, turned up it to the lodge. They recognized him immediately. They fed him, of course, and asked him where he had been. He said he had been visiting, but would not say where. He remained with them a year and disappeared again. They searched everywhere for him but could not find him. One night four years later he returned again. They saw him early in the morning and questioned him as before. Finally his father understood [that the boy had a mystic experience not to be divulged], quit questioning him, and told his wife to do likewise. For he knew that his son had been somewhere safe.

After a time, he married and told his wife where he had been, what he had seen and heard. And he said, "I am going to do it. It is called midéwiwin." No Indian had heard of it before.

He got his father to make a [midé] drum, giving the directions. He had him make other necessary things, too.

His elder brother became ill and his father said, "You cannot save him." The boy said, "I think we can save him." "What will you do to save him?" "Oh, we'll put him through midéwiwin." The old folks were confused, never having heard of it before. He told his parents to prepare the required things [food, tobacco, and furs as offerings].

When he finished with him [his elder brother], the boy was up and around, well as ever, except for being a little thin.

From then on, he [the visionary] taught the old men [the shamans] how to perform it. They claim that this is how midéwiwin was started among Indians. It is a true story. The man's name was Cutfoot. He and his family lived at Yellow Hammer Beach. He had two children.

The origin tale was not a thoroughly trimmed account even when told by one person only. For example, hidden in two versions of Bear's travels with the "pack," there is an Indian girl whom Bear cured by midé rites. But she is not a visionary. This is consistent with the Ojibwa's view of women but not of midéwiwin as a curing originally available only through a direct vision, as with Cutfoot. Nor does this version describe mediation of the vision through purchase. The main intent is again to boast of the midé Bear cure:

Our Grandfather left his pack on the north side of the river and placed a manito there to guard it. He departed, following the chain of lakes. An Indian lived atop the big hill that our Grandfather had burst open [when dashing against it upon emerging from the water]; he had a son and daughter. The daughter had been sick a long time,

111

partly paralyzed, and full of ulcerations. The son told his mother, "It would be good for you to build a wigwam for her some place apart, for she stinks." The girl felt very bad to hear her brother say that. She struggled up, went down the hill, and lay in the shade of a tree with sharp boughs. Our Grandfather was returning from his trip and saw her. He thought, "This appears to be the one I am seeking." He took out his bow, strung it up, pointed it at her, and led her to believe he would shoot. Frightened, she jumped up and ran up the hill and told her father a bear was going to shoot her. [He had shot a migis at her.] After that she was never known to be sick. So he took his pack and went on.

When securing midé origin tales among the Ojibwa at Red Lake reservation and Manitou Reserve in the 1930's, I saw that they differed widely from midé tales of other tribes and from Ojibwa ones W. J. Hoffman had recorded (1891). In 1885–86, Hoffman had studied the Midé Society among the Minnesota Ojibwa around Red, Cass, and Leech Lakes and found it very similar to the Menominee form, especially in the origin tales (Hoffman, 1891). By 1932, I found prominent features of ideology, organization, and ritual not mentioned in other sources. It seems reasonable to infer that the Ojibwa divergences from their recorded older forms were expedited by the people's devotion to visions. Yet the Indians always said that they were transferring faithfully the teachings of past times. They might have adhered to this literally if midéwiwin had been limited, formally or by general inclination, to persons incapable of acquiring visions. Actually, when an experienced midé officer had no visions to back his career, the Indians I knew belittled him in gossip, sneering, "He is just an old man . . . he bought what he knows! He has no [personal] manito!"

ORIGIN OF SLEEP

Important among origin tales was the story explaining sleep. One variant, told me by Hole-in-the Sky, related that Lion or Tiger introduced sleep to the midé world for the purpose of maintaining dignity, peace, and order in the midé lodge. Lion

112

got Moon to aid because Moon puts people to sleep. Other manitos, like Bear, applied brute force to settle difficulties, but applying sleep precluded all quarrels in the midé lodge since the
primordial one when Lion knocked dirt out of Snake's hand and
substituted sand, for fashioning the first Indian.

A variant involved Cutfoot, whose personality, like Bear's, at-
tracted narrative accretions. This tale stressed the guardian spirits' pity. It was told by one of the midé leaders at the close of
each night session, just before the officers filed out of the midé
lodge.

Now then, I will give a little talk. I thank all present. You have
completed the evening's job. You were told that, sitting on the level
Earth, you were to concentrate on the one wishing for life. And you
did. Thus I do. . . . Now then, the Night Traveler has arrived and
stands by. When he appeared [long ago, when Supernaturals were
teaching Cutfoot midéwiwin] he saw the manitos sitting in a bunch.
[He approached] and the olden Indian [Cutfoot] fell back, asleep. All
were hushed. He [the Moon] spoke to them, "Why do you hush? I am
not evil. I come to make the Indian well [by sleep]. Sometimes I will
make him think, causing him to dream about things you tell him. So
I, too, will aid the Indian. He cannot live without sleep. Now then,
after a while, that ball-like one [Sun] behind me will come in sight.
Look behind me and see. His coming wakens everything. Thus will I
contribute to your work for the Indian."

Chapter **6**

THE RITUAL IN THE LIFE MIDÉWIWIN

U<small>NLIKE CURING BY VISION</small>, which was a public performance of one man (who was the sucking-doctor, diviner, blood-letter, or herbal doctor) and an assistant, the midé curing required a group of colleagues working secretly and publicly. During the 1930's, the number of colleagues varied with the locality and the midé grade, being fewer in lower grades everywhere. First grade usually required a band of about ten, second grade had sixteen, third had twenty at Cass Lake (but thirty-two at Red Lake), and so on in multiples or parts of four. The "chief person" (*gitchi webid*) was called in English variously the leading shaman, principal midé, headman, or simply chief; he was, during ritual activities, Shell. At first grade he had one assistant leader; for each successive grade, he added one. He and his one or more assistants might be referred to collectively as "the chiefs." Red Lake increased the number of assistant leaders so that at the fifth grade there were five assistants, and so on through eighth grade. But at Cass and Leech Lakes, count recommenced with the fifth grade, which was the first grade of Sky midéwiwin.

During the rites, the position at the left of the last assistant leaders was occupied by the important *naganid* (or "Bowman" in Ojibwa canoeists' idiom, meaning literally "the foremost one" of the Supernaturals approached by Shell regarding midéwiwin). Bowman was proxy for Bear, the Supernaturals' servitor. He was said to "own" the midéwiwin and had special interest in the sweat rite. On Bowman's left stood lesser undifferentiated midé officers, numbering six for first grade, seven or ten for second (i.e., an increase of one each grade, cumulatively, as at Red Lake, or of four, which is an irreducible ritual unit), and so on; but Cass Lake and Leech Lake recommenced count with the fifth grade. Closing this string of "bystanding" manitos was the *wedaged* or "end man," called "Steersman" in canoe idiom. Besides officers, the assembly at the midéwiwin included the patient-initiate (or the person appointed, under some circumstances, to substitute for him) at the chief shaman's right, honorific messengers or servitors, and witnesses at the public sessions.

Midé curings had secret sessions lasting two, three, or four nights and one or two days, besides the day the public was called to look on. There followed one or several days more of closed gatherings when portions of the original vision were recited. This meant a possible total of seven or eight ritual days. The ritual added the patient to the fellowship of his predecessors in the Society—which must have seemed extraordinary to a people otherwise reared to ideas of each being solitary vehicles of revelation. Recitation of the original vision also invoked the Supernaturals mentioned. The patient was directed to play-act the ancient visionary's experience and to respond to the midé officers or doctors, as in a solitary vision he responded to his manito; this enactment carried "life" or cure.

The secret sessions occupied fewer nights for lower grades than for advanced ones. The public day ceremony was like a miracle play in the Christian world, as the onlookers' responses showed. The days following the public ceremony were for private feast exchanges between patient and curers where also the patient learned further "powerful" details.

A midé "doing," even at the mild lower grades, was held fearful and potent. Casual visitors were shooed off; drumbeats were heard effectively, though muffled by lodge walls and distance; tobacco fumes were sensed, so heavy were the offerings; lights burned on until first dawning. Because of the evil and the secrecy, a patient dreaded the rite as one does major surgery. Surgery fears usually end with the success of the operation, but the Ojibwa's midé fears might lift only briefly when the ritual ended. Then they returned as he offered tobacco for a year or more to the mystic mementos given him to cherish for his "life." These mementos were analogous to the ones made after a personal revelation of power. Midé mementos could be a post of the ceremonial lodge, a rough woodcarving of a midé Supernatural, a hide sack made from the skin of a creature regarded as a midé Supernatural, and tiny sea shells. But the usual midé patient had only a meager understanding of the symbolism; his little knowledge seemed to heighten dread of shamans. However, he could wield his midé status to cow others less equipped.

FIRST NIGHT RITUAL

The first night of a midé curing was secret; its date was set by the patient and the principal shaman he solicited. The patient at that time brought the shaman a kettle of choice cooked food to which was tied a sack of tobacco, or he called the shaman to his lodge for this food. The feast and tobacco were a first payment to shaman and Supernaturals. The principal midé invited his preferred assistants to join the feast and hear the patient's reason for the undertaking. He informed the midé Supernaturals accordingly, "This man, my grandchild named Crashing Thunder, desires midé rites to strengthen him. He will undergo them later [at a specified date]." Supernaturals had to be summoned from far places to eye the patient. Throughout this evening and all following ones, the chief shaman carefully stated the patient's name and identity for the Supernaturals. On the first night, shamans started telling the origin tale.

The patient's problem might require immediate cure but he might lack funds. There was no cure without immediate payment. Hence such a patient would give the private feast at each new moon when he announced that he was deferring full rites until he could finance them. In midé reasoning, he gave the feast to secure the kind attention of midé Supernaturals, borrowing a margin of health on the feast's credit. The shamans would tell little of the origin tale at such feasts. These palliatives might drag on for a year, in the 1930's; no other adjustment was made to the severe financial depression of the era.

When the patient presented adequate fees, regular rites began on the first night of the private feast. After salutations and narration, and after some of the hundred or so midé songs were sung by the officers (who individually selected songs at random, though each one must "own" what he sang through purchase from one or more teachers), the chief shaman dismissed the company saying, "Tomorrow we rest but we meet again in the evening."

SECOND NIGHT RITUAL

Next night, usually, more of the origin tale was told, another few songs were sung, and the patient's needs were urged upon the manitos. Because the patient-initiate paid all shamans present (with food, goods, tobacco, furs), whatever they did in the lodge —everything that they said and sang and danced—became his property; some day he might use these, for a return fee, at a curing. At the moment, this property was medicine for his disorder. However, the very sick often retained little memory of the ritual.

THIRD DAY: SWEAT RITUAL

At the end of the second evening's session, the chief shaman announced that the following day, not the night, would be observed in a midé sweat lodge, undergoing the sweat ritual. Sweating was a sovereign medicine of the Ojibwa, for moral and intellectual power. The Ojibwa boasted of his ability to endure the sudatory's tropical heat: sweat pouring, pulses blasting at his temples, he sang mystic songs. There he might wrest a mystic

117

dream. Before a vision-curing session, the shaman underwent a lone sweat bath where he invoked his personal guardians. The midé shaman also did this at odd times. Besides, there had to be the group sudatory, of all shamans staffing any particular midéwiwin. In the mid-1930's, younger midé shamans ignored the sweat ritual, shocking older men. The traditionalists reasoned, Why attempt midéwiwin at all if you do not prove and purify yourself for the Supernaturals? Ignoring this rule could bring manito reprisals.

The principal shaman directed the patient or his able-bodied substitute to build the sweat lodge. It had to be large and circular: its framework was to be four feet tall, of eight arching sticks or stakes, each six to eight feet long when upright. Eight stones were heated up, water was dropped slowly upon them to create a heavy steam; they encircled a pile of beach sand in the lodge center. Properly, construction of this lodge should follow erection of a small one for the leading shaman at the time his services were first solicited; but this was not generally observed. The small one required only four curving sticks and its steam needed only four stones. As the leading shaman explained in the big lodge, the sudatory was protected by the midé Bear, "for our Grandfather [Bear] told the Indian to get in under him and then he dropped his hide over him," creating a cavernous lodge. Each pair of curving sticks arched over one diameter of the circular lodge or "shadow of the Bear," encompassing cardinal points. So, when one stick was staked at an eastern point, its mate curved over it from the western point; the same held for north and south stakes; and the other four stakes, in two pairs, found places at the semicardinal points. Later, this framework was covered heavily with blankets, to contain the steam. Sometimes the sudatory was built outdoors, sometimes within a large wigwam. Its imagery said it was circular like the earth, the sun, and the moon, and was staked out by cardinal points to invoke their guardianship.

On the morning of the sweat rite, the chief shaman stood outside the lodge with his officers and the patient. Officers had to stand and move in fixed relationships. When the head shaman stood at the south, the others ranged on his left trailing off west and north, imitating the sun's course.

Standing outside the sweat lodge, waiting for the sun to rise and see their good work, the head shaman, proxy for Shell, ritually turned over conduct of the day's affairs to the Bear proxy, the Bowman, saying:

Now I address you. Enter this place I am supposed to enter. Do as you were taught and the midé manitos will regard you [your pleas] with favor. I begin [the song] that drives you in [to the sudatory]. And when ready, you lead the manito-talk as it was done for you [at your rites]. That is all I need say.

Bowman replied ritually:

Well, I am ready. I salute the midé manito [in the person of the head shaman]. I will do as you have told me [literally, "to my existence"]. I say likewise to all you [all the officers present, especially the chief's assistants]. Now I salute Bear [beseechingly], that he give me power when I enter his Body [the sweat lodge]. And I salute our Grandmother [cedar bough], in the fire heating stones for the sudatory, and surrounding the fireplace with her head. May she regard me gently, pitying me for not knowing this [performance] thoroughly. Perhaps another should do this, yet possibly the manito has a reason to prefer me. Well, the manito grows restless, waiting.

Then the head shaman intoned the song that catapulted Bowman into the lodge. It might be almost any midé song; all are alike in eulogizing some midé detail or personage, in allusive language. The melodies commence high in falsetto range, sung to a rapid four-eighths beat, each melody held to a narrow compass; by the time each of the four verses has been sung four times, the voice has reached its lowest range, whatever that is for the individual. The words of one song in the 1930's were:

Wi ah ni ne [comparable to our "la! la!"],
Wi ah ni ne,
My green clouded wigwam [refers to the brush laid on it]
Do I enter.

119

Another song ran:

> My Colleague [the Sun], hear me,
> When I rise.
> My Colleague, hear me.

Singing, Bowman ritually traced an involved circuit through and around the wigwam poles; circuit and singing were conterminous. The circuit represented "eluding the evil manito" and recalled Bear's success in escaping the Evil One tracking him when he emerged from the heart of Earth. As a ritual dance, it mimicked also how Great Snake wrapped himself dangerously around the primordial midé wigwam, to be removed vigorously (by Water Lion). Ontario called the midé lodge "Snake Lodge" and termed the long slim stakes "ribs of the Snake." The ritual of "eluding" also exposed life as a hard conflict of ethical forces, the midéwiwin being a refuge from evil and defeat.

Bowman must start the mythic trail of "eluding" with a sunwise circle outside the sweat-lodge framework, commencing where he had stood in the formal line of midé officers. This was usually to the south or east. Returning to his starting point, he would make four ritually false starts (it was prescribed to make three or four false moves upon entering a place) and at the fifth he would encircle the first post sunwise. He continued around the outside, sunwise to post number two, which arched to meet post one from the opposite cardinal point. He encircled post two, continued outside the lodge sunwise to post three, and encircled it. Post three was to the right of post one; that is, the post next to post one countersunwise. Bowman continued until he had circled all eight posts. Post eight was just to the left of post one; that is, the first next to it going sunwise. Between posts eight and one was the sweat-lodge doorway.

After encircling post eight, Bowman stepped outside to the front of the doorway, backed away from it, entered, stepped over the heating stones placed in the lodge's center, exited from the lodge between posts two and seven (since these were at opposite cardinal points to one and eight where he had entered), continued around sunwise outside the lodge, re-entered between posts one and three, stepped over the stones, exited between posts two and four, continued sunwise around the outside and entered again between posts three and five, crossed over the heating stones, came out again between posts four and six, continued sunwise outside till he could enter between posts five and seven, crossed over the stones, left the lodge between posts six and eight, made a complete sunwise circle from that point all around the lodge till he returned to the doorway where he entered, made a sunwise circle inside the poles, between the poles and the centrally placed stone pile, and ended up inside the lodge at post one. Then he would say, relieved, "It will be done," meaning that now the lodge was purged of Evil and could be completed for midé use.

The unfaltering intentness with which Hole-in-the-Sky depicted this ritual circuit, referring to the markings on his birchbark scroll and tracing further in the dirt near us with a stick, was arresting. It was evident that he had seen it often—but more, he had studied it, perhaps had performed it himself as Bowman. I could not ask, because the priestly account could never be interrupted for such queries, which amounted to personal intrusions. The Ojibwa novice would never interrupt at all, and I can only marvel at the old man's patience in tolerating the many queries I did put.

As the sudatory belonged to Bowman, Bear's votary, no one might enter it without his express invitation. So now Bear invited those sitting outside, starting with the leading officers. Theoretically, in ritual, they were free to refuse the invitation, as manitos. But to act as the Supernaturals did when Bear invited them on Shell's behalf into the mythical midé sudatory, they would enter and seat themselves in formal order, starting at post eight.

Bowman, as master of ceremonies, stood in the lodge center by the beach sand and the stone pile, holding paraphernalia he had been carrying throughout the anti-Evil circuit. These included a pipe of tobacco, two drumsticks, a stone-carrier slung across the chest, and a water-carrier, all indispensable in the sweat rite. They were termed ritually after Bear's image. The drumsticks, which Bowman rapped on a pan of water or on a stone when he sang, were "forepaws of our Grandfather." The stone-carrier, a fork of a flexible wood like ash with arms about two and a half feet long, was "Bear's shoulder strap." The water-sprinkler was "our Grandfather's tail," made of cedar boughs into a flat brush or, for lack of cedar, made of hay or a bunch of leaves. About twelve inches long, large at one end, small at the other, it was said to resemble a bird's tail also and so was used in Sky midéwiwin rites.

Standing by the sand and stones, Bowman told patient and officiants about Bear, his content ranging over any portion of the origin tale not already covered during previous sessions. As Hole said with characteristic effort at judiciousness, "generally Bowman mentions Bear's intention" to have his Body (the sweat lodge) accommodate all midé Indians; this was a Bear invocation. Bowman would appeal to "our Grandfather" to help him level the sand heap, for spreading over the dirt floor. Thereupon the lesser officers approached, stretched out their hands, and leveled the sand.

Ceremonies now proceeded within the sanded area so far as possible. The patient, having collected the heating stones the previous day, now set down the first one he (or she) had picked up, on a line approximately north of, or opposite to, the doorway, if the doorway was on the lodge's south side. Bowman seated himself just behind this stone. Seven more stones (this was the number for a first-grade rite) were deposited at equal distances in a clockwise circle, each aligned with a post. Thus, Steersman found himself seated at the right hand of Bowman (also called, honorifically, Bear). The lodge framework was now blanketed over; a dish of drinking water and a larger pan of water set on stones were placed within Bowman's reach.

Bowman then saluted the lodge stakes or framework as the "Bear's legs"; he saluted the midé stones, the "Bear's tail" of

122

cedar bough, the "Bear's arms" or drumsticks, the "Bear's shoulder muscles" or the stone-carrier; and he saluted all Supernaturals, represented by officers present—all this bound the Powers' willing aid. Bowman's ritual required uplifting both arms to a considerable slant and sometimes, as the arms dropped, allowing the hands to stray in ritual caress and blessing over the object saluted. (The gesture occurs also among Ojibwa lovers, when a man strokes the girl's hair, a palm smoothing down each side of her middle parting.) Bowman intoned, "Now I salute the midé stone [speaking collectively] praying [it] regard me gently if I err. Now I asperse some of this midé water, using his [Bear's] tail." Vapor would rise from the hot stones. "You [Supernaturals] understand our purpose and the reason for this [lodge] structure. That is all. I salute you."

With the cedar "tail," Bowman aspersed the assigned water over his red-hot stone, passed the "tail" sunwise to the second stone, and so on until Steersman had sprinkled his stone. Bowman again took the watering outfit and passed it as before. During the round, he sang a song, or a couple of songs if he was generous to the patient. The words ran thus.

> All over the Earth
> Am I distributed,
> The manito stone.
> Na! [similar to "amen!"]
>
> All over the Sky
> Am I distributed,
> The manito stone.
> Na!

The substitution of Sky for Earth in the second stanza shows respect for Sky. Hole reproduced the song for me, in his aged but true voice, gazing intently, devoutly, at some remote horizon; first, he had offered tobacco, silently. During such mystic reproductions, I felt that he summoned the effort from emotional depths. I could not tell whether his attitude contained some apology for possible blasphemy, singing or praying in this unusual

123

secular situation. Legalistically, he "owned" this material and the "right" to teach it.

As the lodge was governed by Bear, it was his Bowman representative who initiated action within it. Hence, as the dish of water and sprinkler made a second circuit, Bowman directed Steersman, aside, to sing when he aspersed his stone. This focused ritual notice of the stone's significance to the sudatory. Steersman complied with:

> Ah ni a yah ni neh [equivalent to "la! la!"].
> These people [Supernaturals, officers]
> Encircle the stone.
> Ah ni a yah ni neh.

Steersman had to see to it that all the mystic sprinkling-water was consumed, and he passed it around sunwise, sprinkling any or all of the stones until the water was gone. Then he sang, and repeated four times more, to total five:

> My Colleague [midé Supernatural], hear me!
> My Colleague, hear me!

The patient brought in another basin filled with drinking water. Bowman poured a bit on his stone, in offering, then drank from the basin. This continued sunwise around the officers' ring; the last officer was required to use up the water by drinking some and pouring the balance on his stone. The men sat quietly during this interval, a ritual rest.

The sweating lasted twenty to thirty minutes before the ceremony ended. Bowman then thanked his men "for their help," and they filed out in their order, Steersman leading, preserving the sunwise route. The obligations of this session were to baffle the Evil Monster (accomplished by Bear's tortuous circuit), to orientate the lodge in terms of the cardinal points, to establish mystic unity of midé officers and the guardian cardinals by having the officers sit at proper posts, to alert Supernaturals, to fortify midé officers through ritual sweating, and thereby to benefit the patient.

124

Nor had the patient (of either sex) been idle or passive. He, or a substitute, sought sweat-lodge blessing by collecting materials for the lodge, including the vital stones and all related implements; he kept the stones heated high during the rite, taking them in and out of the lodge. He himself was not permitted to remain inside, the sudatory being only for midé personnel (and, otherwise, Bear visionaries). After the officers had filed out, the patient was required to disassemble the framework carefully, straighten the stakes, tie them together, and stand them up against a sound tree, this honorific disposal being regarded as a reverent burial. Stones and other items, except for pipe, drumsticks, pans, and blankets, were treated the same.

THIRD NIGHT RITUAL

That evening, the patient would invite the chief midé and his men to a feast at his home. Actually, a special framework was erected for the large number of guests, oriented east and west. The patient and his family would have been cooking since late afternoon. As night fell, they called the chief midé, who arrived with his dish. He had already invited his assistant (or several assistants, if the ceremony was beyond that of first grade). He was accompanied by an honorific messenger, to whom he gave a bundle of eight (or more, for advanced grades) invitation sticks, each of which the messenger delivered to an officer, as invitation for the night's "eating." Every guest brought the certifying stick with him and handed it to the patient, who returned it to the chief midé. The latter laid the sticks aside, counting them to see that all were returned. Each guest brought a clean food-pail; but the head midé should receive from the patient a fine one with a cover, polished to gleam. The lodge or tent had been decorated with aromatic green cedar brush spread over the ground and propped up a bit against the sides of the structure; the ground was sanded in the middle. Food was brought in to be passed around, and the rituals commenced. Such a feast had to be served

125

on each preparatory night before the public performance and at each meeting for instruction after this ceremony.

The men arranged themselves in ritual sunwise order outside the feast lodge or tent, marched in through the eastern door, circuited the interior, and seated themselves in the same succession. The fees of cloth, blanketing, and formerly of furs were laid in ordered piles at the tent's center.

At the chief midé's word, his servitor (who had delivered the invitation sticks) filled the large midé pipe with tobacco and passed it, by its very long stem, to each officer in succession. Low-voiced or silently, each man invoked midé Supernaturals as he puffed. This was required routine in many situations outside midéwiwin, and the Supernaturals invoked were always the same, but in the present setting they were distinguished as "midé." The smoking over, the servitor filled each one's pail or dish with the fine food cooked and displayed alongside the pile of goods. The chief midé might smoke further, calling the manito's attention to the feast in whose eating he (the manito) participated as a reward for the health petitioned; or this sentiment might have been voiced in the first general smoke. Then the chief midé would tell all to eat and to carry home the leftovers.

After eating, he narrated a section of the midé origin tale, taking up where he had left off last. He stopped where he chose, and the tale was continued by an assistant to any length desired. When the one or more assistants finished, Bowman would take up, and finally Steersman closed the session.

Hole explained that an officer should not speak too lengthily nor too briefly; length is tedious, brevity offends and lacks power. A narrator should not "hog" the talk, carrying the adventure so far that little is left for others. A man wishing to discourse fully should confine himself to a short space of the adventure, elaborating details only. Hole complained that Everwind, Red Lake's chief midé at Ponemah village, talked too much and articulated too poorly for ready comprehension. Everwind's brother-in-law and frequent midé assistant, Bios, agreed. But when Bios led,

Hole and Everwind found themselves agreed over *his* deplorable ignorance and etiquette. Such criticisms seemed rivalrous. For Hole, who never was Bowman or Steersman, found much to approve of in these officers at Ponemah. He said they knew the portions they narrated, spoke clearly and in proper measure, were earnest yet remained correctly in the background.

After all of the evening's narrations, or when one officer ended, the chief midé sang once or twice. As in instances given earlier, the songs were eulogistic and allusive, slight or sparing in verbal content. Then the patient, sitting on the chief midé's right, stood up and walked sunwise to the chief. He (or she) saluted the chief with "Na-ge! Na!" which resembles our "Hail!" and "Amen!" The chief responded "Eh-h-h!" He tipped his drum, which was about a quarter filled with water, to dampen the hide head, rubbed his hand over the head to moisten the hide evenly, and started a new song with usual words but with a special rhythm and melody. As he sang, the patient danced to show the Supernaturals respect and win their care. Finishing, the patient uttered an "Amen," and the officers acknowledged with "Eh-h-h!" Then the patient traveled around the tent sunwise to his seat, again hailed Supernaturals, and was acknowledged. This routine forced the patient on the Supernaturals' attention. Then the drummer, become the principal officer at this juncture, passed the drum sunwise to his left-hand neighbor. The latter had rattled for the drummer who had been singing; now he passed the rattle to *his* left-hand neighbor and this new pair took up, the rightmost singing and drumming, the leftmost rattling only. Each officer had to render a song in this manner, "to benefit the patient," who stood and danced each time.

Patient and officers were plainly exhausted at evening's end, at rites I attended. Each man had to drum, sing, and rattle in turn, keeping a tense, rapid beat for minutes at a time (I noticed five-minute stretches) so vigorously that each pair was in a sweat when their turn ended. The patient, on the other hand, danced only perfunctorily, apparently not the least involved; torso and

127

arms drooped limply, the legs pumped only languidly up and down, knees giving usually with a heel and toe rise, and rarely did the whole foot leave the floor. The 1930's patient often combined this with steady gum-chewing or spitting snuff in a vigorous stream from the mouth.

A conscientious singer, "if not timid," in Hole's phrase, might recite briefly from the origin tale before going into his song. Or an officer might decline to sing at all for some personal reason, like shyness or a cold; he indicated refusal by hitting the drum once, whereupon the rattler threw the rattle once. Usually the person handed tobacco to another who was willing to sing for him. Women officers were driven to this resort, being barred traditionally from active roles such as singing and narrating the midé tale.

After the round of singing and dancing, the chief midé thanked Supernaturals and Indians present, and dismissed all. The last singer rose and crossed to the chief midé to return him the drum, for it belonged to him on behalf of Shell. The officer who yielded the drum saluted the chief with "Hail!" The latter responded, then requested Steersman, "Will you take this drum?" Doing so, Steersman went to the west door, standing there facing the eastern one, with drum in his left hand and stick in his right. He called the six (at a first-grade ceremony) lesser officer-Supernaturals to follow him and they ranged alongside him facing north. Steersman saluted the chief and ritually asked that he bear him, Steersman, no hard feelings for having taken up the drum (so usurping leadership of this rite); and he petitioned the assistant chief identically, for, said Hole, "generally he holds the rattle." Then he sang. Afterwards, they made two sunwise circlings of the inside of the lodge and ended up at the west door in their original standing position. During these circlings, Steersman chanted barkingly, "Wah! hee-ee! hee-ee! hee-ee!" Closing the first sunwise circling, when Steersman reached the lodge center, he cut across to the north side, continued sunwise around until he reached north again, returned to the center, and laid the drum on the ground alongside the pile of goods or fees. This circuit and its barking was to defeat all Evil; the circuit symbol recurs over and over in midé rites. Steersman- and his train next greeted the chiefs, "Hail!", were acknowledged, traveled to the west door, and filed out. The assistant chief's rattle was laid down at the same time as the drum and in the same manner.

When all were gone, the assistant chief thanked the departed officers for their work and said they would resume next morning the rites for stronger life, adding, "tomorrow we distribute the goods and make the manito wigwam." The officers listened to him from outside the framework. Then the assistant directed the patient to take up the goods and place them on the north side of the tent against the wall. Saying "Hail!" the patient obeyed, circling sunwise around the interior to the north side location. Patient again saluted the chiefs with "Hail!" and was answered. Saying a very elaborate "Hail! Colleague!" to Bear, the chiefs left. Patient and family slept in the lodge, surrounded by evidence of midé guardianship.

DISTRIBUTING THE FEES

About five o'clock next morning, the two (or more, if the grade was beyond the first) midé chiefs directed the patient to send invitation sticks to Bowman, Steersman, and the six (or in accordance with the grade number) "bystanding" officer-Supernaturals, summoning them to a feast for ten o'clock in the morning. The guests arrived, returned the invitation sticks, were seated in the order indicated by the chief midé, and were given tobacco and food by the midé servitor. The chief then repeated the officers' duties, thus, "You steer these worthy midé folk. . . . You lead these excellent midé people . . ." and so on. Finally the chief concluded "Hail!" to which the others gave assent; he continued, "I have told you your positions, so be it," and smoked ritually.

Distribution of the officers' fees displayed earlier was central to this—usually the second—daytime session. The ritual had local variations in the 1930's. At Manitou Reserve in Ontario, the procedure was simple, as described later, but at the Minnesota reservations of Red Lake, Cass Lake, and Leech Lake, it was more elaborate.

At Minnesota reservations the rite was called "Sitting by the Sacrifices," or fees, since the officers did this upon receiving their individual allocations, before proceeding to bless the patient further with "life." The lodge was oriented east and west, the entrance being easterly because Bear's travels began in the east. Directed by the chief midé, the patient had erected four posts on the east-west axis, each post representing an Earth layer penetrated by Bear in mythic time. The general pile of goods for first grade was set by the most easterly of the four posts, a black stone was set by the second, a gray stone by the third. The stones were honored as midé patrons, of the original vision and the sudatory.

When the Minnesota ceremony was for grades beyond the first, the general pile of fees for second grade was set by the second post from the east, the black stone being moved farther west. Fees or goods for third grade were set by the fireplace in the lodge's center. Silvery beach sand was heaped nearby, honored for its part in Bear's adventures.

The post for fifth grade was placed between the first and second posts, as it represented first grade of Sky midéwiwin. This reasoning dictated placement of posts for more advanced grades.

For the distribution of fees, only chief officers were seated in the lodge, and in their usual succession. For first grade, the two chiefs (i.e., the head midé and his assistant) rose and walked to the pile of fees. The first chief, representing Shell in this Earth midéwiwin, circuited sunwise around the goods, lifted them, circled the place again, carried the goods to the doorway, and said, "Now, I have taken up this that [the patient] hands to the midé manito." The assistant chief followed him to the doorway, rattled while the other drummed, "helping" the other to sing:

> I am seating him [the male or
>   female patient], my Colleague,
> I am seating him, my Colleague,

I am seating him down
On this Earth.
I am seating him, my Colleague.

Shell-chief circled sunwise around the lodge's inside and threw down the goods. He circled again, straightened the pile, counted the pieces. By Hole's reckoning, there should be at least four major items to fee first grade, eight for second, twelve for third, sixteen for fourth; smaller pieces were added for each lesser officer. (Serving at a Ponemah midéwiwin, Hole earned two new patchwork quilts, handworked so well that they are used daily in my home over thirty years later.) Each chief midé laid tobacco on each piece, for the Supernaturals; in midé theory, unsmoked tobacco essence (like a Platonic epiphenomenon) or smoke of burning tobacco carried fees to the waiting Patrons. Then the goods were spaced around the lodge, one at each officer's seat.

There were variations to this stage of the 1930's Minnesota practice, which Hole reported earnestly. Thus, when the sweat ritual was ignored, as could happen improperly in the 1930's, only the chief and his assistant(s) might have been appointed and operating. In that case, the chiefs each gave four eagle feathers, tail or wing, to the patient for delivery to the expected Bowman, Steersman, and lesser "bystanding manitos." The feathers, used in lieu of mundane wooden invitation sticks, carried midé symbolism: Bear was said to have resembled Eagle partly during a stage of his negotiations; his tail was "just like an eagle's tail"—the basis for the symbolic brush-sprinkler in the sweat lodge—for only later did his tail dwindle to its present stub; and Eagle replaced Bear in the Sky midéwiwin as honorific servitor.

As each officer gave the patient a feather-invitation, he named the midé person to receive it: Hole averred strongly that "every chief [including assistants] has the same right to issue four invitations," giving the specific names. But this procedure followed deliberations during which the chiefs agreed on selections for Bowman and Steersman; the one who first named a final choice sent out the feather to him. As there could be numerous appointees, the chiefs prepared the patient-messenger by having him lay down a feather while naming the intended recipient. The whole business was preluded, interspersed, and concluded with "Hail . . . so be it . . ." and assents. If the patient appeared to stumble, a relative was sent to escort him and alert his memory. The patient, not a servitor, went on the errand in order to force him upon the Supernaturals' attention, for he summoned their attendance in the persons of the officers who received the feathers. As officers arrived with their invitations, they returned the feathers to the patient, who passed them on for tallying.

The ceremony for distributing fees was open. Servitors never were invited formally; villagers were expected to appear at the lodge, having long heard rumors of the doings. Inducement for general attendance was that servitors of the occasion received fees from the patient and might also claim as their own all ritual picked up this way. A chief shaman might have a favorite servitor, in which case a personal though not formal invitation was extended.

The invited officers filed into the lodge, to sit in the usual succession, each by his fee, already distributed at officers' seats. The chiefs, Bowman, and Steersman sang several times, and the drum passed also to the so-called bystanding officers for their handling, since this invoked mystic aid for "life." The chief might sing the last-quoted song, above. Bowman might sing:

> From the daylight land [the east] I walk.
> [*Sung four times*]
> Like a white bear [considered most powerful],
> I look in my walking.
> From the daylight land I walk.

Or he might sing:

> Nee-ee wah heh-eh [nonsense syllables].
> [*Sung eight times*]
> I [the patient] am to be kissed,
> I am to be kissed.
> Nee-ee wah heh-eh.

132

Plate 5a. Log cabin of Maggie Wilson's mother, Mrs. John Bunyan, at Emo, Ontario. It was built to resemble the traditional lodge or wigwam. Photograph by Ruth Landes, 1933.

Plate 5b. A midé lodge. This lodge, a style used also for dwellings, was built by Chippewa (Ojibwa) Indians in Wisconsin, about the turn of the century. Courtesy of the State Historical Society of Wisconsin.

Plate 6. A birchbark midé scroll. Courtesy of the State Historical Society of Wisconsin. Unrolled, this scroll measures 11 × 57 inches.

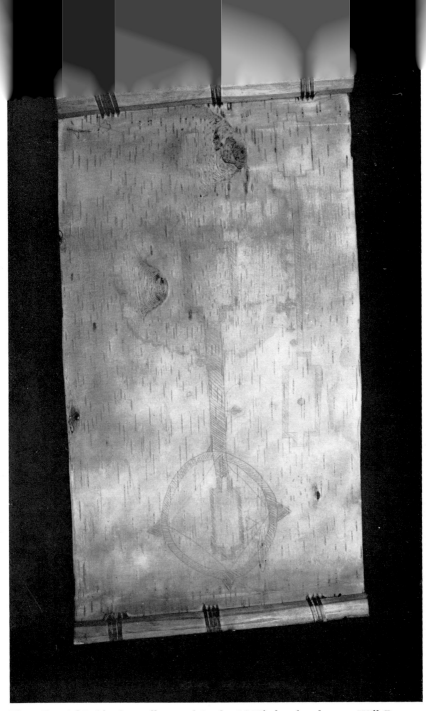

Plate 7.   A birchbark scroll owned in the 1930's by the shaman Will Rogers, for the Ghost midéwiwin. The pictographs on this scroll, which measures 8¼ × 16½ inches, are reproduced by line drawing in Figure 3. Courtesy of the Milwaukee Public Museum.

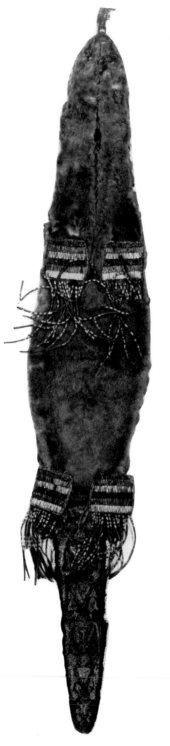

Plate 8. A midé migis sack, or wayan, made from an otter skin. Courtesy of the State Historical Society of Wisconsin. The sack is 32½ inches long.

The kiss was one of blessing, bestowed on hand or face by Bow-man.

Bowman now directed Steersman to sing, and told him how many songs, for Steersman was under his command, as the whole company was under the chief midé's command. Bowman esti-mated the time available for this ritual by glancing at the sun, as rituals should be completed with the sun's setting. Now Steers-man sang any song, as did the others in their subsequent turns, provided there was no repetition. To repeat another's song was condemned as withholding power from the patient. However, each officer enjoyed displaying his ritual skills and versatility. Oc-casionally Steersman had no song to sing. As he carried least re-sponsibility among the major officers, he could then beg another "chief" to sing for him, offering the necessary tobacco; so also he learned a song, as Hole pointed out to illustrate how midé in-struction might proceed indefinitely.

The bystanding officers generally did not sing, having no pow-ers to transfer, and no vital roles in the origin tale. It was their duty to pass around the drum, each man striking it one or more times, up to the number of the grade being ceremonialized. Yet occasionally Bowman might direct them, as his subordinates, to sing, saying, "I will sing once, then each of you will." This oc-curred when only a few such subordinates were present, when the rites had begun early and were proceeding well, when Bow-man cared about the patient's welfare, and when Bowman did not insist on executing the several songs of his responsibility.

The drum rotated among all officers for its "voice" and "song" (in Ojibwa idiom recalling the mythic splintered old Indian) to invoke every Supernatural in turn. Finally a servitor carried it to the chief. Bowman observed, "Again our Grandfather [drum] re-turns, having made the round of midé manitos. So now we shall rise and lift up our goods to the midé manito." (Lifting the goods carried thanks and reminded the Supernaturals that the pa-tient had credit for their "power.") Bowman started circling clockwise and the "bystanders" followed him around four times, each carrying goods that were his fees; if he sang while circling, the subordinates followed in a dancing walk. At the doorway he halted, and the string behind him halted, each time. As the fourth circuit began, each officer dropped down his goods before the chiefs, who added their own fees to the pile, and arranged all neatly. Every officer returned to his place and sat.

The chief midé stated then, or earlier when saluting Supernaturals with the goods, "Well, now I will try [for the patient's benefit]. I salute the midé manitos, every one. I salute this pile of [wealth] before me. These things are set down for the manito to see. Carefully does he examine [the pile], to see how much it is."

Here the chief, or an assistant, directed a servitor to count the items in the pile, to establish their sufficiency, and check that nothing was stolen during the nights they lay in this preparatory lodge. Usually someone remained with the goods, watching. Nonetheless, goods were known to disappear, for no sanctions controlled this theft. Red Lakers told me that six out of twelve pieces were stolen from an unguarded lodge, in the 1930's, commenting only, "That was a pretty bold trick."

The chief observed the verifying count and proceeded:

The manito sees how much the patient pays, as [the patient] owes for his life. [The patient] did not promise a firm date for [the midéwiwin] meeting his needs. He vowed only that he would do it when able. . . . Now the manito is seated [so signaling Bowman to sit by the pile of goods]. Bowman will sing, Steersman will then take it up. They will be the only ones to "talk" [mystically]. This is all the time that need be spent on [the patient's] preparation. So now we lift up the goods for the manito to see.

All circled around for each to pick up his respective fee. After one or two rounds, the chief dismissed the company by saluting them and receiving the usual acknowledgments. He remarked, "Thank you all, manitos, for your fine work. That is all for today. Tomorrow we lead [the patient] into the manito wigwam [for the public rite]." They filed out in ranked order, Steersman first to preserve the sunwise course. Steersman and Bowman might return informally to discuss the next day's business, for they were the chief actors.

On this ritual occasion of accepting fees, some aspects of the origin tale were elaborated upon—or any other proper mysteries, fitting the grade. Portions of the tale omitted inadvertently at earlier sessions were told here by any leading officer, with two particular "pieces" being reserved generally for higher midé grades. One concerned the practice of issuing invitation sticks, which had to be of cedar, about eight inches long and one-sixteenth of an inch in diameter, split from the mother piece, whittled, and colored red, from native pigment. During preparatory midé sessions, these formal sticks were made and issued by the patient to the chief officers, at the head midé's direction. Thus, four sticks were issued at first grade: to the head midé, his assistant, Bowman, and Steersman. Eight sticks were issued at second grade: to the original four and besides to the assistant that each one now engaged. Twelve sticks were issued at third grade and sixteen at fourth. For later stages, and always for the public ceremony, a large corps of "bystanding officers" was engaged, composed of each chief officer's further appointees, and additional invitation sticks were made and delivered to each of these at the direction of his appointing officer.

The origin tale explains that before people knew to issue sticks, they pointed a finger at the person invited, but often found that the pointing was forgotten. Shell and Bear feared that this would cause neglect of midéwiwin. According to the tale:

When the midé manito commenced, he knew the Indian would not remember invitation by finger, that directly the Indian turned away, he would forget. "I guess this [stick] will be better" [thought the manito]. Therefore [Bear] reared and bit a piece off the midé Tree [cedar] so that splinters fell about. He dropped down, picked them up, counted, and there were eighty. Shell said, "Too many." Bear answered, "We will set a number for each Layer [grade]. This is what

135

the Indian will use and henceforth cannot forget when people give sticks to him. Indeed, this will the Indian use."

A second "piece" elaborated on Bear. In the lodge of sacrifices and in the sudatory, Bowman (impersonating Bear) held a small, rough-cut profile in birchbark of Bear. At the public rite, this image was replaced by a freshly killed dog termed "midé Bear" (more than one above first grade) which was placed briefly at the lodge's east entrance and was then boiled for the feast. It was laid at the east entrance because Bear commenced his travels in the east; Bear was said to be "the one who opens the midé lodge door." The dog was also an offering to Bear for purchasing entrance to the midé life from this Guardian of the portals. Thus, the cooked dog simultaneously represented the birchbark image, the animal and manito Bear, and an offering. His ritual potential did not protect a dog from neglect and abuse in ordinary circumstances—as midéwiwin's fine intentions and uses did not bar the most evil sorcery.

Bowman or the chief midé told the Bear story, waving the image. The interpolation fits at that point in the origin tale where Bear has broken through to Earth's top layer:

Shell said, "I am going to talk about our midé Bear. He is the one to go ahead [receiving the Indian's first tobacco and food offerings and opening the midé lodge so that the Indian's requests reach Supernaturals seated there] when the Indian requests anything. And he said he would receive it [the dog offering] direct." Now I [the midé chief speaking] do not recite this for mercenary reasons [as did some midé chiefs, demanding further fees for the "piece"] but only to explain this provision of the manitos for man's life on Earth. . . . So all the manitos could do was answer, "Thank you!"

Such "pieces," and the entire origin tale, seem extremely slight on surface merits, in a foreign language and setting. But the Ojibwa's focus put the verbal product in its far richer context, as suggested by the explanations and parentheses. The tales' slightness was partly a literary form, even a religious one, for value was laid on great understatement. There existed a general injunction against public displays about mystic matters. There should be little open talk about mystic personalities' names and deeds; circumlocutions of phrase and thought were preferred, and these too should be brief, no matter how elliptical the consequence. It was meet to glance seldom upon mystic objects or symbols, to employ the mystic only in extremities, and briefly. Supernaturals were said to resent public familiarity and importunity. The individual's pursuit of his vision harmonized with this view that the public religion had much that was tacit. Tacitness, taciturnity, and vicious jealous secrecies coexisted in all Ojibwa life's aspects. Even today Canadian authorities complain of these traits among the reservation tribesmen.

In Ontario, apportioning the fees and exhibiting them to Supernaturals was much simpler in the 1930's, possibly reflecting recency of the midéwiwin there and geographical remoteness from the center of influence. After smoking ritually, the Ontario chief midé directed the patient to distribute the goods (which had lain against the north wall all night) among the officers, who were all present. Complying, the patient moved sunwise from the chief midé to all the officers, giving each one his allowance, stroking down the sides of each one's head in loving esteem, thanking him for giving longer life, leaving each one with "Hail!" When the patient finished, the chief midé saluted his officers and thanked them for their "aid to the patient." He rose and told the other officers to rise, and he sang.

The officers complied, dancing in place to the chief's singing, each with his allowance on his arm. The drum went the round of the men and each sang in turn, the patient holding one end of the drum, facing the singer who held the other end in his left hand, as he sang and danced, and the patient accompanied with a jiggling dance. The shaman's rattle was always one officer ahead of the drum. Drum and rattle were returned to the chiefs and all sat silently a few minutes until the head midé spoke again, telling his colleagues to make four circlings of the place. Singing, he led a sunwise walk; ending the circuit he placed his goods in the

137

lodge center and the others followed suit in order. Each returned to his place and stood there. This ended the portion analogous to the Minnesota rite of "Sitting by the Sacrifices."

SHELL-SHOOTING CEREMONY

Climaxing midéwiwin in dogma and drama, the ritual of each shaman "shooting" a mystically powerful migis shell into the patient followed the distribution of fees. In Minnesota in the 1930's it was done separately, after being rehearsed the night following the rite of "Sitting by the Sacrifices" or during previous night sessions. The migis shells were declared to have originated anciently in the great "ocean" (Lake Superior?) and were presented as a materialization of the Earth Supernatural who conceived midéwiwin. To them was attributed a life so vital that they were said to multiply as they lay in a shaman's mystic hide sack. Shooting one from the sack into a person injected a dose of vigor. The ailing patient-recipient found the dose unbearable, ritualistically, and "fainted" or crumpled, to be restored by secret techniques. (The conception seems to mimic vaccine inoculation.) The shell had to be coughed up, ritually, from the patient's body, but its mystic vigor remained behind. This notion recalls the body "spot" of all visionaries—the tiny replica of the guardian manito. The actual shells were used over and over, their mystic vigor never fading, being that of Shell manito.

In the public shooting ceremony and in rehearsal, actual shells were used, but the chief midé never pretended to colleagues and patient that the shell was shot literally. That image was a mystery preserved for laity. The 1930's chief said that he and his colleagues ritualized the shooting to cause spiritual change in relations between patient and midé Patrons. The Patrons took their cue from seeing officers shoot and then actually sent their mystic charge of life into the patient—"because they said they would." The patient must *act* struck to help effect the change.

At rehearsal, each move was coached by the chief midé. As the

138

patient was handicapped by illness and fears, he was coached even during the public ceremony.

When a patient did follow directions clearly, he might grow skeptical. This happened at Emo with Katie Namepog and her brother John, who assured me that the shell never truly was shot in, that they had never felt penetration or after-effects, that the whole rite was fraudulent, "a racket" for midé officers. Another woman, Redbird, decided that she would get in on this racket, had herself engaged repeatedly as a "bystanding manito," and kept herself in shells at the Hudson's Bay store, buying them in gross.

The shooting was preluded by a number of smaller ritual moves, comparable stylistically to the ritual hesitation of three missteps before entering a doorway. Thus, the shells were first placed singly by a shaman on certain of the patient's joints or elsewhere, considered as entrances of life and vulnerable; and the patient was coached that when one was placed on a joint or elsewhere, he must snatch at the spot as if in agony from the Supernatural's potency—he must appear ritually pitiable. Finally, when an officer aimed a shell, the suffering patient must simulate collapse.

Local variations in the pattern of shell placement were regarded as gravely as are doctrinal disputes in Christian dogma. Hole-in-the-Sky, with his Minnesota views, was outraged at the Ontario version of shell placements. In Ontario, the 1930's midé chief walked the patient ahead of him in the lodge, leading from the east towards the lodge's west door, making two sunwise circuits around the lodge as officers sat and watched. The chief sang while holding a rattle and throwing it on beat, during this. Then he seated the patient atop the pile of fees in the center, facing east, dramatizing the despairing appeal to Shell, armed with goods for purchasing "life." Thence the chief circled sunwise about the lodge back to his own seat against the eastern wall. He directed the officers, "Now we ask you for your shells. Hail! Now arise, midé men!" Thus Bowman led lesser officers sunwise around to the eastern door, marching the circuit twice, stopping at the north while Bowman sang and directed them to prepare their shells. Bowman approached the patient and laid a shell on patient's right toe; the next man laid one on the left toe; the next, on the inside of the right ankle; the next, on the inside of the left ankle; the fifth man, on the right knee; the sixth, on the left knee; the seventh, on the right hip; the eighth, on the left hip. This pattern of starting from the lower body belonged to first grade, which was nearer Earth's "bottom layer" than advanced grades of Earth midéwiwin.

But Hole-in-the-Sky assured me that the first grade cure required four shells placed solely on the heart, for the heart is the seat of life! He asserted that Earth's second cure called for shell placements on right and left ankles and knees; that the third cure demanded placements on right and left little toes and hips, plus one on the pubes and one on the navel; that Earth's fourth cure located shells on right and left sides, including the soles of feet, the space between the big toe and the next, and in the kidney region but placed ventrally. In addition, he said gravely, there were Sky aspects to these cures which Ontario people ignored but which should not be ignored, for every person consists, like the world, of a region above as well as a region below. Therefore second grade added "above" treatments invoking Sky powers by shell placements on right and left wrists and elbows. Third grade required additional "above" placements on right and left, including the little fingers, shoulders, and ears. Fourth grade "above" placements went on both sides, including nipples, collarbone, inside of the mouth, palms, between thumbs and index fingers, on upper lip, and on top of the head.

Hole diagrammed also a system of shell placements in cures of midéwiwin's Sky grades. These locations belonged above the belt, generally in the breastbone area. The fifth cure, being first of the Sky grades, required four placements, one in each corner of the area. Sixth cure required eight placements, right and left, on parallel lines within the area. Seventh needed twelve, placed right and left on parallel lines in the area. Eighth had sixteen such placements. Hole found that Red Lake made the "dreadful error" of laying shells for Sky grades on spots assigned to and already "cured" by Earth-patterned placements.

Starting the shell-placing ritual, Bowman set the example for the officers following him, saying, "I put this [shell] on your ankle [or elsewhere] to strengthen your life on Earth. . . . I give you this shell with which I keep myself strong and healthy." When the last officer, Steersman, applied the shell, he admonished, "And now I caution you. Cherish most carefully what we tell you. That is all. We have told you everything, given you our shells . . . eight shells we have given you [for first grade in Ontario] to strengthen your life. Hail!" The chief supported with his assent.

After each officer placed his shell, he moved aside west and stood waiting on the others, facing them behind Steersman. Then the band circuited sunwise twice, after which each in sequence removed his shell from the patient's body and returned it to his mystic hide sack made from an animal whose Spirit patronized the rite. They returned sunwise to their places and the patient did also.

The chief midé set down the drum, rose and faced south, and addressed the Supernaturals: "Thanks for strengthening [the patient's] life. That is all. By putting these shells in his body, not ever again can any injury touch it, I tell the midé people. Hail!" All assented formally.

BUILDING THE MIDÉ WIGWAM

In Ontario it would now be about three in the afternoon, the ceremony having been proceeding since mid-morning, interrupted occasionally by food and tobacco. At sundown everyone departed. The patient's family started to cook again, preparing two large kettles of food for the ten or fifteen village women invited by Bowman and Steersman to construct the wigwam, or lodge, for the following day's public ceremony. (Informants often

141

used the word "tent" in English for the midé lodge.) At about five in the afternoon, the women entered the large preparatory wigwam with their food pans. Bowman served each with a pipeful of tobacco and food, saying, "Eat, all of you, this midé food. Now the manito wishes you to help build the manito wigwam where our lives are to be strengthened. There we villagers go tomorrow. That is all I have to say. Hail!" The women gave assent.

Following Bowman's instructions, the wigwam was built near the preparatory lodge. Ash poles for the frame were cut by some women, brush by others. The wigwam would be about 50 feet long, 12 or 13 feet wide, and 7 feet high in the center (see Plate 5b). The brush was spread around the base of the lodge, to the height of a seated person. Bowman waited in the preparatory lodge until a woman went in to tell him the job was done. He stepped out to address the women, "Thank you! Already you have completed the manito wigwam. And tomorrow we come to it! That is all I say to you. Hail!" The women responded, "Eh-h-h."

Meanwhile, more food had been cooking. Bowman returned to the preparatory lodge where the four chief men were seated, together with the patient and the latter's spouse and children. The patient set food and tobacco before the chief midé; the servitor then distributed these to all the officers. The patient did not eat, as the food was midé fees. The chief said, "Thank you for filling my 'shell' dish. . . . Now [to his colleagues], eat! Hail!" They gave assent.

The patient, wearing ritual paints on scalp and face identical in colors and pattern with what he would wear for the public rite next day, sat and waited while the four officers ate. When they finished, the chief midé said, "I bless my [brother-in-law or sister-in-law, or some other kinship term for the patient]. Now I will take the drum and have him dance—this one for whom we midéwi. Let him rise, come out, and stand before me. That is all I need say. Let him rise and come forth to dance. Hail!" He picked up the drum, rubbed it to dampen the hide head, and started a song. After two verses, he signaled the patient, who rose, walked around sunwise unaccompanied by song and drum, halted before the chief's seat, said "Hail!" All assented. The chief struck his drum the number of times that corresponded to the midé grade and said with violent exhalations, "Wé! ho! ho! ho!" repeating three or four times.

Then he said, "Hail, Colleague!" and started to sing. The patient danced before him, bending the knees regularly and slightly, arms spread out. When the song ceased, he said "Hail," thanked the officer who had been dancing and so curing him, and returned sunwise to his place. The drum moved to the chief's assistant, who said, "I too take the midé drum. That is all I have to say. Let him rise and come forth, fellow manitos. Hail!" Like the chief, he sang two verses. Then the patient traveled sunwise around the tent to the singer's place, as before, stood greeting him "Hail!" and received his benign assent. Then the assistant struck the drum briskly with the "Wé! ho! ho!", sang, and the patient danced. When finished, the patient returned sunwise to his place, with all midé courtesies.

Transferring the drum to Bowman, the assistant chief said, "Greeting! I pass the midé drum to you!" Bowman acknowledged, "Thanks! I take up the manito talk. I will perform the [traditions] transmitted to me by the colleagues who put me through the rite. Those outside [lesser manitos and possibly the women who worked on the lodge] may enter and dance. Some midé food remains, so when you finish dancing [in worship], you may eat. Hail!" He sang. The same business with the patient was repeated. Outsiders entered ("just for the meal," I heard a woman mutter resentfully) and stood behind the patient, dancing with him. This over, these guests squatted around to receive the leftover food. In the quiet lodge, only whispering would be heard. The chief addressed the eaters, "We thank you for coming in to dance. Hail!" They assented, showing good will; they were supposed to eat everything and then depart, with formalities.

Bowman passed the drum to Steersman, "Now, you finish the manito talk. Hail!" Steersman answered, arms spread in blessing,

"I greet you all. You who own the midé rite, pardon me if I err. That is all I can say. Hail!" He sang, then addressed the chief, "I have finished this [business]. Now I rise with the drum. Twice [or whatever the grade number] I strike the drum, and twice I circuit, then I leave the drum to you. Hail!" He did this with all the formalities, returning the drum to the chief. The latter spread his arms in blessing and said to all officers, present and absent, "Thanks for concluding this. We try [our best]. That is all. I thank you all. Hail!" Turning to Bowman and Steersman, he continued, "I salute you! Tomorrow we lead this one [the patient] into the manito wigwam. You lead in, I ask, all the midé men, women, and children. Bear will give that one [Bowman] power to open the midé lodge door. Hail!" They left, in formal order.

That night, patient and family slept in the preparatory lodge. Sometimes the chief midé would sleep there too, if his home were distant. An important officer had to be on hand before sunrise, as the goods were then displayed—hung indoors on a rack, at the lodge's north wall—for the Sun to see as it rose. The supervision was considered onerous and the chief officer liked to delegate it to a subordinate, who was in no position to refuse. The officer had to get up before sunrise and waken the patient and his family; none would have slept more than a couple of hours. All were already painted.

THE PUBLIC RITE

The chief stood by the bundle of goods lying at the north wall, stretched out his arm, and said, "I salute the goods. Colleagues, hail!" He told the patient, "I salute you [for] going through the rite. Rise and follow the manito path to the manito wigwam. Hail!" People assented ritualistically. The patient rose and, like the chief, faced south. The chief said, "Now you go." He threw the rattle and barked, ritually cheering up the sleepy people and scaring away the Evil Spirit: "Wah! hee-ee! hee-ee! hee-ee! hee-ee! hee-ee!" The patient, scared and dazed, but considered brave-looking with rosy paints, walked as directed before the

144

chief, facing east. After some paces inside, the chief told him quietly to stop, but he continued his own cheering and scaring bark, "Weé-e! ho! ho!" They resumed walking, patient before chief, until the sunwise route brought them opposite the pile of goods. The chief's assistant joined them and both walked behind the patient, the chief rattling and singing. When the patient was opposite the goods, the chief had him walk over and bundle them on his back "for the Sun to see him working for the manitos." The courtesies of hail and assent always preceded and followed any communication, song, and new ritual detail.

They continued south, rattling and singing in a full sunwise circuit to the west door where they stood in file, facing it. A dog had been laid there, alive if a puppy, killed if full grown. He represented Bear, the door's guardian. There were also two invisible Snake guardians, one on each side of the door. If they objected to someone's entrance, the Snakes rose too high to be stepped over; if they approved, they flattened themselves on the ground. Hence, either at this time or on the previous night, the chief begged these "barrier manitos" to stoop low on the public day to admit midé members but to rise again after the midéwiwin ended. He chanted:

Now, I salute you, door-tenders. Tomorrow [or, today], all day, draw in your breath for us, called Indians. Yes, let this door-stop, this stick [Snake] across the door, sink low all day for those we call Indians [humans]. Now [to Bear], oh, manito [if this is the dawn of the public rite], open the door. Here are his [the patient's] offerings [goods and dog]. Kindly open the door for him! Hail!

Different animals guarded doors of the different grades. The Great Lion seemed to supervise the door-tending at all grades. Otter, in particular, seemed to guard the first-grade entrance; Weasel, the second; Mink, the third; and Bear, the fourth. Sometimes Bear was said to supervise generally all the grades. The two Snakes always flanked the doorkeeper. Lion assisted each keeper by blowing fiery breaths across the threshold. The valued hides of these animals were made into sacks for storing the mystic shells

145

and midé medicines; they were regarded simultaneously as weapons, since the shells were "discharged" from them.

With the chief's exhortation to the door-tenders, the patient picked up the sacrificial dog and, cradling it, walked to the midé lodge. Rattling and singing accompanied the two chiefs and the patient. The chief called a halt at the lodge door, extended his arm in ritual salute, and said with ritualistic speed, "I salute you [door-guardians]." He faced north: "I salute you, manito." Facing south, "I salute you, manito. And you who tend the door, open the way for this one holding the dog." The patient set the dog on the ground before the door, and the chief midé repeated, "Hail!" The patient, followed by the others, circled sunwise about this place with the dog. The chief resumed, "I salute you, doorway. Hail! Thank you, manito for opening the door to him. Hail!" This was said to guardians of north and south directions. No obeisance was made to guardians of the east and west, perhaps because they were thought to be covered in salutes to the doorways, which faced east and west. "Now the midé door is open. Hail!" The chief rattling and barking, they moved upon the door and went through the lodge sunwise. On the second circuit they stopped at north center, as the chief directed, crossed to the south side center, recrossed to the center of the lodge floor where the patient deposited his bundle, undid it, and, aided by the chief, hung the individual sacrificial pieces on a rack standing near the center of the floor. They hung first the chief's goods, then the assistant's, then those of Bowman and Steersman, and finally smaller pieces for the lesser officers.

Now the sun would be up, and the people left for breakfast. Hole explained that the Sun had seen the patient was ready for him, having worked since dark. So Sun blessed him with his pity. The concern with Sun was practically unspoken; this manito received no speeches, no feasts, no tobacco, and in Ontario did not figure as a personal vision patron. But Sun held the foreground of people's thinking, more prominently than Moon, who figures in the midé origin tale, and more so than the Great Spirit who received frequent lip service but little thought at the feasts.

Having breakfasted in the preparatory lodge, the two chiefs walked into the manito lodge—"because the way in has been paid for." The head midé brought in his drum and rattle, setting these by his place. The others stood outside, usually at the eastern end, waiting for Bowman. Though ceremonies could not start without him, he often behaved as though it was never too late for him to arrive. Neighboring women carried kettles full of cooked food to offer midé Supernaturals upon entering the lodge. With some drunken exceptions, the women were dressed nicely and had painted red on cheeks and hair-parting. Waiting for Bowman, the chief counseled the patient how to live properly. The chief handed his servitor a number of invitation sticks, traditionally fixed at eighty, and told him to deliver these to Bowman, besides repeating to Bowman, "Bring your midé paraphernalia [shooting sack and shells] and repeat what was done to you when you were last put through the rite. [Hole explained, 'Paint yourself and put feathers in your hair.'] Do thus."

"Then he will walk up to the manito wigwam," Hole said. "He will wait there until our Grandfather [drum] has sounded three times [for the duration of three songs]. Then we will look for him to arrive, entering the manito wigwam with the manito people."

Waiting, Bowman stood practically alone at the east door, most people falling away toward the west door to yield him the stage. He lifted his arm and said, "All you midé people, I salute you." He moved about among them, extending his arm over their heads in blessing. "All you midé people. Hail!" He circled sunwise outside of the lodge, barking ritually. At the east door again, he said, "I salute you. The door bars our way. Open, you [two] midé manitos, for I wish to lead in the midé men, women, and children. Hail!" He circuited sunwise and continued to the west door where he barked in the two monosyllables, barking each three times successively. He circled sunwise in place and barked again, continued to the east door, turned sunwise again, directed three barks at the door, continued barking on a further circuit to the west door, and stopped short of it. The servitor handed him the sacrificial dog. Bowman walked up to the west door, rattle in right hand, dog in left, shook the rattle at the door and barked three times. The dog now in his outstretched right hand, Bowman said "Hail!", carried the dog inside the east door, laid it on the ground, and repeated "Hail!"

Thus the door was opened to all; the outsiders now entered. Officers sat in fixed places, but ordinary midé folk sat anywhere. Guests set their kettles of food under the patient's hanging goods. Sticks and stones were nearby, placed as in the "Sitting by the Sacrifices."

Once the people were all inside, the patient and his family, directed by the chief, led the chief and his assistant once around sunwise, ending up at these officers' seats. The chief intoned:

I salute you all. Hail! I must talk [ritually] about the food, all the fine food brought into the manito wigwam. Again I address the midé manito. We put all in your care: we beg to trade these eatables for midé life [for the patient]. We greatly desire life. Whereas, you want for nothing. We would trade for the life we desire so greatly. Indeed, grant us life! Hail! . . . Now the servitor takes his spoon to serve each midé man, and midé woman, and midé child. Hail! Four times the midé officers will sing [at first grade, so that each of the four main officers sings once for the patient to dance]. Then [the patient] goes to the center of the midé wigwam and they [the officers] will give him the midé shells. Hail!

When the chief and his assistant finished singing, Bowman addressed them before commencing his own turn. If it was fourth grade, and the chief had several (four) assistants, Bowman said:

I salute the manito, and the next, and the next, and the next. . . . Now our Grandfather [the drum] has come and seated himself by me. Carefully I salute all manitos, all whom I represent. Now I begin. Hear me attentively [addressing the patient who would hear the powerful song Bowman would sing for his health and instruction].

The song is not borrowed [a strong assertion, meaning that the giver, Bowman, bought it and owned it entire] and I am not merely lending it [but giving it outright to the patient]. Now I take up our Grandfather [to strike the drum accompaniment]. I do not request the other manitos [to participate]. What I do now [the singing] requires no strain by the others [they need not sing]. Only *I* will sing. Finally, when it [the ritual] gets to him, the End One [Steersman], he may take it up, if he considers it needful.

So Bowman sang a song and sometimes another. The patient came to dance before him. Bowman declaimed:

I was taught that, where you stand before me [or, "before the manito"], are four strips of iron. [The number of strips is that of the grade.] Iron is *strong*. You stand on the fourth strip and there must dance to the mystic talk [mystic songs]. Thus you will lose all that ails you, never more to suffer.

He sang and the patient danced, as rehearsed in the preparatory lodge. This declamation was a major one and in the 1930's was appraised jealously by adepts. John Wilson, Maggie's husband and son of old Chief Namepog of Manitou Reserve, considered the version above, given me by Maggie's stepfather, to be inadequate. John was a recent Protestant convert, one of the few at Manitou, still steeped in Ojibwa tradition. His midé father and uncles had trained him assiduously; he had been an able and responsive pupil. His Christian conversion merely evidenced extension of his mystic interests; he was absorbed in "cures," especially for his own chronic ailments. As a valued servitor, he attended midé rituals constantly, acquiring detailed knowledge of them. He appreciated his wife as much for her mystic talents as for her character, and discussed mystic matters with her.

Though Maggie had arranged for her stepfather to give me his usual Bowman's declamation (so he could earn a little), she arranged also for her husband to register his objection. John did not intend to challenge his father-in-law openly on this occasion (probably it was an old, known bone of contention between them) but to set me straight. So he offered this speech instead of the other, his version coming of course from Namepog practice; it

149

was made in the nearly empty lodge before patient and family only, the villagers having sent in their foods:

Hail, Colleagues! First and foremost I offer thanks for the tobacco I take now; and for the food prepared by the [other] people, which they will take later. *These* people [patient and family] seek renewed life on this occasion. I salute the midé chief, who will take the tobacco and food. "Oh, thanks," he will say, "surprisingly, they remember what they were taught." I beg the midé people to regard me with indulgence. Soon we will call them in. Soon invitations will be carried from lodge to lodge. I salute them tenderly. And I salute the one [manito] who takes care of them. [Addressing the servitor, waiting at the chief's side for directions:] Now, go about inviting the people. For tobacco smoke spreads over the skies [in ritual invocations] and the food too is known there [so the Supernaturals are prepared to heed Indians' requests]. Indeed, he [collective manitos] is grateful that the Indian remembers how to gain life. Tenderly does he say, "Thank you. From here I am pleased to grant you what you beg for. See me: never do I ail. That is why I was set here, to watch over Indians and listen. And I too gain, receiving tobacco and food. Yes, for this was I set here, from afar to give Indians what they request, from afar to give them strengthened life. That is all I need say."

I will take up a song [Bowman informs the Supranatural] and you will understand why.

The chief had the villagers enter the lodge to hear the song. Then the chief's assistant declaimed, before singing in his turn:

Colleagues, hail! I now salute you, midé manito, and you colleagues. May they regard us kindly—the midé manitos, the midé posts [wood spirits], and the midé stones [used in the sweat lodge]. At this moment the manitos take [our] tobacco, food, and fine sacrifices. These Indians have worked to gain life! Indeed, may the manitos approve—the manitos of the four directions from which the wind blows and protect us. That is all I will say. Let the manito regard most leniently the errors I make. Colleagues, hail!

Before, during, and after this routine, the chief and his officers interspersed bits about the Supernaturals, saluting, and telling portions of the origin tale in general terms. At any point in the ritual, the head midé observed:

150

The Ritual in the Life Midéwiwin

I'll say this little thing. The manito wigwam is filled throughout with Supernaturals—I salute them. This talk does not exaggerate or ignore anything. An old Indian [the speaker's teacher] taught me to say this at some stage. [To the Supernaturals:] Regard me kindly, pity [credit] my sincerity.

Then he would start the mythic portion:

Now when he [Bear] got his manito thing constructed, then he, our Grandfather, came up and looked in. He saw no caretaker guarding the manito entrance. He gazed around and saw a midé manito [Lion]. He told him, "After he [the Supernaturals collectively] arrives [in this primordial mythic lodge to consider the Indian requests], will you not stay on guard? Perhaps the Indian will be confused [and so wander where he should not]. But he will see you and you will know how to handle it."

Our Grandfather continued the journey, piling up life in Earth's center for the Indian to draw upon. It was like piling up food in one dish for many people to eat from. At Earth's center [sometimes identified with Lake Superior], he piled up the pack of life.

Coming over the hill from the daylight land [the east] he heard manitos discuss this wonderful thing designed for the Indians and they said, "Perhaps we can own it." [They were the red, or heated stones of the sudatory, anxious to patronize the first midé grade. Bear was supposed to have responded, "Yes, you will own it."]

Heading for a door that faced him, he went right through the manito wigwam, south towards Earth's center. On the way, he heard sounds of talk and stuck his head in [a midé lodge]. It was a full meeting of seated Supernaturals. They said, "We wish to own what is being planned for the Indian."

These Supernaturals were the cedar boughs, wishing to patronize second grade. Bear later replied, "Yes, you will own it." These mentions invoked present support of the Supernaturals. But lay hearers remained confused, for clarifications were withheld, usually. Special terms, perhaps obsolete or borrowed, and mystifying periphrases were legion. Speech constructions that appear odd in this English version were often odd also to Ojibwa laymen. Shamans did not mind saying that the mystification was developed to intimidate.

151

These were the blue [or green, cedar] supports of midéwiwin. Heading for a door, he walked in straightway, never slackening. "Yes, you may own what is being planned for the Indian."

Again, coming from the south toward the place whence the wind blows strong [walking west, for the cardinal points require mention on the sunwise route], he heard sounds of talk, "Perhaps we can own what they design for the Indian." A manito lodge door facing him, he entered straightway and saw the lodge full with a meeting of Supernaturals. They were the midé hides [or animals whose hides became shamans' sacks; their recorded color should have been yellow]. He thanked them [for offering patronage], passing right through the lodge, "Yes, you will own what they are planning for the Indian."

Again, there whence comes the cold air he was walking and heard sounds of talk: "We think we want to own what is being planned for the Indian." A door of the manito wigwam facing him, he poked in his head, saw that those within resembled icicles, and thought, "So it looks like this—these are the manito shells."

The white color should be named, to salute the fourth, top layer of Earth, identifying it with the mystic shell and the cardinal north. Here the chief's ritual portion-telling ended. The final incident varied in small details of Bear's wonderment.

The officers went through a round of singing; the patient, the attendant round of dancing; and all returned to their places. The chief rose, faced the patient, and declared, "Colleague, hail! I salute you!" Patient responded. The chief directed him to arise and approach. Agreeing, "Hail!", the patient circuited the ovoid lodge sunwise from the east, the chief fell in behind, rattling, barking, directing in undertones, until they pulled up at the east door, when the patient said, "Hail!" The chief assented, then added, "Greeting, colleagues! I salute these sacrifices to the Supernaturals. Hail!" With the patient slowly stepping ahead of him, the chief resumed rattling and barking, both circling sunwise around each of the two poles supporting the horizontal that held the fee-sacrifices, oriented east-west. The chief stated, "Thanks, says the midé manito." The chief's arm spread in blessing. "Now the midé manito accepts the sacrifices. Hail!" There continued further slow sunwise pacing around each of the two supports of the sacrifices and around the whole piece too, until at its west end they halted and the chief barked three times. Eyes slanted to catch the chief's motioning and other cues, the patient took down a blanket—a main fee-offering, and intended for the chief—laid it on his left arm, saying "Hail!" and repeated this with the other nine (at first grade) pieces he took down. The two resumed sunwise pacing around the poles till they reached the center of the lodge. Here the patient neatly piled the blankets and other goods, concluding with "Hail!" when he and the chief returned sunwise to their respective seats.

All others, except the four chief officers, sat relaxed during the preceding ritual, eating and smoking. The chief rested only briefly, then resumed with the patient a sunwise circuit around the lodge, barking and rattling away the Evil. They came to the pile of goods, the patient turned sunwise around it, and sat on it facing east, legs outstretched. The chief made a ritual circuit to his seat and smoked. He saw the patient and his goods as a whole, before the Supernaturals, since both pleaded for "life."

The chief rose, arm outstretched in blessing, to say, "I salute you, midé people. Hail! . . . Now prepare your shells, for the one undergoing this rite bought them for his life. Hail!" He directed Bowman: "You begin, with your midé wayan [sack]." To the first lesser officer: "You, too, prepare your midé wayan. Hail!" He directed the other officers likewise and added to Steersman: "You will complete what it is the patient desires. Hail!" He sat, smoked, stood again, addressed Bowman: "Rise! Begin the work! Hail!" Unless the hour was too advanced, the chief then dramatized his transfer of ritual direction to Bowman by picking up his drum and snaking around in the tortuous fashion called "eluding the evil manito" while he sang a group of songs or verses called "Moving the Drum."

With the drum, he proceeded sunwise around the lodge, stopping at the east end to sing the first verse of a song:

> The eastern land [where Bear started his midé travels].
> [*Sung eight times*]

> The manitos walk at Earth's middle [referring to the shells].
> The eastern land.
> [*Sung four times*]

He continued sunwise halfway around to the western door and halted to repeat the song. He finished his circle and halted at the east end to sing another verse of the song:

> The southern land.
> [*Sung seven times*]

This invoked the cardinal South Supernatural in the sunwise circuit.

> The manitos walk at Sky's middle.

This was to honor Sky Supernaturals, equally with those of Earth.

> Oh, the south land!
> [*Sung three times*]

The same business was repeated; then the chief sang the third verse:

> We-e-o heyo heyo.
> [*Sung seven times*]
> Lion's hide contains my shell!
> We-e-o heyo heyo.
> [*Sung seven times*]

He circuited around sunwise, crossed sunwise (left) and continued so, crossed again (right), singing steadily. Then he fell quiet but continued around sunwise to where he had made the (right) sunwise crossing, and stopped. He began a fourth verse, this number and its multiples being favorite sequences:

> We-o he-o heo.
> [*Repeated from four to eight times*]
> The Snake's hide contains my shell!
> We-o he-o heo.

He turned sunwise around a midé pole at his stopping-place, and continued singing towards the door, where the singing halted, but he went sunwise around a pole there and halted. He said a few

154

words about the drum; he had the option of doing this earlier, too, when starting new verses. He made several more tripping sunwise courses around the lodge, the number corresponding to that of the grade, halted opposite Bowman, tripped sunwise in place before him, and handed him the drum, then sat down.

Bowman rose to address his six followers:

Salutations! Prepare all, withold nothing from him [the patient] who depends on us! Let him feel strongly that which he desires [i.e., strength and life]. That is all I have to say. Hail! [Then, to Steersman] Salutations! You be rear man. You were taught much by the midé people. Use today all that you learned. Do as you were taught: teach him, this purchaser of midéwiwin. Hail! [He sat briefly, then rose.] I salute you men once more. Let us all rise and on with our work! Greetings to midé manito! And to the midé wigwam, the midé sticks [for invitations and other "useful ends"], the midé posts, the midé stones, the midé brush [usually cedar branches, rimming edges of the lodge], the midé food, the midé tobacco, the midé Skies [or Day], and the midé Earth. Let all judge me kindly. So be it. I salute too the midé people now starting the work of guiding our colleague [the patient]. Hail! I will begin to sing.

He struck the drum the servitor brought him from the patient's side at the lodge center; the rattle also might now be given to him, though preferably it was given to the first officer standing by the servitor. Bowman tripped quickly sunwise around each of the two midé posts, barking in the two different ways; he returned the drum to the chief, resumed his place, and sang unaccompanied after throwing out his right arm four times in blessing, barking each time. "Hail!" he said, and opened his song:

Manito, they are flying.

Here, "they" refers to the mystic shells that the men now prepared to shoot into the patient.

Manito, they are flying.
[*Sung twice more*]
The shells of the midé people [officers].
Manito, they are flying
[*Sung twice more*]

Meanwhile, if the sacrificial dog was still alive, it was knocked to death on the forehead by the servitor and singed for cooking. The servitor distributed food, the people smoked. Inside the midé lodge, people behaved decorously, but outside there was much roistering by people who turned the occasion to drinking and gambling. Midé officers might join them for relaxation.

Bowman ended his song, walked sunwise to the west door, rattling and barking, and the servitor drummed. Lesser officers lined up behind. After halting briefly, with barking and "Hail!" Bowman continued sunwise to the east door, his band behind him. He barked again, cried "Hail!" and addressed the patient, "Greeting! Now I'll talk to you and show this that you beg of me—my migis. I will conceal nothing, I am ready to give you all you wish of me. That is all I have to say. Hail!" Privately, he told the patient that he addressed him from the east to imbue him with strength that would rise as surely as the sun rises daily in the east.

Listen to me, look at me: all I say, hold in your heart for I give you good advice. Swallow your saliva and you will understand all. Never speak badly of others, the worthy midé men, women, and children. For your strength is so great that if you speak badly of them [i.e., curse them], they will be killed [by your midé society]. Be kind to all, love all living things, and the worthy midé men, women, and children. Never speak evil—be as kind as possible. Share your food, no matter how little [the speaker illustrated with half of the index and middle fingers], give half to the worthy midé. . . . Now I prepare my shell. Hail! You too, reveal your shells to this one buying midé life. Hail! [To Steersman] You finish this, he depends on you to complete the rites. You are the last to aid his search for life. Hail!

Repeating "Hail!" to the patient, he started rattling, singing, drumming, barking. Both hands grasped his midé sack full of shells, right hand before the left, aiming it like a gun. The sack's fur depended on the grade into which Bowman was last initiated: otter for first grade, guardian of the doorway; weasel for second grade; mink for third grade; bear or bear's paw for fourth grade. The chief and his assistant (or more assistants, beyond first grade) stood, one with the drum, the other with the rattle.

Watching the band, Bowman walked sunwise to the south center, barking. From there he directed the sack-weapon at a fixed spot on the patient's body, the number and location of spots varying with the patient's grade, as told above; and he barked. With him barked all others in the lodge except the patient. Bowman concluded "Hail!" and proceeded silently to the west door; his band remained behind at the east door.

The first of the lesser officers said "Hail!", walked barking to south center, as his leader had, directed his midé sack at the patient's body, and proceeded to the west door behind Bowman. All lesser officers repeated the business, each shooting at another, stipulated spot, so that couples covered opposite sides of the body.

At his turn, Steersman spoke from the eastern door: "I want to give you advice. In your blessed fine life, never speak a bad word to your fellow men. In all things, be kind to the worthy midé men. That is all I have to say. Hail! And like Bear, I will use my limbs." He sang a song in which he said he would walk like Bear (resembling a song of personal vision power). Before shooting, he proceeded sunwise to south center with big clumsy steps, pretending to use his hands like paws; the midé sack was shoved in his belt; at each step he barked and rattled. This opened one of the most exciting acts of the ritual, underscoring the previous shootings. Steersman stopped at south center, pulled out his sack and "threw" it—making a violent throwing motion with his arms but never actually letting go of the sack—at the proper spot on the patient, barking. At his shot, the patient pretended to collapse, falling flat on his face, head to the east, towards the land whence Bear came with the pack of life. Steersman saluted, "Hail!" and joined the others at the west door. All gave "Hail!" to the scene of "cure" and started sunwise towards the patient. Four stood on each side of him, awaiting the chief and his assistant (at first grade), walking sunwise to them. The two men halted on opposite sides of the patient, one facing south, the other facing north, watching him. Both held their sacks, the chief holding also

157

the drum, and the assistant holding also the rattle. The band of men barked twice, aimed their sacks, then laid them on the patient's back, stroking it. They barked steadily a few minutes, shaking the sacks at each syllable. Barking, they helped the patient sit up, pulling at each arm; when he was up, they breathed thankfully, "Hail!" The chiefs and the band sang and rattled while Bowman and Steersman also pulled up the patient slowly, for he was "weak."

When the patient collapsed upon being shot, people said that he was overcome by the transfusion of "power," by awe of midé Supernaturals and the whole business, and by especial fear of the migis, which could be fatal in sorcery. The patient was revived in various styles. At times, shamans feinted withdrawing the shell. At times, the patient rose of his own accord, "regurgitating" the shell. Sometimes midé officers "extracted" the shell and then simulated regurgitating it from their own bodies. When the shell was finally "out," and the patient up on his feet, he was held to be well and strong again.

At this time or before he shot, Steersman sang this song praising Bear:

> I am in sight,
> [Sung four times]
> Coming from the daylight land.
> I am in sight.
> [Sung three times]
> It is as though you could see me,
> [Sung four times]
> Coming from the daylight land.

At the patient's side, officers dancing the invocation, the chief sang a song, addressing the patient, that might be:

> You will see our shell.
> [Sung four times]
> In two days you will see our shell.
> [Sung three times]
> You will see our shell.
> [Sung two or three times]

158

The chief's assistant then sang, the others danced, and the words might be:

> There I [the flying shell] will alight.
> [*Sung five times*]
> I am your shell.
> There I will alight.
> [*Sung three or four times*]

When the chief had two assistants (at second grade), the second one sang here such words as:

> Do you hear me? Do you hear me? [shell speaking]
> [*Sung eight times*]
> Oh, midé folk,
> Do you hear me? Do you hear me?
> [*Sung three to five times*]

Bowman and Steersman had been guarding the patient. Now Bowman told the patient to face north and proceed sunwise to the east. The band followed in order. The patient halted at the east door with all behind him, said "Hail!" (being so directed in undertones by Bowman), continued sunwise, the men barking behind, turned at the west door for the north center and remained there. The band went to the chief's seat and waited in file. Bowman, on a ritual "Hail!", proceeded to his seat sunwise, and the others followed suit, the chiefs barking, lowering drum and rattle gradually to the ground, saying "Hail!" and assuming their seats.

The patient had remained standing in the center. The chief rose, addressed him, "Greeting! Now deliver your offerings. Hail!" and walked sunwise to him. The patient laid a blanket for the chief over his own arm, saying, "Let this be it!", and repeated with the blanket or other fee for the assistant "bishop" (in the translation of Will Rogers and others for this midé rank). These were the only two offerings that the patient held, the chiefs carrying the others. The patient led a sunwise turn to the chief's seat and laid down the blankets, saying "Amen" or "Hail!" and hearing the responses. Followed by chief and assistants, he proceeded to Bowman; there the due fee was laid over the patient's left arm and the patient was directed to turn sunwise before Bowman. Complying, the patient smoothed down the sides of Bowman's head in reverence, saying, "Thanks for strengthening my life. Hail!" and gave him the offering; and all assented ritually, "Eh-h-h!" The patient repeated the same business with all other officers.

The patient returned to his seat on a sunwise circuit, saying "Hail!" as everyone did when completing any ritual act. The chief rose to say, "Now all of us will arise, to dance and display the goods offered to the midé manito," meaning the fees. All officers rose with their goods, and danced, singing, sunwise once around the lodge, and resumed their seats. The servitor drummed and rattled for them at his place, which might be anywhere. All smoked and ate.

The chief rose and directed Bowman, "Greeting! Prepare as many shells as you wish to use, eight or ten [at first grade rite]. Hail!" Bowman agreed, "Eh-h-h. Among us, we have only eight shells. So we will use only eight men." The eight rose, saying "Hail!" Bowman directed, "Take the shells out of your midé sacks," and all went sunwise to the east door. Bowman sent the chief to the patient seated on brush and mats at the center, facing east. Bowman walked sunwise to the patient and laid a shell on his right foot. (This account holds for Manitou Reserve, Ontario, in the 1930's. Placement patterns varied locally, as told earlier.) The chief barked. Bowman saluted "Hail!", went to the west door, stopped with "Hail!" The same business was gone through by each of the others, who finally lined up behind Bowman.

All this accomplished, Bowman directed his band, "We go now." They circled sunwise to the east door, thence to the patient in the center, where each in turn picked up his shell from the patient's body. They continued sunwise as before, lined up near the east door, shell in the right hand, sack in the left. Bowman directed his men to watch him: he turned about sunwise, the others did also, all saluted "Hail!" They proceeded sunwise, barking, until at about halfway on the south side, each put his shell in his mouth, squatted down, and pressed his hands over his mouth. Now the chiefs took up the drum and rattled. They undertook the barking also as the other officers had their mouths stopped by shells. Bowman and his men rose and went to the west door, the chiefs barking. Bowman continued alone from the west door, sunwise, barking, until he reached the mats and blanket in the center where the patient had been, where he mimicked a terrific gagging, bending far over. The chiefs pacing him with barks, the gagging Bowman expelled the shell upon the mats, barked, saluted "Hail!" and proceeded to the east door. His followers went through the same mimicry, elaborating at will, as by pretending that the gagging was hopeless and demanded rubbing the mystic sack on a desperate gagger's back. But inevitably, each shell was expectorated. The symbolism was that the manito shell was the body's vigor, integral to the body, as hard to separate as a limb— and it was this strength that the patient now received.

The chief and his one or more assistants barked and sang; the band danced up to the patient near the east door; the patient danced in place. In this round, Bowman feinted throwing the midé sack at the patient and shooting him with the shell it contained. As he had been taught in previous secret sessions, the patient responded by formally enacting a drama of injury: he threw his torso down from the waist and moaned or made some crying sound of hurt. (I heard a disbeliever say at this point, at Manitou, "It doesn't hurt at all!") Then the patient straightened up erect—indicating that the shell inoculation was functioning, restoring his strength. Each member of the band now went through the same business of dancing to the patient, shooting him and enacting the test and transfer of strength. As each finished, he danced back to his seat. Only when all finished did the chiefs cease singing.

The principal midé addressed those watching from outside the mystic lodge, "Now you may all enter, for in here do your lives belong. Let each one enter this midé wigwam, each with his midé sack. Hail! Here is your life rooted fast, like a pole driven hard into the ground. Let all enter! Hail!" The watchers crowded in through both doors, in festive mood, all dressed nicely. "It is like a celebration for them," said Hole. "They think about getting a gift of life."

The two chiefs (with additional assistants above first grade) crossed sunwise to the drum on the floor at the center, each took hold of the drum, facing each other, and they started a song, preluding it with barks. This cued the patient to rise, and he barked for the first time, being now a midé with the eight shells "inside" him. He danced sunwise around, halted at Bowman's seat, threw the sack at him (having been directed in the secret sessions but also being guided now in undertones), keeping Bowman's shooting as a model, barked, uttered "Hail!" Bowman fell "wounded," and the onlookers now understood that the patient had received mystic power, enough even to best a seasoned officer of the rite. The patient repeated this with each of the band; the onlookers stood and shuffled a dance in place, the dance being a response like "Amen!"

When the patient had bested the last of the band, Bowman followed and shot his sack at the first onlooker (guest) standing in the sunwise circuit next to the last one of the band, barking, saying "Hail!" This opened the assemblage to formal symbolic dueling, a unique feature of Ojibwa midéwiwin which ostensibly demonstrated ritual kindliness but actually emphasized shamans' threats and covertly permitted shamans' attacks, as described earlier. The first member of the band followed Bowman's example, and so did each succeeding officer. Each officer shot at only one guest, returned sunwise to his place, and shuffled there to the drum song in the middle of the floor. When the patient and eight (at first grade) officers had done their turns, singly, the eight (at first grade) guests, having been shot at and now recovered, carried on the dueling, acting as the officers did, shooting eight more guests; this moved around sunwise until all guests had been treated in sets of eight, or in sets of whatever number of officers the band contained.

When the officers started shooting the first guests, the chiefs transferred the drum partially to others. While Bowman dueled with his first guest, the chief midé traded his drumstick for his assistant's rattle; then the assistant drummed and the chief threw the rattle to the song he now sang. As the second band official was shooting the second guest, the assistant chief passed the drumstick to Bowman dancing by; and the chief returned the rattle to his assistant. Bowman drummed, the assistant rattled and sang and grasped the drum with his chief.

The two chiefs (larger numbers at higher grades) held on to the drum throughout the ensuing business. When Bowman ended his song, the first of his band, having shot the second guest, took the drumstick from him, and drummed and sang for the next in the band, who handled the third guest, while Bowman danced back to his place. The procedure was repeated for each member of a band, whether the band was of eight officers or of eight midé guests (a larger number at higher grades). Those refusing to drum, from shyness or ignorance, requested a chief to sing instead, feeing him with tobacco.

This ritual shooting lasted hours, a kind of orgy of "fun" (a word occasionally used in English by arrogant Ojibwa and Potawatomi, during my studies), its mystic overtones suggesting analogy with the religious overtones to Catholic Carnival. Everyone had repeated chances to shoot, eating and smoking never stopped, tired ones took time out for rest, gambling never ceased on the green outside and in adjoining woods. When a chief wearied of holding the drum, the patient relieved him but might not sing; if both chiefs sought rest, the patient held the drum alone. But the drum, seen as a personified manito force, must never be deserted.

The chief midé indicated to the last singing guest that the ritual should end and had the guest remain at the drum, salute "Hail!" and return the stick to him. Ritually positioned, the chiefs stood now at east and west ends of the drum, the patient stood on the north side of the drum, and the final singer on the south side. As the chief barked, sang, and danced, the four danced up a sector on the compass, carrying the drum. Handing the drumstick to his assistant, the chief saluted "Hail!" and so signaled the latter to sing. The assistant concluded with bark and salute and all moved another sector on the compass. The chiefs barked in concert, danced around four times, bending progressively lower, and so deposited the "Grandfather" drum on the ground. Each of the four bowed himself away from the others with "Hail!" and went sunwise to his place.

Now there was a rest period, which all felt to be well earned. The servitor handed around tobacco and food. The boiled dog was brought in or, wanting dog, whiskey substituted.

The chief stood, looked skyward, and told the Supernaturals:

All of you I salute. And to all you midé folk I give thanks for visiting the midé wigwam, by intention [not casually]. Hail! I bless the food and tobacco. I imagine he [Supernaturals] has already taken our bear [cooked dog]. Hail! And also has taken the eatables and tobacco. Hail! Hail! Let midé folk and outsiders too enter now and partake of this midé food. Hail! That is what I have to say. Hail!

He sat and the servitor brought him a kettle of food, with a sack or plug of tobacco tied to its handle. He thanked the servitor who then gave the assistant chief a kettle, and a kettle each to Bowman and Steersman. A few more kettles remained in the center, with food for general distribution. The chief extended his arm to bless his kettle and started a song of praise, his assistant rattling for him. Bowman and Steersman blessed their respective foods and each sang. In conclusion, the chief rose: "Enter, midé folk. Bring in your dishes." Many visitors had left the lodge with the end of the ritual dancing and now returned to the summons. The chief directed the servitor to apportion the dog among all the midé people, even if each were to get only a taste.

The servitor used a foot-long stick as a fork to thrust into the dog's body when he carved the meat with a knife. The chief supervised the slicing, checking for the desired number. The servitor began with the chief and proceeded around sunwise to all with the kettle of dog. The chief watched until all were served, then signaled them to eat by doing so himself.

164

The dog's head remained in a pail and was reserved for the four men present who had undergone the rite four times; failing such adepts, it was offered to those present who had undergone the rite oftenest. When the dog slices had been distributed, the chief summoned the men to be honored with the animal's head, calling them by name to eat of the symbolic Bear. They did so apart from the rest, near the chief or in the center of the lodge. There was no further elaboration about this point, possibly in keeping with the belief that the Supernatural of whose substance the adepts partook belonged not to them individually but to the corps of shamans, that they were being blessed thereby instead of issuing that power actively, in the visionary's way.

Having eaten, Steersman and Bowman went to the drum at the lodge center, picked it up, and started "tracking around" in a route "taught by Bear." They barked, walked sunwise around to south of center and on to the west door, saluting "Hail!" and barking, on to north center, to south center, back to north center, proceeded around sunwise to south center, on to north center, finally to the dead center where they deposited the drum, then rattled and saluted.

Here the chief stood and directed Steersman to conclude the rite by leading the people out just as Bowman had led them in: "Greeting! You must guide the midé men outside, and the midé women, and the midé children. I will not teach you how. You have learned this from your colleagues. I greet all, I bless all now within the midé lodge. Hail!"

Steersman rose from the seat to which he had returned after the Bear circuit, stepped forward, and declaimed:

Colleagues, I salute and bless you, all of you here. To you who crowd this place, I say thanks. We have finished our search for the life this patient so desires. Colleagues, do not fail to heed the good advice given here, for the manito witnessed it. Now, all the manitos thank you [to the patient]. The shells, each bearing life, were placed one by one all over your body. The offerings were made during the rites; the manitos accepted them. I have said all I need say. I salute the Skies [motioning with his right arm, as he did with each subsequent mystic designation] and the midé Earth, and as far as I can see, and as far as you too, my colleagues, can see. I salute the midé posts and the midé stones and indeed all midé people. Salutations! Colleagues, hail! [He walked sunwise to the west door, the present exit as it was in mythic times for Bear.] Hail! I salute all you here.

The servitor returned dishes and cutlery to the individual owners and now handed drum and rattle to Steersman. All rose. The last officer of the band was signaled to join Steersman and help him with the rattle. Steersman saluted "Hail!", marched sunwise to the east door and barked through it; all followed him and the band. He stood at the door drumming and singing until the servitor relieved him of the drum and took it to the lodge center. Observing Steersman resume a sunwise trek, the servitor moved the drum apace; Steersman sang to his own rattling. Observed by the seated chiefs, the assemblage was led over the tortuous route of "tracking around," crossing back and forth from north center to south center and back three or four times, in a weaving dance, all in the single line holding babies, kettles, spoons, and other personal belongings.

Reaching the west door, Steersman faced west, the crowd dancing behind him, and he halted to say, "Colleagues, hail! I salute the One above watching us, Sun manito who visits us daily. He requested to be the last mentioned in the rite. So, Colleague, hail!" The people departed, but as they moved out, they were cautioned by the seated chief to thank the Supernaturals. Each one then responded, "Hail!" Then Steersman spoke: "All are gone, oh midé manito! Hail!" He too went out, singing and rattling.

There remained inside the midé lodge the chiefs, the patient, and his family, all seated near one another. The principal midé rose and said, "Thank you. Greeting. I bless you. We have finished and will leave. Hail!"

He directed the patient to rise and proceed west, the chief following with further directions; the patient carried the pail and the brush on which he had been sitting, as the chief rattled behind and panted "like a bear." Thus, the chief panting and singing, they went sunwise to the west door, on to the north central section of the floor, crossed to the south central, recrossed to north central, on to the east door, concluding at the west door. Here they were joined by the assistant (or assistants) and, behind him, the patient's family. Leaving the lodge, all circuited sunwise, then went to the preparatory tent, where the chief ceased singing.

AFTER THE PUBLIC RITE

For patient and chief midé officers, the day ceremony did not end the rituals but was largely a high point and a brilliant break in the still ongoing sequence of curing days and nights. Next day they resumed, brushing up on parts essential to the grade but which the patient failed to grasp clearly during the preparatory training.

By ten in the morning the patient had a feast prepared and sent or carried invitations to the chief midé and his one or more assistants. These guests sat in the center of the patient's lodge and had their dishes and pipes filled. Relatives stood watching but did not participate. The chief directed the patient to invite the other officers, and during the wait for them, a sweat lodge was built inside this dwelling lodge; the servitor heated stones and prepared utensils. When the new guests, or officers, arrived, the servitor gave them food and tobacco, the chief directed them to eat. Later the chief rose and addressed Bowman, "Greeting! You lead those who put [the patient] through the rite. Once again, here you lead, taking charge of the sudatory. You may sit there with your colleagues. You do not require my instructions. You know all about it and how to enter. Hail!"

The chief directed the patient to take from him the cedar-brush sprinkler and the ash-wood stone-carrier. The patient approached him sunwise saying "Hail!" and took the articles. Chief directed, "Go, give [Bowman] the brush sprinkler, to use repeatedly on the stones you set in the sweat lodge." The patient obeyed.

167

Bowman disrobed to his breech cloth and addressed his "by-standing" men, "I greet you all! Not everyone need enter this sweat lodge. Those who do not wish to, may give tobacco instead to the chief who sits there." Often the men did not enter, and it was tabu for women, even when midé officers. It was usual for only Bowman, Steersman, and a couple of others to enter.

Bowman circuited, brush in hand, saluting and barking. He and Steersman walked sunwise to northwest of center, then to the west door of the sudatory, where Bowman entered, said "Hail!", walked around inside, sat, saluted again. Behind him, Steersman did the same. The others filled the space in this tiny lodge or tent, omitting the routine for lack of room. Bowman handed the ash carrier outside to the patient, who lifted heated stones (usually eight of them) with it into the sudatory, then rested the carrier honorifically upright against the tent's outside. The patient piled quilts and other thick coverings on the tent. Then, or earlier, he brought the sweat-bathers brush to arrange matting for themselves. Inside, the officers sang and "talked mystically" while the patient stood close to listen and learn. When Bowman had sprinkled the stones and sung, he was heard to say, "Tough as these stones will your life be, hard as this wood will your life be. Therefore, offer tobacco to these, hail! also to water you make offering. Then never will the manito regard you harshly if you err. That is all I have to say. Hail!"

Steersman sprinkled and sang but did not "talk." Then the lesser officers sang. "But these songs don't mean anything," Maggie Wilson said, "they're just to let [the patient] know that these people own songs, which he can buy if he wants. These songs don't give power, they're just like hymns."

Bowman sprinkled for the last time, barked, and saluted. The chief sounded assent, men stripped the tent of its coverings. The ritual, lasting one or two hours, was ended. The patient handed a pan or cup of fresh water into the tent. Bowman drank, uttering ritual thanks, returned the cup, which the patient then filled for Steersman, and then for the lesser officers. Bowman rose to leave the sudatory, saluting, leading the others in taking a sunwise half-circuit to their seats. The chiefs thanked them for their "work." Then all rose but the chiefs, Bowman led them in a full circuit, and they departed by the west door. It was now late in the afternoon.

That night, once more, the patient prepared a sudatory and the same business was repeated, but now only with the chiefs. Four stones were used instead of eight, and were steamed all at the same time instead of in single succession. Possibly these differences reflected status, but they seemed connected also with everyone's fatigue and the limited night hours.

The chiefs worked up a good sweat, sometimes lying on their bellies, other times squatting, to expose all sides to the vapors. They wiped off the sweat and dressed, with repeated "Hails!" Chief directed patient to pull out the sudatory's poles and pile them aside for honorific disposal at a "clean" place in the woods or on the beach. The patient was told to allow the midé lodge poles to stand, being too potent to touch; they would stand until they rotted. Patient was to keep the colored midé posts, the colored birds carved atop them, and the colored stones, for they symbolized Supernaturals and received seasonal invocations. (Maggie Wilson sold me the weathered wood bird of her husband's grade, when both became disillusioned with midéwiwin, as told earlier.) The chiefs left. All retired early, for the first night in nearly a week, to rest.

The patient arose at dawn or only slightly after, breakfasted, cooked another midé feast, secured midé posts and stones as directed, invited the chief and assistant(s). Again he served them tobacco and food, and was directed to summon the lesser officers and the servitor. The latter, favored for his alertness and earnestness, was being groomed for high office, learning the principals' roles as he served and observed.

The chief invited his colleagues to eat. After resting briefly, the chief directed each officer in turn, "Now give him [the patient] your shell." They did so. Henceforth, when the patient was called to a part in subsequent rites, he used the shell given by the one who exercised the same function during his curing. Bowman explained this when giving a shell. The lesser ones implied this, each giving a shell. Steersman repeated the direction, in his turn. Each shell was believed to be immortal, reproducing young, so that a midé person never ran out of shells. (Despite dogma, these individuals bought and traded for shells.)

A new detail appeared at this session: over his breast the patient wore a black cloth about four inches square, on which human outlines were embroidered, full-face, in white beads, following the chief's directions. At each joint of the figure, corresponding to the patient's joints shot at in the public rite, appeared a tiny pocket. Each shell was put into a pocket, which was then stitched up; so the patient would not forget where a shell belonged and would know it existed within him. Wearing this mannikin at midé dances, the patient called it his "Shell Person." It suggested the tiny creature most visionaries "carried" within their bodies, replicas of their patron Supernaturals and repositories of their "power." Dr. William Jones had studied Minnesota Ojibwa some years before his death, and he left notes describing a similar embroidery that a sick visionary pinned on the wall above his head, representing the strength of his dream patron.*

After receiving a shell from each officer, the patient should say, "Thanks. I salute you all." Usually too "shy" to speak, he might need prompting from the chief, who followed with, "Thus his life is strengthened when shells are laid over all his body. Hail!"

Steersman then took the rattle, throwing it as he sang loud and shrill in place. Steersman's act always closed the band's preceding routine; in this case, they were through for the day. The band rose and followed him to the east door where he sang again, throwing the rattle three times and barking each time. They pro-

* These unpublished notes were among those Jones left with the Bureau of American Ethnology, Washington, D.C. They were shown to me by Dr. Truman Michelson, their custodian, about 1940.

ceeded sunwise to the west door, Steersman barking at each step, the barks thrown alternately right and left as salutes to north and south cardinal points, and as dissipators of evil. Facing the west door, Steersman stepped back and forth three times, barking through this ritual hesitation. Then he laid down the rattle to one side of the door, saluted "Hail!" and walked out, followed by the band, who each took leave in the same way.

Inside, the chief told the patient, "Now we too will leave." He and his assistant(s) rose, he received the rattle from the patient, and he sang as he walked around sunwise inside, followed by the assistant(s). They departed with "Hail, colleague!" to the patient, still sitting on the ground.

The following dawn marked the sixth day, often, of continuous curing rites, if reckoning from the day of the sweat ritual. The patient dismembered the preparatory midé lodge, taking the birchbark sheets to his dwelling lodge for mundane use in covering the frame. Maggie Wilson, in her dry, often derisive manner, indicated clearly how much work was laid on the patient and the family. A conservative Ojibwa, no less so than Will Rogers, she expressed skepticism and even jeering so openly and often that I take the attitude to have been authentically of her tribe, carrying a special bite from her own genius.

On the succeeding day, the patient received formal invitations, or a collective one, from the lesser officers to join their feast. The ritual band met, each bringing his own cooked food, fee of printed cloth, and midé sack. The patient, carrying his own dishes, received a portion from the pan of each "manito" officer. The food had to be traditional, including rice, berries, maple sugar, and dried meat. Bowman stated, "This is our [the officers'] feast and you are invited because of the fees you set before us." All assented. The patient left with full pan, saluting, and invited fifteen to twenty-five others to this feast, as directed, the number depending on the supply of food. He himself did not return but ate with the family at home, of the food given by the officers. Back at the feast, the new guests were served tobacco and food

171

by the ritual waiter who had been serving the officers throughout the ceremonial days. The feast over, Bowman said, "Now we can take the goods that were given to the manito." The pattern seemed to be that, as the migis shells were finally given to the patient, so the goods were finally turned over to the officers. Describing this to me, Maggie Wilson twitted, aside, "They worked six days and five nights for those goods. . . . My! I wouldn't! Of course, there was lots of eating . . ."

The principal midé and his assistant(s) invited the patient to their feast also, where the chief stated, "Your dish has been filled. Now I give you a midé shell." The assistant(s) followed with, "I too give you a shell. Hail!" As before, the patient exercised the privilege of an honored guest and invited a number of others, possibly ten, to the chief's affair. When they had been served formally, the chief directed one of the guests to walk out sunwise, barking, taking his food along. Other guests might not wish to remain eating with the "old men" (shamans) and were entitled to depart in the same way. Concluding, the chief stated, "Now we may take the goods that were given to the manito."

Next day, probably the eighth, the patient prepared young birchbark for a writing tablet, which he would take to Bowman, as directed days earlier. From bark collected in the spring, when sap ran, and the bark's inner side was pink, firm, and fleshy, he made a strip about eighteen inches long and about six inches wide. Hole showed this to me, handling the beautiful material with love, smoothing it firmly and slowly, contemplating it reflectively. This was the Ojibwa's own vegetal parchment, durable indefinitely under proper care. Such bark was used chiefly to record mystic songs by means of pictographs. The pictograph patterns were familiar, generally, to all Ojibwa, employed traditionally by hunters, trappers, and travelers for blazing trails, boundaries, and other notices, such as gentile eponyms on grave-markers. However, the specific bearing of any pictograph in a mystic song or other notation was the secret of the shaman who wrote it. He must teach this explicitly to another before the notation was usable. More esoteric and expressive of the writer's secret intentions or knowledge was a sequence or combination of pictographs.

Taking the virgin bark to Bowman, first, the patient petitioned him to write down the song or songs he "gave" and to teach the notations. The song or songs were vital to the patient's life; also he would sing them at others' midé rites. As the patient petitioned by offering tobacco and saluting "Hail!", Bowman assented, "Ho-ho-ho-o-o . . . Thank you." As directed, the patient said, "I ask you to teach me the songs, as many as you wish, as many as you want to give me. Teach me exactly as they come in the rite. That is all I've come to say. Hail!" Bowman acknowledged, "Prepare the birchbark for the songs." This required opening out the curling length and flattening it with weights, like stones.

Bowman sang repeatedly until the patient knew the song, and then he told the patient how to write it. The patient scratched the symbols on his bark with an awl, as he had been shown briefly days earlier in the preparatory lodge. The first-grade pictographs were simple; at higher grades they became more complex but followed the same principles. The song Bowman taught might be one sung *to* the Bird carved on the midé pole, at the same time as it was considered to be sung *by* the Bird as well. Its representation on one scroll that I saw started with a form resembling a rooster drawn in profile facing right, followed by three more such birds, one before the other, as if written from left to right. (However, others made notations from right to left.) Each bird signified start of a new phrase. Lines were drawn between birds, three connected horizontal ones, each indicating repetition of the Bird-phrase. If one asked the shaman why he wrote in one way rather than another, he would respond, "That is how it sounds to me. Someone else might hear it differently." The words of this Bird song run:

> Oh, Colleague, Preceptor,
> [*Sung four times*]
> He, ho, ho, ho, ho!

173

> Oh, Colleague, Preceptor,
> [*Sung four times*]
> He, ho, ho, ho, ho!
> Oh, Colleague Preceptor.
> [*Sung four times*]

Then the words change, keeping the same pattern, to words of linked meaning such as, "I am your guide."

Now the patient departed for Steersman's tent and repeated the same business, using another strip of bark for this song. Steersman might say that his song "belongs to trees, to all things of wood. Listen carefully."

> He-e o hi-i na ne.
> [*Sung seven times*]
> If you wish, you may use this,
> He-e o hi-i na ne.
> [*Sung seven times*]
> Wé ho ho ho ho ho [*barked*]
> Hail!

Steersman sang over and over until the patient had learned; then he drew. He explained, "There is no special picture, just lines. First draw the tree, then lines curve out from it."

The patient left for the chief midé, carrying a fresh bark, to repeat the same business. After being told of the morning's work, the chief said, "I too will teach you a song. This one is about Mink. I give you Mink for a song and also for your midé sack." He handed over a mink fur for the sack. He saluted, puffed tobacco smoke to all Supernaturals, and sang:

> Mink hide,
> [*Sung four times*]
> He-e o hi-i na ne.
> [*Sung four times*]
> Mink hide,
> [*Sung four times*]
> He-e o hi-i na ne.
> [*Sung four times*]

174

This drawing, like the others, started from the left. It was the profile outline of a mink; lines, each indicating a phrase of the verse, led out from the mink.

The patient departed, saluting, for the assistant, giving the latter the tobacco of request. The assistant responded, "Thanks for filling my pipe. I too will give you something to use in the rite: it is Owl. For he too is a midé medicine. Hail! Listen well."

> Ko-o ko ke o-o-o [meaning "owl"],
> [*Sung four times*]
> He-e o hi-i na ne,
> [*Sung three times*]
> Ko-o ko ke o-o-o.
> [*Sung three times*]

Saying, "You are to use this, my Colleague," the assistant gave the patient the feathers and skin of a night owl, for a midé sack.

Now the patient had materials for two sacks. Often the chiefs did not give the actual materials but rather the right to kill such animals for mystic use as midé sacks. In the latter event, the woman, whether herself the patient or the spouse of the patient, sent her husband for the materials which she then sewed up and decorated in traditional beadwork. Sacks might be richly elaborate, made of prime furs, elongated and broadened with rare beads, shells, eagle feathers, and fine Hudson's Bay cloths.

From these officers the first-grade patient had secured all the songs to which he was entitled. He secured more for more payment, by financing another rite or by going to a midé officer and purchasing more songs, without a full midéwiwin, not offering sickness as his excuse this time. At more advanced grades, the patient secured the same number from each principal officer as at first-grade but these totaled up to the larger number because more officers were engaged.

With the songs noted on his birchbarks, the patient took them home to study. Before each practice, he smoked tobacco over them, for each song was the essence of a manito. When the barks were idle, the patient wrapped them carefully and laid them in a trunk or hung them beyond the reach of children and dogs. The birchbarks that Hole gave me remained in the muslin bag that he always used, and were stored in a cardboard box. No one was allowed to open barks casually. Nor was this feasible, for as each lay rolled, it dried and hardened into a scroll that had to be steamed before each opening.

If the spouse happened to be a midé of advanced grade, he acted as instructor and sang with the patient. The two practiced the migis shooting also and discussed ritual steps to further their competence.

Some individuals appeared indifferent to the rite, going through the motions like lay figures controlled by parents and officers. In the 1930's I observed this at Ponemah. E. S. was a handsome young woman of about twenty, a mother, divorced, noted for "wild" drinking and sexual promiscuity. She was an only child, silent, considered sullen and intractable. To better her disposition, her parents arranged successive midé curings. In her twentieth year, she was undergoing her sixth, together with her three-year-old daughter for whom the grandparents had arranged *her* third rite to cure her fierce tantrums. E. S. sat apathetically through the joint rituals, barely muttering the salutations when the chiefs prodded her. Could she have been shy also? She never learned the songs but her mother towed her around and learned the songs for her and the grandchild. (See Appendix 5, where the public rite of this particular midéwiwin is described in detail.)

Chapter 7

VARIATIONS IN THE MIDÉWIWIN

THE MIDÉWIWIN did not occur among all Ojibwa bands in the 1930's, and it does not seem possible to date its oldest origins among the bands that did practice it. Probably it took root much later than the guardian-spirit complex that is universal among Ojibwa. Nonetheless, midéwiwin was considered an Ojibwa feature by neighboring tribes who themselves had Midé Societies. Besides among the Ojibwa, the midéwiwin still existed in the 1930's among some Central Algonkian tribes: the Winnebago, Menominee, and Sauk practiced it, and I knew two midé priests among the Kansas Prairie Potawatomi, but they did not function. The midéwiwin existed also among the Omaha and perhaps other southern Sioux tribes in the 1930's, and it was still clear in memories of the Santee Dakota I studied at Red Wing, Minnesota. General organization and ritual were basically similar at all localities, though details were elaborated variously; hence there were intertribal visits to midé affairs and even participation of shamans from other tribes. One of the Potawatomi priests I knew (then in his early thirties) enjoyed telling me and writing me about these, incidentally appraising the Sauk "dances" (rituals) as very skilled, the Ojibwa ones as filled with alarming sorcery, and his own "power" as unbeatable.

Among the Omaha, Reo Fortune reports, the Midé Society was split into two independent structures, one devoted to secret shamanism, the other confined to the prestigious class of high chiefs. Both of these Societies were supposed to enact the same ancient revelation from the Water Monster (Fortune, 1932, pp. 85 ff.). Among the Menominee and Winnebago there was only one Society, whose membership tended to remain hereditary (Hoffman, 1896; Skinner, 1913, 1920; Radin, 1923), which observed gentile affiliations, cured illness, and sped the ghost of a deceased away from this life. These two tribes had substantially the same origin tale, telling how the culture hero, badly wronged by some Supernaturals, received the midéwiwin as consolation from the Great Spirit and then brought it to the Indians for their comfort.

Canadian Ojibwa generally were skeptical of midéwiwin. This agreed with their isolated location on the northern outskirts of the midéwiwin spread. In 1933, Ontario's Manitou Reserve Indians remembered that the Midé Society had been brought to them not much more than thirty years before by the Ponemah villagers at Red Lake reservation, Minnesota. In 1934–35, the Ponemah and neighboring Cass Lake reservation Ojibwa spoke to me of a remembered time when forebears lived without the institution. Still, that was "long ago."

With small variations, what is described in Chapter 6 was the pattern of every midé performance in Earth and Sky grades, for a living person or a dead one represented by a kinsman. In the four Earth grades, the variations appeared in details of lodge furnishings, the colors and patterns of ritual furniture- and face-paints, the fur of the shooting sacks, the number of officers and shells, the number of offerings, the amounts of food prepared, and sometimes the kinds of food. (Canned goods were criticized in Canada of the 1930's as being "white men's" and therefore improper for midéwiwin; but the same reasoning did not preclude imagery of shooting nor the ritual posture of holding the sack-weapon like a rifle.) The variations were local, and adepts held to them tenaciously in discussions, bolstering them with symbolic elaborations.

The indispensable lodge furnishings were posts and stones.

Their color patterns varied like face-paintings. Thus, Manitou Reserve's first grade used two stones, half of each painted red, the other half painted white with blue dots. There were two posts, the top fifth of each painted white; across the white of one was painted a blue horizontal bar and below it a red bar; across the white of the other the same bars were painted in reverse order. Manitou's second grade painted the stones blue with red dots. One post was painted red, for Earth, with a carved wooden owl atop it, its body painted blue, for Sky, and its head red. (Maggie Wilson's yard had this post and owl standing in the weather when I came, the crudely carved bird having lost its paints and the wood its quality from neglect. She sold me the dreary creation for a pittance, having discarded her midé convictions, she said.) The other post was red on its lower half, blue on its upper, with a blue-bodied, red-necked rooster carved atop it—colors and carving giving the Earth and Sky motifs. Ontario's third-grade post had become a cross. One post was red from the horizontals down; the horizonals and the vertical above were blue; and a red-bodied, blue-necked rooster or owl was carved atop. The other post-cross was entirely red, with two vertical blue bands at the end of each arm and at the top of the post's vertical, on which rested a red-bodied, blue-headed bird. The stones were white, with red dots painted on one, blue on the other.

Such variations differentiated the grades of a locality but were recognized and interpreted significantly only by adepts of the particular location. Certain color values were possibly universal, however, in the Ojibwa midéwiwin range. Thus, red in Earth grades usually referred to "the second layer," while in Sky grades, it referred to clouds. Blue in Earth grades referred to "the bottom layer"; in Sky grades it referred to the heavens. Combinations of colors referred in Earth grades to the successive "layers," in Sky grades to the rainbow. Higher-grade furnishings varied from lower-grade ones in showing additional color units.

Except on the human face, the color patterns were applied in forms that seemed to repeat the shape of the object decorated.

179

So, posts always had lines or smears running horizontally and vertically, never showing such possible alternatives as spirals or diagonals (though diagonals appeared, arranged as rhomboids, in beadwork and porcupine-quill work on hides, in my own 1930's Ontario collection). Again, the round stones were decorated by dots, by an all-over color, or by two colors that each covered half the stone in a semicircle; lines were never used, not even as circles. The local peculiarities in patterns left a stranger, a midé adept from elsewhere, feeling uncomfortable with arrangements of a foreign lodge, as these were "wrong," offensive to the Supernaturals of his schooling. Hole-in-the-Sky, of Cass Lake, expressed bewilderment constantly over such departures during the months of his residence at Red Lake. Mrs. Wilson felt so intimidated by the variations, when I brought her down for a long visit, that she seemed to shrink physically, shoulders hunched, head drawn down into them, eyes hooded.

The midé patient wore ritual paints on scalp and face. Formerly such paints were worn by men on a range of occasions, mystic and profane. Visionaries painted for mystic services, in patterns dictated by the respective guardian spirit. On profane occasions, such as social dances and courting, paints were chiefly red. Paints worn at the midé rite belonged to or denoted the midé vision dogma. Only the patient could wear them, signifying his blessing by the ancient vision, become his by purchase. Paints varied with the midé grade but not systematically even in a given locality, in the 1930's. The colors used were the only ones the Ojibwa knew in paints: red, white, black, and green or blue. These were not of native make and seemed never to have been so among these Ojibwa although in the 1930's the people could still manufacture their own dyes for porcupine quills. The paints were powders, bought for generations at Hudson's Bay stores. No one knew if the color range was limited through Company awareness of Ojibwa requirements or if the Indian accommodated himself to the Company's ideas. Actually the Ojibwa appreciated a range of additional shades and deliberately chose these when buying commercial beads for embroideries on hide and velvet. Also the Ojibwa native manufacture from grasses and herbs produced stains and dyes (not paints) of additional shades, including brown, orange, yellow, and a kind of pink.

A midé patient wore the paints, as a single color or in a combination recommended by the chief midé, to symbolize the color changes experienced by Bear upon emerging from Earth's deeps. The paints also symbolized the strengthened patient's joy and vigor from the cure. Women were not to color as freely as men but confine themselves to round red daubs on the cheeks and one on the central hair parting; I heard that some women took exception to this. The patient's relatives (especially spouse and children) also dressed up, though less than the patient; and formerly midé officers painted if they chose to.

Hole-in-the-Sky had clear ideas about colors to be worn at the first four grades, which were Earth ones. Referring to the origin tale, he explained:

Our Grandfather [Bear] was black in color at Earth's bottom layer, representing woods and sticks lying there dead and bare. At the next layer he turned red, being surrounded by growing things—flowers and leaves. At the third layer he was yellow, for the growing things had changed color with the changing season. At the fourth layer he was white, for snow. Also, the colors represent the cardinal directions: east winds are black, south winds are red, west ones are yellow, and north winds are white. We midé folk paint ourselves after them, for their "pity."

Hence, Hole argued, a first-grade patient must draw two horizontal bars across the forehead, one red, one blue, the top one being red to symbolize Sun and Earth's upper layer, the bottom one being blue to symbolize Earth, especially the bottom layer. A second-grade patient needed two bars painted at an oblique angle across the right eye and continuing on to the forehead; these also were red and blue. A third-grade patient had three such bars, the top one being yellow to correspond with Earth's upper layer. A fourth grade patient painted red on the center hair-parting and stuck downy white feathers in his hair, symbolizing "the Earth layer on which we sit" and also the mystic promise of living until white-haired age.

Dr. William Jones, himself of Fox ancestry, left his unpublished sketches of Ojibwa-seeming midé face-paintings among his other notes. Dr. Truman Michelson examined them with me at the Bureau of American Ethnology, and could not say definitely that the first sketch was of an Ojibwa but believed that this seemed certain. This painting of a "second degree member" and officer shows a vertical blue line down the middle of the chin, a small blue circle on either cheek surrounded by a large red circle, green lines painted vertically on both lids of the right eye, red lines painted vertically on both lids of the left eye, and alternating red, blue, and green lines painted obliquely at the top central portion of the forehead. The man wears a blue necklace. Jones's note explains that "the paintings on his face are a prayer that the day [of the public rite] will be clear, the idea being that his power for healing will be better on such a day. The blue necklace represents the . . . shells which will be given to the [patient]."

The next sketch also depicts "a member of the second degree of the midewiwin." The Indian's hair is colored red on the top. Diagonally across his face, from the top of the forehead above the right eye to the farthermost side of the lower left cheek, run rainbow bands of blue, red, green, and yellow, the colors descending in the order given. On the man's neck is a bear-claw necklace. Jones's note says, "The red is said to be given by a bear that rose from beneath the earth. The rainbow was handed down from ancestors far ago in the past. The giving of the red and the rainbow is told of in a story peculiar of the midewiwin alone."

A sketch of a fourth-grade chief midé carries Jones's translation of the native title as "Fourth-time chief." It shows the upper two-thirds of the forehead smeared over in red; the lower half of the face, down from the nostrils, is smeared solid in blue; on the left cheek under the eye is painted a bear paw, designed as a black center surrounded by a red line from which radiate red claws. Jones's note reads, "The red is for the idea that his prayers and wishes have been heard by the manido. The sign that the prayer has been heard is seen in the red glow of the dawn on the morning following the prayer. The green [blue, in Jones's sketch; Fox and Ojibwa use the same word for both shades] really stands for black paint or charcoal. This means that he will talk earnestly to the manido beneath the earth in order to get his aid as he confers the degree on a neophyte."

A sketch of a fifth-grade painting shows a man with a broad band of blue smeared across the upper forehead, the lower edge being outlined slightly in red; from it, red and blue lines radiate vertically onto the hair, the blue ones massed on the right side of the head, the red massed on the left side. Across the width of the face straddling the middle of the nose is a rainbow band of blue, red, and green, the colors descending in the order given. Down the middle of the chin runs a vertical red line; downwards diagonally from the mouth's corners radiate red and green lines. The forehead paints "represent a clear sky. . . . The lines upward are for feathers which represent prayers to the manido birds above [this being the first grade of Sky midéwiwin]. The lines are not feathers but representations. The lines from his mouth represent the prayers he makes to the underground manidos when he asks them for help in giving the degree."

A sixth-grade painting shows a man with hair colored red. A solid blue smear runs diagonally across the left side of the face, from the hairline at a point outside an imaginary extension of the nose's right margin down across the left eye and cheek. Around the neck is a medicine sack of eagle skin, worn with the eagle's head down; the eagle skin is colored blue and its head yellow. Jones's note states, "Raven is the name of one who has the power to confer the sixth degree. This refers to the idea that a man of the sixth degree represents a huge raven as large as the Sky above. The blue is for the clear sky. If a clear day comes, then the prayer for power to heal is said to be answered."

The Manitou Reserve Ojibwa of the 1930's had simpler paint-

ing styles. Perhaps this was consistent with their simpler culture
and scanter economy. But the paints were used in the same ways;
and in midéwiwin they were applied on the patient by Bowman.
The Manitou Reserve bands had been brought there in 1914 from
seven villages strung along the Canadian side of Rainy River. According to old John Bunyan, his stepdaughter Maggie Wilson,
and his other stepchildren, all these villages had the same style of
face-painting, which they shared with Minnesota's Red Lake
Ojibwa, just over the international boundary. Accordingly, those
at first grade streaked red on the middle hair-parting and painted
a red circle, for the Sun, on each cheek; the pattern was retained
for the four Earth grades. Those at second grade, besides, painted
a blue band horizontally across the forehead; at third grade they
added a red streak painted horizontally under the blue one on the
forehead for the rainbow; the fourth added a red streak painted
horizontally above the blue one on the forehead and blue-rimmed
the red circles on the cheeks. Fifth grade red-painted, "for red
clouds," the whole face except chin and upper forehead, smeared
blue on eyebrows and perhaps on upper eyelids. Grades six,
seven, and eight painted the cheeks blue, for the Sky.

The lodge or wigwam sheltering Earth Supernaturals and creatures during Earth ceremonials took on modifications of language
and different stylistic arrangements for Sky ceremonials. Thus,
the wigwam structure became a vast "nest" of brush for Sky Supernaturals and creatures. Because brush for the midé "nest" lay
on the ground, the Sky fee-offerings were set there, to contrast
with their Earth position on a tall rack. Earth-grade furs for the
wayans, or shooting-sacks, were replaced by birdskin sacks.
Though I never saw the bird sacks, Hole told me of befeathered
eagle and hawk skins that were used, with feathers intact. At Red
Lake's Ponemah village, I saw a midé wayan of wood carved as
an eagle profile. For Sky grade, Earth's shells were replaced by
claws of predatory birds, including owls, hawks, and eagles. Hole
said Cass Lake used seven (a ritual number) kinds of claws. Red
Lake used besides some pretty, round cartilages found in the

head of a buffalo fish or sheepshead; possibly they were replacements during a scarcity of bird claws, justified by the symbolic logic of water mirroring sky. In Sky grades, the Great Spirit was mentioned oftener than Shell, who was Earth's overlord; and Bear of Earth grades was replaced by Eagle as servitor to Sky Supernaturals. But in Sky grade talks, the special Characters are mentioned only rarely, leaving the ordinary officer and guest vague about the differences between them and Earth Characters.

My elderly informants said midé therapy once stressed herbal ministrations. In the 1930's these were no longer practiced. They are mentioned in older published works, especially W. J. Hoffman (1891, pp. 197 ff.). In the 1930's the chief midé, or any other officer he designated, made out a prescription which the patient followed as blindly as laymen follow medical prescriptions in our own society. However, Hoffman states that the officer *taught* his patient the herbal properties. In the 1930's, this did not belong in midé cure; the nature of a prescription was taught separately at that time, upon special application and payment of a separate fee. (The situation was exactly as among whites.) Hoffman also leaves the impression that herbal medicine was particular property of midéwiwin. In the 1930's, rather, herbal pharmacology (*mashgigiwaboge* is "herb-brewing") existed apart from midéwiwin, chiefly monopolized by the category of men and women called "herbal curers"; they prepared a considerable number of compositions, prescribed to treat nearly every disorder attributed to congestion of body fluids, ranging from nosebleed to uterine, pulmonary, and alimentary disorders, with or without Supernaturals' aid. Midé officers drew upon this.

Hole said that, anciently, the midé officer gave herbal prescriptions to the patient during rituals before or after the day of public ceremonial; or he might forget to give them, or do so weeks later. Sometimes formulas were recorded on birchbarks. Originally, informants thought, herbal knowledge was revealed in private visions that long antedated midéwiwin. Hence the separateness of the two in the 1930's was a return to the ancient

185

model of conduct. In the 1930's it was never difficult to buy herbal knowledge; and it was not considered basic to midé curing.

When a chief midé was solicited by several prospective patients, he might put them all through the rites simultaneously, though they had made independent arrangements. This was because traditionally the Ojibwa assembled summers in the villages and were all accessible only for this short season. Patients of the same grade were handled alike, in the 1930's, as though one. When of different grades, they were addressed and sung for at different times, and they danced accordingly but sometimes were told to work together. At these group rites, the degree being worked upon was marked by the number of beats the chief midé gave the drum before starting a song, and by the numbers he mentioned during the midé narration of Bear's turns or of the old Indian's upon becoming a drum.

Hole and others told me that the tcisaki's kind of juggling tricks had been introduced formerly at certain Life rites. Possibly this occurred at higher grades, where fees were very large. They were not performed in the 1930's, probably because the young were not taught them. The tricks had two purposes: display of mystic power and of actual divination. I gathered that midé juggling differed in no way from poltergeist and other stunts executed by the visionary diviner and the sucking-doctor. Hence, the skills probably were sanctioned by personal visions of midé leaders. This contradicted midé dogma about purchase of the primordial definitive vision but was nevertheless frequent. The divinatory aim was to discover if the rite would cure the prospective or actual patient. In the 1930's, divination outside midéwiwin would recommend the rite, at Manitou Reserve, but would not prognosticate cure in exact terms; possibly such prognostication was a midé officer's prerogative.

There were said to have been many juggling tricks. W. J. Hoffman (1891) describes some in his account of Ojibwa midéwiwin (pp. 204–6), showing the shaman's "power" to make wood beads, wood dolls, and the mystic sack move and dance. The dolls' dance was a staple of Ojibwa love medicine, generally.

Hole told me of two other tricks, with fear, actual trembling, and braggadocio. He would not reveal the inner secrets, perhaps because he thought them tawdry by my outside standards. (Considerations of payment could not have barred the revelation, since he knew I would always provide appropriate offerings.) One trick followed upon "shooting" the patient: the chief midé, if he knew "this trick" (a designation Hole never used for other midé routines), placed one shell on a mirror he held, where it stuck fast with a secret herbal "medicine." As the chief circled once around the lodge with it, he carried the mirror shell-side down; if the shell dropped off before the chief had returned to his seat, the patient would die. The routine was called "the testing-out" and was watched breathlessly. However, there must have been skeptics about, as shown in my observations and in the published reports of many other observers; and it is not inconceivable that their pressure discouraged such devices.

In Hole's other reported trick, the "tester" employed a rifle containing a large bullet and much powder. About halfway down the length of the lodge, he set up a thin cedar-wood figure, possibly a quarter of an inch thick and four feet tall, a rounded prominence on top for a head, the whole figure tapering to a point on the bottom. (The Ojibwa pictographs often represented humans this way, full-face or in outline.) When the chief passed on his return round, holding his rifle down and not bothering to sight with it, he fired. Then: "the powder explodes with oh! a terrific noise," and enough violence to have exploded four such slight figures. If the one in the lodge remained intact, the patient lived. Hole's cousin executed this "trick" and once led Hole up to the figure to examine the miracle: it had only a small bullet indentation in the back. Hole assured me, in his measured speech, "Now *that* was medicine! Because with the force of that powder, the shot should have cracked the figure but it didn't . . . it just grazed it. And that was a good sign. Otherwise the patient could not have lived."

Both tricks contain arresting ethnohistorical details: they both employ traditional and modern materials and instruments, notably shell and cedar in the first category, the mirror and rifle in the

187

second, herbs and midé logic in the first category also, the rifle-shooting in the second. I have often wondered at the complete absence of archery in Ojibwa midéwiwin, actual and symbolic, except for an incident in Manitou's Ghost mythology (told below, in Chapter 8). Unlike the Minnesota band, Ontario tribesmen could still use and make bows and arrows in the 1930's; old Chief Namepog, Maggie Wilson's father-in-law, showed me archery techniques with his own huge equipment and made me a toy set. Except for the bow and arrow, almost every traditional detail of Ojibwa material culture was introduced or could be introduced during midéwiwin. Nor did archery appear outside the midé lodge, in company with the gambling and other non-midé pursuits.

Chapter 8

THE GHOST MIDÉWIWIN

THE WEIGHT OF THE OJIBWA religion was addressed to procedures for living, but some thought was given to schematizing a
postdeath sphere. The midéwiwin recorded its rituals for the living in one birchbark scroll, its rituals for the dead in another.
Will Rogers' midé Life scroll was many times more voluminous
than his postdeath or Ghost (*djibai*) scroll, both of which he
gave to me. (See Figures 1 and 3.) The difference in volume followed partly from the view that the rituals were actually a con-
tinuum, the Ghost scroll being an addition to the other; and both
were embraced within the same concepts of manito authority.

The Ojibwa said that they learned about the after-death at first
hand, usually from old or sick Indians who "died" temporarily,
their souls being released to the after-death sphere—that is, these
Indians learned from their visions. The midéwiwin preserved
such an ancient revelation about how to control the sphere of the
dead. Hence it denied access to those who had not gone through
its Ghost rite, or who had been Christianized. Consistently, a
midé shaman conducted funerals, for the next world was a
"midé world."

The Ghost rites of midéwiwin were held after the death of a
promised patient, whether the death occurred during or before
the ceremonials of his appropriate Life grade, in Earth or Sky di-
vision. The Earth "lodge" or Sky "nest" became oriented north and

189

south instead of the Life's east and west, which records the direction of Earth Bear's mythic travel. However, the origin myth was narrated as in Earth rites, perhaps yielding somewhat to formal discussions about the soul, the soul's journey to its own world, and the origin of death. The world of the dead was not conceptualized as differing essentially from this one; it was believed to lie beyond the western horizon because the sun dips there nightly. Birds were mentioned and were carved on midé posts oftener in this version than in the Life version because the souls' world after death is located in the skies. The circling routines, the gesturing, and placement of food, offerings, posts, and stones were rearranged to conform with the north-south orientation.

The talks about the soul and about death were the prominent elaborations at Ghost rites, as discussions of belief and as manifestations of dread before death. In the Ghost lodge it was explained that death befalls man's fleshly component; and that flesh houses a perpetually vital soul or spirit, which the Ojibwa termed preferably a "shadow." Perhaps an apter term, had they known it, would be "aura." Upon death, the shadow wanders, searching after old haunts and habits. It takes to the water pail to drink and to wash its face; it demands attention from close kin and retaliates violently when ignored; hence it "kills" or injures the surviving spouse who takes a lover; it haunts enemies in dreams. The ideas and actions surrounding burial and Ghost rituals were aimed at placating the restive, angry shadow and removing it definitively. For the shadow pursues a dangerous path to its final haven, one beset by evils insurmountable without midé aid at burial and at the Ghost rite. Further, the afterworld is a midé one, which looks for midé credentials gained in the Earth sphere.*

* Dr. William Jones left unpublished notes taken soon after 1900 on the Ojibwa of Bois Fort, Minnesota, that offer local views of the soul, or shadow: "It is believed that a person has two souls. One leaves him at death and goes to the spirit world. The other remains with the body and makes the grave its abode. The soul of the grave goes out and comes in. For it is placed food at the entrance of its home. The soul of the spirit

There were several traditional ways of removing the corpse itself, keyed to isolation of the family and the season of the year.
In winter, a corpse was burned; or it was blanketed in birchbark
or mats and laid on the high branches of a tree, since the ground
was too frozen to dig for a grave; or it might be laid on the
ground and covered with rocks, to protect it from depredations of
beasts. In the 1930's, however, ground interment was universal,
though people said they remembered how the corpse's juices
would drip down from the tree-bed on arrival of warm weather. I
saw how, above a shallow grave, they built a small, wooden,
gabled house, like a toy, with a ledge on which mourners set food
and tobacco for the "shadow," and a flame that was kept burning
four nights; after this, the shadow was to have gone. The flame,
or light, was to guide the shadow in its stumbling forays; the food
and tobacco were to feed it. In coming years, food would be left
occasionally to sustain the shadow afar. And for the whole year
immediately after death, at mealtimes the family would throw
food and tobacco into the fire for the lonely shadow. At all midé

---

world is said to return, and when it does, the person comes back to life.
It is said that once a man was supposed to be dead. But before burial, he
opened his eyes and rose and told where he had been and what he had seen.
He told that he had gone to the spirit world, but was told to return for his
time had not yet come. After that incident, people fell into the habit of
keeping the dead four days, in the hope that the soul of the spirit world
would return and the person come back to life." According to other notes
by Jones, "a person has as many as four souls. Often he may know as much
as a year in advance that he is going to die. In that case he lets go of one
of his souls. It goes about in the form of some animal or bird. A person may
see this animal or bird one moment, and the next moment it is gone. . . ."
Animals too have souls. "The dewlap of a moose or caribou is the seat of
that animal's soul. It is hung up to please the soul of the slain animal on a
limb or bush. It is said that if the dewlap is not hung up, the hunter would
find it difficult to kill another such animal; the soul would always warn the
animal of the approach of the hunter. It is claimed that the soul is like the
form of a small, swift hawk. It is said that a man once got between a moose
and its soul. The soul flew past him and made straight for the moose. Whereupon the moose looked straight at the man. . . . When a man lets one of
his own four souls out, it takes the form of some animal or bird which
roams about giving him knowledge of things."

rites, a mourner served dishes he prepared of choice meat, berries, and rice to officers and guests, to be eaten in honor of the mourner's deceased kinsman or spouse; for the shadow was said to eat with the humans. The Ghost midéwiwin strengthened and guided the shadow on its journey and in the new abode.

Not every leader of Life rites was competent to handle Ghost rites, for they demanded particular instruction. One with less than perfect knowledge of Ghost content trembled to speak familiarly of it, on pain of courting death. Hole put this explicitly. Yet Hole and other masters of Life rites surely knew the Ghost material, for they heard and watched the rites year in and year out; besides, they gave the same talks at burials. But the knowledge could not be employed in midéwiwin unless it was paid for as a midé property. (See Landes, 1937a, chap. 5, for the Ojibwa rules covering property.) The right exercised by Hole and others to give the burial talks at the grave rested on experience, on eminence in midéwiwin, and on the invitation of the mourning family. The invitation carried no fee, so there was no technical invasion of property. Presumably the mourning family accepted the possible risk in return for speeding the soul on its way at burial.

Hole explained that the midé officers conducting Ghost rites were titled the same as for Life rites. However, the patient was a "shadow." Hence someone was chosen to represent the deceased, or his soul, as the human officers represented midé Supernaturals. The person enacting the deceased sometimes was adopted by the mourners to replace the deceased permanently in their family affections; this development followed kinship practices, not midé requirements, however. Also the surviving spouse could enact the person of the deceased; this too satisfied kinship and sib practices, for the ceremony then stressed paying heavy compensation to ritual officers who were chosen from relatives of the deceased, the surviving spouse's compensation for the "murder" or death giving him the freedom to remarry (see Landes, 1937a, pp. 44–52). For example, I heard of a widow at Manitou who underwent the Ghost rite for release from the obligations of her spouse's death, in the 1930's. Chief Namepog told me that such compensation and release, which returned the mourner to normal existence, were always done anciently through the Ghost rite, as was also the reinstatement to normality of all other mourners, if the deceased had vowed to be cured by midéwiwin. The Ghost rite freed mourners of every category from further responsibilities to the deceased they represented, relegating the ghost or soul completely to the shadow-world.

In the Ghost ritual, as earlier at burial, the chief midé would tell how Death came to the world when Nehnehbush caused man to lose his enamel protection. The speaker might stress Nehnehbush's pique and also his Malthusian fear of overcrowding the world. A variant presents him as creator of the otherworld's town of Indians, or for Indians, before the Supernaturals had established midéwiwin, in competition with it. In such variants, he avoided the council called to discuss the new rite, and he hid, with his brother.

Hole said, evincing no criticism of this trickster and culture hero, "Nehnehbush did not like the manitos' plan to have the Indian live indefinitely, until he would just die off naturally, like the leaves. He considered some alteration necessary. So he traveled southwest, to the town of shadows [the dead], to ask his brother to aid his plan. His brother said, 'That cannot be.' "

Nehnehbush had brought to his brother, Keeper of the Hereafter Town, the corpse or soul of his son, whom he had killed to demonstrate human death. At his brother's refusal, he proceeded south to ask aid of a manito related to the mythic Great Snake. There he dropped his burden "like a ball of fire" (symbol of evil), and it burned down to the bowels of Earth. Nehnehbush called to Bear to bring up his dead son but Bear could not. He called to Hawk and to other great-billed birds but they also failed. He called upon Fly and Bumblebee; they refused at first, outraged because he had done his son to death. Finally they agreed to aid him. (Ojibwa folklore delights in achievements of the weak and young.) Twice they circled around the spot, fruitlessly; twice

193

more they circled; and "the pack [corpse] commenced to rise." After his son's return to Earth's surface, Nehnehbush waited out a year. Then he held a Ghost rite and so got his son admitted to the world beyond the westering sun. Hole offered this justification of Nehnehbush:

He did not really invent death. He shortened life. And he created the Ghost world. His was really the best plan, for everything is pleasant there. The manitos came to approve of it, in this way: when Nehneh-bush's son was returned to Earth's surface, Bear went angrily to Shell to report and to ask for the boy's restoration through midéwiwin. Shell answered that [Life] midéwiwin was impossible for such a case, that the spirit must be taken to the afterworld for a Ghost rite. They called upon the Great Spirit, and they all counseled with Nehnehbush. The Great Spirit approved of Nehnehbush's idea. All were pleased that the Indian was provided for.

At Minnesota burials and Ghost rites in the 1930's, the midé dignitary invoked Otter, one of four "Grandfathers." Otter was said to approach the footloose or footless shadow with an offer to conduct him, on his own back, to the "land where midéwiwin sounds forever, without end," in Hole's deep-felt phrase. The soul climbs to a "nest" on Otter's back (surely reminiscent of the baby-carrier on an Indian mother's back), and somewhat later Otter propels himself violently forward, to slide the remaining distance into the next, midé world. But during this travel, Otter and his burden are interrupted by four evil Supernaturals who each seek to divert Otter to some byway. The first Evil is easterly and offers the allure of its strawberry appearance. The second is southerly (the telling observes a sunwise circuit) and offers the lure of its blueberry appearance. The third is westerly, an allur-ing raspberry. The fourth is northerly, alluring as a Juneberry. (The succession of red and blue colors characterizes midé sym-bolism.) At each point of temptation, following ritual advice of the midé shaman—and so of Otter—the shadow would drop to-bacco or another offering and avoid the danger easily. But if the

194

ignorant shadow, called also "he who disappears," went his way unescorted, he would be destroyed by the four Evils.

This was reported, in the 1930's still, by Indians who had "died" briefly (seen the Hereafter in visions) and then returned to life. They said that the Evils' territory showed trees gnawed and the ground clawed by desperate captive souls misled by the summer-fruits illusion to this barren of starvation. The shadow paid this penalty when a midé officer sermonized mistakenly, as he then heeded the siren calls that sounded like, "Here! Come over here!" In the myth, Otter passes the fourfold hazard and carries his charge to the threshold of Nehnehbush's world.

—One clear October twilight, Hole took me to an open spot in the woods around Red Lake from where I might glimpse the Nehnehbush world; or at least view the starry universe that long before had come to him in a vision. It rose palely above the western horizon, and Hole said quietly, "That is it, the brightest star in the southwest. My [manito] brother told me, and he should know. These Indians have no idea about it. Doubtless they're not supposed to know. They claim Nehnehbush's world is on Earth. But that cannot be, or the midé manitos would have said where he was hiding."—

Otter and the shadow enter the afterworld and walk up sunwise a little to the lodge of Nehnehbush's brother, Keeper of the Dead—"it's a kind of registry," Hole explained. The Keeper returns Christian Indians to life to be put through midéwiwin. Nor does the Christian Supernatural or God allow Indians of any creed into his Heaven, not even Christian converts, according to individuals who had died and come back. He tells them to go where Indians belong, for Indians were created in a location separate from that of whites. A soul cleared at the "registry" is directed to the village of souls arrived earlier, to decide among which kinfolk he chooses to remain.

At the center of this village is a permanent midé lodge, where souls forever sing, dance, eat, smoke, dress and paint beautifully,

195

and play games at will. (The games include gambling.) There is
no need to hunt, as each shadow receives food, drink, and tobacco from the tiny portions mourners toss into the fire for them,
offerings conducted with the smoke. Running short of food, a soul
borrows from fellow souls; and he also appears in his relatives'
dreams to protest the neglect. Hole gave a vivid picture of the
bonds between the worlds, the living struggling to maintain distance while contributing both the ghostly peopling and their
sustenance, the shadows struggling to maintain contact through
dreams and omens.

The soul of a nursing child travels through the same hazards
confronting the adult soul. At the entrance to the souls' village,
however, the infant is welcomed by a woman manito who bares
her breasts for milk to spout forth, beckons the baby to her,
nurses it, and then takes it to its nearest soul relative.

Ontario's Manitou Indians depicted shadow affairs more grue-
somely in the 1930's than did the Minnesota Ojibwa, including
discomforts in "the forever-happy land." They were much visited
by Christian evangelists, who may have influenced the tribe with
their vivid pictures of purgatory; yet Minnesota also had evangelists. The Manitou bands appeared to suffer greater economic de-
privations than the Minnesota bands, who profited from President
Roosevelt's New Deal programs, such as the Civilian Conserva-
tion Corps in the forests. The Ontario woodlands were scantier
than those of Minnesota in a number of resources such as timber,
rice, and berries. To me, the Manitou bands seemed remoter from
centers of population and creature comforts than did the closely
related Minnesota ones. This may have intensified their awareness of struggle and insecurity. Certainly they talked of death as
a culmination of life's mounting fears.

"Oh, I hate to die!" Maggie Wilson and others said, explaining
in terms of what they heard at the Ghost lodge and at burials.
They said that when one closes his eyes in death, his shadow
leaves this sphere and body for another sphere and body, feeling
its way through a tortuous dark unknown tunnel, emerging into a

196

ghostly land through which it must race so madly, to elude ghostly terrors, that the wind whistles in its ears. It races on until it meets an old woman, "Our Grandmother," who directs souls further. Then it comes up against four old men, "Our Grandfathers," one after another, the last of whom warns the soul about crossing a water, half red and half blue, that will be met. The soul finds a pole or log, also particolored, standing on the near shore of the water and gives it a pipeful of tobacco, whereupon the log drops across to the other shore as a bridge. Some say that sinners fall into the water, to wallow miserably forever. (This seems to be a Christian intrusion since the Ojibwa usually exclude ethical judgments from the ghost world.)

When the soul has crossed to the far shore, the log rears upright as before. The soul should not turn back to watch this, but sometimes does. A road from the far bank, leading to the soul village, is blocked by a log that rolls aside when offered tobacco. After this, the soul comes to a "Grandfather," offers him tobacco, and so receives a bow and arrows colored part red and part blue. The shadow shoots the arrows toward the ghosts' village and races after them over a gradual incline until it sees the village. There all appear happy. The female ghost, Shell Woman, who greets women souls, is covered with tiny midé shells that tinkle delightfully as she moves. The male ghost, greeting men souls, is similarly shell-bedecked. These official greeters direct the entering soul to its kinfolk.

Here too the midé drum sings constantly, illness and starvation never appear, those who were drunkards and sinners in life share equal standing with all others. The midé officer said to the shadow at burial, "You suffered enough in this world. Now you are dead and going to a place where there is no misery." The shadows are forever young in their final village, living as in childhood, never marrying or rearing families. All are as sisters and brothers, children of the ghost manitos.

Yet there is sadness in this glad village, for no youngsters are admitted from the life world. These are kept apart in a gleaming

197

white town where the Great Spirit, or God, keeps the souls of white people. Hence, living adults grew frantic when a child fell ill. Parents strove fiercely to arrange a midéwiwin for a sick child, to carry him past the excluded age. When a child under the age of ten died, the parents cried inconsolably although this excess was forbidden at an adult's death. "Oh-h-h, the Great Spirit is taking him!" they would wail. This deep concern over children echoed the general interest showered upon them and also the high child mortality, so threatening to adult security in the scattered hunting economy still functioning during the 1930's.

Manitou Ojibwa believed that not all adults were admitted to the ghosts' village. Thus, people who were burned to death (chiefly, evil windigo shamans) kept burning forever; those who drowned remained so forever, with the Water Monster probably. These examples express ancient conceptions about punishing evil shamans, in the first case, and fear of mythological manito underwater creatures in the second.

Hole knew the Ontario version of the route to the shadow world but considered it too "dangerous" to narrate. Not only in this instance did he have the attitude of "let sleeping dogs lie" so as not to evoke their terrorism; generally, the Minnesota shadow concepts were milder than the Ontario ones. Above all, Hole feared the "dangerous logs," though he could mention them after describing the four Evils seeking to mislead in the guise of summer berries. He explained, "Suppose I made a mistake in my [mystic] talk. Then the shadow would be destroyed forever, because the log would upset it in the water." His preferred Minnesota scheme did not abandon souls of the burned and drowned. Yet it did let the souls of those scalped or beheaded in war continue so eternally.

William Jones's Ojibwa notes from Bois Fort, Minnesota, taken shortly after 1900, seem close to the 1930's Ontario version:

The soul is said to come to a river with a swift current. The path leads to a bridge which at first looks like a tree fallen across. The roots lie on the side where the soul is, and the tops are on the other shore.

198

The bridge moves up and down. The soul finds on approaching it that it is a huge serpent, the head of which is on the soul's side of the river, and the tail on the other. The soul of a person who was a member of the midewiwin will find no trouble in crossing because it knows what to say to it; and what is said is a formula taught in the midewiwin. But the soul of one not a member of the midewiwin is likely to find some trouble getting across. The serpent lies still for the soul of one, but not for the other.

These notes also reveal ethical judgments similar to those in Ontario:

It is said that the soul starts on its journey to the spirit world laden with the sins committed by the person in life. For every sin committed, there is an obstacle to impede the progress. The overcoming of the hindrance must follow, else the soul cannot proceed. To overcome an obstacle is to pay off the debt of one sin committed. It is said the worst sin is fornication. A soul of a man with such a sin against him goes its journey with the vulva of every woman he has lain with. In like manner, the soul of a woman goes along with the penis of every man she has lain with outside of wedlock. The obstacle in the way is some hardship, some peril.

Remembering my discussions with shamans and others in the 1930's, the variant versions seem stamped with marks of the individual informants. All recognized one another's outlines and details. Emphases shifted with the personalities speaking, perhaps with the occasions, and with the localities. The departures seem traceable more to individual perferences than to other single factors. This is not surprising in a small, wandering population, given to the solitary communion of visions, relying solely on oral transfer of tradition, prizing individual assertions of worth. But all recognized the common store of tradition on which they drew, such as the values (e.g., power), the plots (e.g., competitive pursuit), the details (e.g., avenging souls, guilty lives), the traditional referents (e.g., beast Supernaturals), the culture borrowings (e.g., use of rifles and separation of Indian souls from white ones).

Consideration, by Ghost rites, of the soul's experiences em-

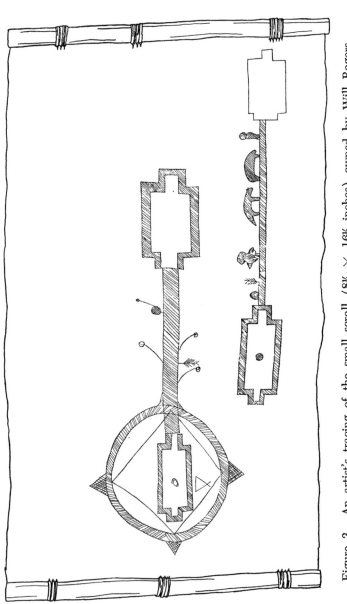

Figure 3. An artist's tracing of the small scroll (8¾ × 16¾ inches) owned by Will Rogers, recording songs for the Ghost midéwiwin. Courtesy of the Milwaukee Public Museum. See Plate 7 for a photograph of this scroll.

ployed some concepts and expressions not found in Life rites. Ghost midéwiwin officiants spoke of "the overlapping world," which was other than the world on which the living dwell. The latter was called "the Earth with four ears" (because the manitos of the cardinal points "heed the Indian's pleas") and "This on which we sit." The "overlapping" universe might signify the hereafter or a condition special to a soul freshly released from the body by death. My informants thought it named the location whence Otter starts out with his burden of shadow. In the midé origin tale, it coexisted with our mundane earth, overhanging it, and casting a shadow that caused Indians to sicken and die. The Supernaturals had to remove it to a distance that rendered it harmless, as Lion had to remove the evil Snake from the midé lodge. Hole asserted that "the overlapping world" had been the Hereafter but, since it shaded Earth, Nehnehbush shelved it for the present one; however, Hole's supporting tale ran thus:

Well, now I'll tell you what the manitos did. They could not arrange the Indian's life on Earth to their satisfaction. They were displeased with the overlapping of the two worlds. They said, "It is not good for the Indian to be shaded. It would be well to remove it so the Indian can see his way around, at least. It is not at all suitable for Indians to live in shadow. The manito will select a place for the Indian to live and will show the Indian how to live." So the manitos said.

Nehnehbush was not a Supernatural but a mythic Character who often spoke an Indian's mind—notably in daring and rebellion—so it is possible that the removal was thought too important for attribution to the Trickster alone and his daring had to be atoned for or concealed by exalting the Supernaturals' might.

The Ghost rite introduces a Dreamer who parallels Cutfoot in the Life rite but has no name. Nehnehbush revealed Ghost proceedings to him, and he then took his revelation to Cutfoot, who rejected it, "saying he had not been informed of it," as Hole told me.

Ghost rite shamans also described a white-haired manito who sits by the westering sun. No Indian has ever known or seen him.

201

The Great Spirit assigned him there to receive those who die of great age, whom he adorns with snowy hair and directs to the hereafter "world of beautiful sounds." Anciently, the Great Spirit directed him, "Now, I place you here. Probably no one will be able to reach you. The Indian will fall short of his goal of old age. But when one does reach you, make white his head and show him the right [or safe] way to the world of ever-beautiful sounds. Here is your obligation to the Indian."

Sometimes this figure is "talked of" ("talk" being an Ojibwa idiom for religious invocation or supplication when combined with the idea or term "manito") in Life midéwiwin, as the head midé prays that his patient may be strengthened sufficiently to reach "the manito in the west." The rite itself reflects the Ojibwa preoccupation with survival, against hazards of illness especially, and implicitly against the hazards of the precarious dependence on weather and the food pursuit. Ojibwa mythology and conversation reveal, besides, high admiration for the unusual white or silvery shades in prime game animals, such as a rare silver-colored moose, readily perceived therefore as manito.

The Ghost midéwiwin further echoed adventures of the shadow-soul in procedures it added to the basic Life rite. Thus, Bowman at intervals passed around a dish of food, telling people to eat a little, so that all the souls might eat. Then, the posts were supplicated directly. Again, the mourner, regardless of whether he enacted the deceased in the ritual, was re-arrayed by the close of the ceremony and adorned with fresh rosy paints, to symbolize the soul's successful journey, its new life, and the severance of living kinfolk from it, releasing the living to normal interests. Further, Bird or Sky symbols took over, as in the identification of Bowman with Eagle, in the figures carved on midé posts, in the blue and green paints of water and sky.

Management of Ghost proceedings could strike difficulties when a representative of the same grade as the deceased patient was not ready at hand. A lower-grade representative would have to be raised. This happened with Hole's daughter, Ruth, for whom he officiated. Herself of third grade, she wished to substitute for her daughter who had been fourth grade and had died before the ceremony that was to advance her to fifth. Now Ruth had to be advanced to the Life rite's fourth grade. Hole saved costs, he told me, by "skipping" his daughter, devising an irregular procedure of "talking" (mystically) about two curing degrees in one midéwiwin. He explained why this was improper. The condensing or intensifying lays double duty on Supernaturals; it exposes the patient to excess dosage of "strength"; it angers midé colleagues who feel cheated of their due fees; it overburdens them with onerous ritual; above all, it is never done.

When the substitute was of higher grade than the deceased, or the shadow, grades would have to be "skipped" for the latter. The equalizing of grades raised concern because a Ghost curing benefited the substitute also, who was credited in the Life rite with the one or more additional grades of the Ghost rite.

Occasionally a ceremony treated several souls at once. Here, there arose the problem of handling multiple substitutes. These would all be "talked about" together, the one of highest grade being sermonized over first, in both the public and the secret or preparatory lodges. Thus, when a fourth-grade man had a curing at the same time as a second-grade one, he was treated ("talked about") exclusively during the first two of the four preparatory nights (or another similar proportion was devised); thereafter the second-grader was treated simultaneously with him. The same arrangement was followed in the public ritual.

Tense and uneasy as the principals felt during Life rites, there seems to have been more hysteria during Ghost rites. All the mourners, not merely the ritual substitutes, were understood to be woefully sad over their loss, a sentiment burdened with fear of death in general and with guilt over desiring the release that the rite gave. I heard this quality affectingly at Manitou when Joe Bluesky "talked" for the burial of his beloved adopted son, admonishing the shadow, "You are ready to leave me now; be sure not to look back [or the glance draws us with you]. Look straight ahead as you were told [by the midé shaman]. We live here as long as we are supposed to. Never wish for us to hasten and join you. For you will find your brothers there, and your mother, father, and grandparents also. Do not trouble us; we will do all you requested before you died." Withdrawing, he seemed broken with grief.

REFERENCE MATTER

Appendix 1

A WOMAN'S WAR VISION

IN ONTARIO of the 1930's, the Ojibwa pursued Supernaturals with traditional intentness. Necessarily, the war complex was interrupted, but at the opening of World War I, Maggie Wilson, the Ojibwa-Cree who was also an English-speaking Christian, had received a series of spontaneous mighty revelations, totaling one vision, which were well known at Emo. I still possess a few of the emblems that she made under vision direction and had discarded just before I met her—she had "abandoned" the vision earlier.

Maggie Wilson's vision presented auditory and visual details about a great war dance to involve all the Ojibwa Manitou Reserve villagers for "the benefit" of relatives fighting overseas in World War I. The dance was a mystic rite affirming the Thunders' patronage of the Ojibwa in the armed forces; this included endowing the soldiers with shamanistic powers of disguise. The dance recalled a traditional ceremony bringing villagers together for a dance of several days' duration when a war party was to be sent off, in the era "before we had law," as Maggie put it, meaning before governmental supervision. For a long while, Maggie did not understand her vision, obeyed it only reluctantly, and found its whole atmosphere painful, especially during the first weeks. Contradicting the usual strict secrecy enjoined upon the visionary, Maggie's Supernaturals had told her to promulgate their message, to aid the tribe and other Canadians in the Great

War. Maggie herself had a son-in-law with the Canadian forces overseas, though she was still in her early thirties.

When the vision installments invaded her nightly rest, her husband was disturbed and told her that she moaned in sleep and then sang songs, war songs being taught her by the Thunders; so he made her disclose all. The Thunders assured her, she reported, that they meant to console and "amuse" her and the village; but for some time she feared announcing the message. The Thunders threatened, "If you do not tell, something will befall your family and all the people. Now will you accept the dream, learn from us, and teach the others?"

She had nine long vision sessions with the Thunders, besides irregular daytime snatches. The patrons taught her eighty songs in all, with accompanying dances, and taught her designs of a drum, of ceremonial staffs and pipes, and of costumes. Because sixty Thunders shared in the dream, she engaged sixty villagers to represent them in her dance. At first she called the undertaking the Star Dance, from its heavenly origin; then she called it the Union Star Dance because the United States joined Canada and so could also enjoy its patronage.

This was how she described her unsought vision to me, in English:

I dreamt when the War first began, in 1914 in the fall. We were living in a wigwam on Manitou Rapids. It was the first time I had camped on the Manitou; perhaps that was why I did not have the dream before. So I had this dream about a dance and disregarded it. But it returned to me nine times. The Ginyu [arctic owl? it is an especially valued Thunder] came with the head Thunderbird, saying they were going to take me somewhere—and I did not want to go. I heard them singing. I wakened, got out of bed, thought about the dream, returned to bed, and dreamt again. They repeated that they wanted me to go with them, to a big mountain [home of Eagles and Thunder]. If I went, they would show me all the other Thunderbirds. I went; it was like looking at another portion of a stage show. I saw things like the Northern Lights, dancing—it was Thunderbirds. They asked me if I would learn eight songs; then I would live till my hair turned gray; and they would teach me one song at a time.

Each time I had a dream, I awakened, then returned to sleep and dreamed the same dream. I was scared to dream more, which was why I wakened—because I did not know if it was a good dream.

The fifth time they came to me they brought a drum and showed me how to make it and how to use it in the dance. Everything was so clear. Ginyu and Thunderbirds brought the drum.

Next day when I was sitting quiet, John, my husband, said, "Don't you know you were singing in your sleep last night?" Maybe the dance would never have come out if John had not made me tell. I said I had no dream. He said, "You must have had some kind of dream or else you are crazy." So he made me tell him. Then he told his father [Chief Namepog, a noted good shaman] and his father asked me, and others came to ask me. Anything like this had to be told because it was a dance, not a secret dream. I had to tell it to get all those to help me. They [Thunders] wanted me to bring this dance into the world.

I felt shy about teaching others. It was my first time. I had to remember everything. It was hard on my head. I was so shy I taught John to speak for me. [Ceremonial spokesmen were traditional.]

At the second dream I saw that woman along with them. She stood at one side of the Thunderbirds. I do not know if she was an angel but she had feathered wings and was veiled. Or, it might have been a he—it never said anything. [Ojibwa cosmology has a glorious woman, covered with gleaming migis shells, who receives ghosts and souls of women entering the happy afterworld.] Leading them were Ginyu and the head Thunderbird. They used to sing a lot [teaching Maggie] but she did not. Sometimes this one with the wings was not with them. Those two [Thunders] who were talking to me said, "She comes down just to see that we teach you correctly." She had long hair [i.e., was beautiful] and her feathers looked like flowers on her head.

At the first dream they just wanted to take me to the mountain, where I saw sixty Thunderbirds in a bunch. They kept saying I was not to tell my dream but to make a drum. It was at the eighth dream [contradicting her earlier statement that it was the fifth dream] that they brought me the drum, marked as you see it now. [The head of the drum was divided into red and blue by a center line of yellow; a white figure of the Thunderbird was painted across the whole.] They brought the bells to be attached to the drum and staffs, and the beads to be used on the dresses and headbands. So we made everything as they directed.

People were glad to help and join the dance for I dreamt that the soldiers would come back if their relatives danced.

I dreamt so much that at last it seemed no longer like a dream but like a person talking to me. It was so plain!

Now I think the angel did not come the first time [she had earlier said the second dream] but only the four last times. She looked so bright: her veil swayed, her huge wings of white feathers shone. After they told me the dream, she would be the first to fly away. She flew west [the afterworld] and the Birds followed.

All who came to me were kind, petting me with their paws [*sic*] and feathers. Sometimes I was scared of them in my dreams but they told me they were bringing joy to me and the others, they were giving a nice thing to amuse me; they said they would teach me a dance with nothing harmful [i.e., having no sorcery]. The Birds said the old dances were all war dances. This would be a new war dance. The head Thunderbird told me to name the dance the Union Star Dance.

The sixty birds all came in a flock, flying with a tremendous noise, like a rattling train. They would tell me [repeatedly] how to lead the dance and how to fix things. I would dream and waken and return to dream from the place where I had left off. They said, "Count us—as many as we are, so many will you have in the dance." I would sit awake for the dream to leave me alone—I couldn't understand it for a long time. But it would come back. I do not know what would have happened if I had not obeyed the dream. Maybe I wouldn't have lived. [This was the classic sanction.]

Each of the nine dreams lasted six to ten nights. That was what scared me, that the dream hung on. I did what they told me because I was afraid my husband and children would die [otherwise]. Anyway, I had no luck. People got jealous and destroyed my child [with sorcery] about a year after we began giving the dance.

But the Birds were kind and friendly. They even laid their heads on my arms. Sometimes I saw shadows of [these] People on the sky.

At the second dream they commenced teaching the songs. They came many times because they had to teach me eighty songs. Some nights only the two leaders came and sang. When the other Birds came, still it was only the two who sang; the other Birds danced, to show me how. Yes, the voices were like Indians'. And the Birds wore headbands.

After the fifth time, my husband had *his* dream about my dream!

By the ninth time, I made up my mind to [act upon the vision], as the Birds knew. So the ninth time, they showed me the uniforms for the dance, and wore them. I thought, Where am I to get the feathers? They said they would have someone dream to bring me feathers. I never told anyone. But after the third time we'd given the dance, an Indian who'd lost his child came from Lake of the Woods with feathers for me. [Mourners seek visions to relieve their sorrow.]

After the ninth time, I gave the dance. More dreams came but I cannot say how many. Then they told me how to bring the drum into the dancing-place: it had to come through the roof [symbolizing the sky] because it was from Thunderbirds.

After I started the dance, eight men [manitos] came now and then to teach me more songs. Ginyu and head Thunderbird came occasionally to help me over difficulties. But the great bunch of sixty never came again. About three years ago [speaking in 1932] I stopped dreaming and stopped giving the dance. Still, I dream occasionally, even last summer. They never say they are paying the last visit.

During the seven or eight years that I gave the dance, other people had dreams about it. They would not understand their dreams and talked to me about them. Several people dreamt songs that I put into the dance, because that was why they were given. In September, 1918, I gave the first dance. That winter Billy M'Ginnis [an ambitious shaman] dreamt two songs for it, the following fall he dreamt two more. When he was teaching them in fall at our house, lightning shot out. That was from Thunderbirds, because we were talking so much about them.

Only four of my eighty dance songs had words, the others consisting of airs alone. Words of the first song went, "Would anybody ever talk to you as they talked to me?" Only the dance leaders [Maggie and John] sang this. I learned it from just one Bird; he sang it with me till I knew it; I would wake up singing it. Everybody wanted to learn it.

The second song was sung by the leading women to Ginyu. He was always the head one and I had to talk about him all the time. [Maggie said he had shorter legs than the true Ginyu and a heavier body. He had few feathers on the face but many fuzzy ones around the eyes. He was seen only in dreams and alarmed people with his hurtful lightning. Her description suggested a bald eagle.] The Ginyu sang this song first, and then the head Thunderbird: "It is a precious jingling sound, the sound of Ginyu." I would sing repeatedly until I knew it. I would have known more songs if I had kept on dreaming but the [Anglican] missionary scared me saying the devil was after me.

After starting the dance, I would dream about the eight Thunderbirds who would sing me new songs. They claimed that where they came from, the eight drummers were the singers. So I had my eight drummers sing. [This was quite customary.] They came as Thunderbirds, then turned into men, and before they left they turned again into Thunderbirds.

These are the words of the third song they taught me: "The eternal

211

Ginyu gave me the power to speak about him." Ceremonial waiters sang this.

Everyone sang the words of the fourth song, looking to the skies, arms upstretched, "I raise my hands towards Ginyu."

All who danced and who came to the dance brought tobacco, food, some print [cloth], which we offered to the Thunderbirds, asking protection. I taught John to offer because women do not talk [ritually] at manito affairs. He had to say, "We offer this food and tobacco, brought here to the one who owns this dance for her to teach others. We thank them for this dance, we enjoy this dance, let us have a good time, may he [Ginyu or Thunderbird] bless us all."

The dance was given fall and spring because Thunderbird leaves in fall and returns in spring. You seldom hear the Bird in winter. But sometimes we gave the dance oftener because the Birds told me to commercialize it. The Indian agent helped. We gave it at the ball ground near Fort Frances and charged twenty-five cents admission. We all shared and did well. Sometimes we gave the dance five times a year: at Christmas, New Year's, spring, summer, fall. The dance had to run two or four nights.

But after seven or eight years, the people became mean and jealous, and the whole thing too expensive. If anyone sickened or died, it was blamed on me. [They regarded her possibly as an evil shaman.] Then my leg became too sore to dance. [She limped badly when I knew her and seldom walked.] And about four years ago we turned Christian. So we gave up the dance. We laid all the furnishings in the bush to rot. [This was usual respectful interment of mystic equipment.] But I still dream of Thunders and I do not think they are angry at me for having quit.

Like some male shamans visited by sickness and death in the family, Maggie had discarded her paraphernalia to block further evil visitations. She told me of even great midé shamans known to have done this.

Maggie affirmed in her usual quiet way that her dance saved Indian soldiers' lives but that many died, including her son-in-law, because she delayed presenting the dance. Delays arose from Maggie's reluctance to act on the vision and subsequently from time spent recruiting and training personnel and securing facilities.

Appendix 2

COMMON DREAMS

ORDINARILY, Maggie Wilson spent her imagination on the women's arts and crafts, such as tanning deer and moose hides; embroidering them in traditional patterns that she evolved as she went along using porcupine quills (which she dyed by native formulas) and commercial beads; biting the same graceful patterns into new inner birchbark; cutting and sewing hide moccasins and other clothing; collecting and drying rice and blueberries; making and using herbal cures; and telling vivid stories about village life, which I recorded elsewhere (Landes, 1938a). All her life she had vivid dreams; she made a clear distinction, however, between common dreams and the vision of the Star Dance, with its manito figures and mystic affect.

Maggie's common dreams were exceedingly detailed, as were the village stories she related, and the other tribal information she told and wrote me for years. The Ojibwa freely narrated their common night dreams, which were considered a kind of human companionship, though some were appraised as prophetic after the event. The actors and backgrounds were usually familiar, if not always known personally; there were no mystic creatures or other phenomena, and no mystic promises or threats. Compared with visions, they seemed simple. But their affect could be pitched high. As with Maggie's visions, her simple dreams showed worry, reluctance, questioning, and an occasional onrush of satisfaction or joy. They amplified her sense of living. The following dreams she dictated to her daughter and sent to me. Their secularity seems evident by contrast with her patterned Thunders vision. The comparison highlights traits distinguishing each of the two dream categories.

I dreamed of all my four children and their families and of my old man. We were camping at Lake of the Woods, doing nothing special. We all had canoes. Right back of our tents was a high rock. And all at once as we were sitting, we saw ten canoes come around the islands. The people in these canoes wore big feather hats. The canoes were queer, bent lots at each end, not made like regular canoes. These men had spears in their hands, and guns too. Very much afraid, we crawled back into the bush and up on the high rocks, to watch the people. They seemed dangerous. They came up to our canoes and stopped to find if anyone was in our tents. Then they paddled away behind the islands. We watched them get out of their canoes, crawl to our side of the island, and watch our tents from there; some of the men walked along the shore.

My son-in-law said, "There's a road nearby, not too far. You would be able to walk there." [Maggie was lame.] So we agreed to go, being afraid of those people we had never seen before—they looked awfully dangerous.

My two sons-in-law and two sons and my old man said they would try to sneak back to our tents for clothes and the things for my daughter's newborn baby. They returned with big bundles on their backs and we all changed clothes. My older son's wife said she was returning to our tents for more things and my son went along.

While they were gone, we saw one of those men standing on the shore, spear in hand, eyeing our tents. My younger son said, "I guess he sees those that are gone back to the tents." We were scared. My young daughter put her baby on her back, her husband put their little girl in a packsack, and they said they were ready to leave. I was ready too. My older son, Leonard, returned with his wife and we started off. Two men stayed behind to see what those men would do. We walked quite a while, reached a road, followed it, and soon reached a house.

I told the woman there about those men. She too got awfully scared and told her husband. He hitched up a horse, put the children in the wagon, besides me, my two daughters and daughter-in-law. He said the main highway was only one and a half miles off.

Then I remembered my little black pup left at our tents! Before we started, I heard my little dog barking. Oh! I dreamed I was glad the dog had found its way after us. I told the driver to hurry with us. The men went on ahead. Soon we reached the main highway, found a gas station and sat in the shade. The white men asked us where we came from, we told them, and they said they would see about the strangers. So my two sons and my son-in-law, Janet's husband, said they would go along. All had guns.

We waited. The men returned, said they had found the strangers and asked them what they wanted. The [strange] men answered they were just traveling but had stopped many days because it was awfully windy on the lake, so they had eaten up all their food. That was why they had come to our tents. They were waiting for people to appear. They did approach our men and ask for something to eat; and they got a lunch. One man gave Leonard a leather jacket, besides a pair of moccasins to my other son and a sweater to my son-in-law; and he asked for more food. Our men gave what they could spare. Leonard told me, "I gave them some of your flour too."

Then I dreamed that my husband got right mad with my son [who was his stepson, lazy and poor, and had taken flour, as he did other things, that was not his, without asking permission]. He said, "What business did you have to give our flour away! Now you give *me* some of the things, then, that they gave you for the grub!" My son said, "Why didn't you come along? But you're too much of a coward! [The old man suffered from chronic asthma.] You didn't have the heart [courage] to come back with us!" My husband said to me, "Well, you wouldn't let me go back." So no one said anything more.

But I dreamed I heard my children saying they would return to their tents. I dreamed I did not feel a bit like going back. I saw a car coming down the road toward Emo and I got up and waved at it. I asked the driver to put me on and he said all right. I took my bundle and the [white] boy I adopted and got in the car. As we drove off, one of my sons yelled at me, "You're foolish to go home! Don't you know there's a war in Emo?" I asked the driver if there was and he said he didn't know. At Sleeman, he said that was as far as he was going. I said, "I'll go right back with you then because it's too far to walk to my house from here." He said all right, I rode back with him, and he left me at the gas station.

I asked the man for my family and he said they had returned to our tents. So I returned along the way we had come. But it was getting dark and soon we lost our way. We walked on and on. My little boy got tired and wanted to sleep. It was very dark, I sat on the ground and he lay on my lap and slept. All night I sat up trying to remember which way we had come and just how it had looked. Morning came, the boy awakened, and we started off. I was tired and awfully worried. Then we heard a shot and I knew it was they [her family] who had fired it. We went in that direction, after walking a long time we reached the Lake, and then I knew where we were.

But the tents were gone—they had already moved away. I dreamed that, oh! I felt so bad and tired and the boy was hungry. So we walked along the shore, found a house and rapped on the door. A woman opened and invited us in. I said we were lost and also that I could not find my children. She gave us a nice meal and asked where we were from. I said I lived on a reserve between Emo and Barwick. She said, "I'm going that way as soon as I finish and I can take you along." I dreamed I was very glad and thanked her. So we ate a good meal and started off. I dreamed we drove along the Lake shore to the mouth of the [Rainy] River. I even recognized the places we had stayed before. We drove onto the main highway and home. She stopped the car, I got out, and she said, "I suppose you're thankful now to be back in your own house. Now you're all right, nothing will worry you." I said yes and thanked her. Then she told me, "Now come back in the car and thank the good Lord you're safely home and also ask Him that the way be open for you to get Home up yonder." Then I knew she was a Christian. I got in the car again, we knelt together, and she prayed a long time. Then she told me to pray. While praying I started to cry [this accords with the Ojibwa form of asking Supernaturals for "pity"] and woke up and so that was the end.

The following dream shows vivid imagery and affect; it describes good fortune in pursuing fur; but it remains a common dream for want of manito intervention.

"I dreamed about my younger daughter [who was inseparable from Maggie], her two children, a friend of ours named Gentle Woman, and some men. I dreamed we were on a river with lots of otter and we were trying to kill them. The water was very low and I dreamed we were running in the water [after the fur]. The men had gone ahead. The otters that were returning were the ones we were after. I dreamed we were killing them with mallets that had iron stuck in the end. When we got close to an otter, we hit it on the head and it died. I dreamed my daughter killed seven, the other woman killed ten, and I only four. While busy talking and running after these otter, we heard rushing water. We knew the dam upstream was breaking so we ran up the banks and soon saw the water rising. Lots of floating logs showed that they had broken the dam. Now I dreamed we saw lots of otter sitting on the logs floating downstream. All at once a beaver swam near us. I struck with my mallet and killed it. I dreamed I was very glad to know I would have money [from selling fur] and so I wakened.

Another simple dream reports Maggie's hardships with a female ward and appears partly to reflect her children's violent resentment over the white boy waif Maggie adopted and cherished. It lacks the stereotyped images and phrases of the manito vision but it seems to hover self-pityingly on outer edges of Ojibwa mysticism.

I dreamed that my [younger] daughter Janet and her two children and I were living in a house near the River on a high bank, near Manitou Rapids. A man came with his daughter, about twelve years old, and asked if I would adopt her. I said I didn't know and my daughter said, "Don't adopt another." So I told the man I could not take the child. Then he asked me to take care of her for a while. So I said she could stay for a while, and he left his daughter.

For four days she was fairly good. A tent stood outside the house and there were all kinds of flowers planted about, and I was looking after these flowers for the people who owned the house. On the fifth day the girl began to climb around and I tried to stop her. But no! She climbed the house, fences, trees—and here I was telling her to come down, worried she might fall. I told her girls did not climb around and after a while she came down.

When I was busy watering the flowers, Janet yelled, "Mother! That girl is down at the Rapids, wading in water up to her neck!" Oh! I dreamed I was awfully scared, knowing she could not swim. I went down the bank and called her to come ashore. No! She would not listen though I talked and talked. So I took off my shoes and stockings and my top dress and I waded out in my underclothes. I took a switch and chased her around the water a long time. I made her get out but when I got ashore, back she was in the water again. So I coaxed her more, but oh! she was stubborn. At last I took her arm and dragged her ashore. She dragged me back right to the water's edge and then I dragged her away. I talked nicely but she wouldn't listen. She was getting mad and had me tired out. So Janet ran down, took her by the shoulder and pushed her up the bank and into the house. And I went in.

I dreamed I forgot my dress and shoes on the shore. In the kitchen the girl scolded me and hit me. When Janet saw this, she said, "I'm going to Mrs. Hayes [wife of the Government Farmer, resident on the reserve] and tell her to phone the Mounties to come and fix this girl and take her away. I won't have her fighting my mother!"

Out she went, locking the girl in. The girl jumped up and recommenced fighting me. I dreamed she was very strong, throwing me on the floor, kicking, hitting, and biting me, and pulling my hair. When I got up, she would knock me down. I dreamed I was bloody all over. [In a sacred dream, this would have been experienced with some evil Supernatural, like windigo.] She knocked my wrists out of joint and tore off my clothes down to my petticoat and bloomers. She grabbed a washboard and hit me with it. Just then I dreamed that my other daughter, Christina, came to the window and saw this girl fighting me. She ran to the door that Janet had locked and said, "Oh, I'm going to smash this window and come in! That girl is killing you!" Finally I got the girl down under me. [This was also the way of closing a windigo fight.] She still clutched the washboard but I had one of her hands and I held her by the waist, too, and I stood back of her, so whenever she tried to hit me with the washboard, she hit herself on the back. Then she let go of the board to scratch on the floor until she nearly reached the stove poker; but I held her back.

Just then Christina called, "Janet, hurry up and open this door! That girl is killing our mother!" Janet came and put the key in the lock, but the door would not open. I dreamed I was getting tired and weak, and then I heard a crash: Christina smashed down the door, ran in and kicked the girl and was just going to jump her, when I said, "Oh, Christina, don't do anything to her! We'll let the law handle her!" She said all right. Then I told them to hold her so she could not get away. They held her while she bit and scratched. Just then I saw a car coming and it stopped right at the door. A Mountie came in and said, "What's the matter?" And I answered, "I don't know, but I guess this girl is crazy. She has been fighting me for a long time." Then he said, "Let her go." So Janet let her go. She ran to the Mountie, jumped him and started scratching. He took his club and hit her on the head, and she fell on the floor. He took out his handcuffs and put them on her hands and legs. She screamed and rolled around on the floor. The Mountie told us to get out of her way and the doctor came and the

Indian Agent and the Farmer. The doctor examined her and said, "There is nothing wrong with her brain, she is in her right mind, she is just stubborn and angry."

I dreamed I told the Mountie how it all happened. He asked her why she was trying to kill me, and she said, "Just because I don't like her, because she is too ugly and old and gray. I don't like to stay with anyone who is ugly." The Mountie said, "Well, then you have to come along with me and go to the giddy giddy girls' school." I dreamed that she said, "Giddy giddy, my bum!"

The Mountie looked down and smiled. She made him shy. He picked her up and carried her to the car. She said those words over and over and the Mountie drove away with her. Then I dreamed that the doctor pulled my joints into place again, bandaged my cuts and both my arms. I dreamed that Mr. Spencer [the Indian Agent] said to the doctor, "You had better take Mrs. Wilson to the hospital, for both of her daughters are busy." The doctor said he would take me, but I did not feel like going to the hospital. And then I dreamed that my husband came in; I asked him if he would take care of me, and he answered, "Sure, I will take care of you! You won't have to do any work. You will be all right and I will take you home." So I dreamed I got into the Hayes's car and they drove me to my own home. I dreamed I was very glad to get to my own home, and I lay down on my bed. Everyone came in.

As we were talking, I dreamed another car stopped at the door, and out jumped a man, the father of this girl. I was scared; I thought he would be mad. But he was not. He just came in and asked how it had happened. When I told him, he replied, "I tried my best to train her, but I could not succeed. She is not a bit like my people. There is other blood in her and that blood is cursed. She takes after her mother and her mother's people. . . . I have failed to find a place for her where she could get along." Then I dreamed the Agent spoke to him, "Well, don't worry. She has found a place for herself where she will have to behave. She won't carry on like that any more. It won't be as easy for her from now on, and she will have to do as she is told." The man said nothing and went out with everyone else. My old man and I were alone.

All at once we saw a man running down the hill. He was dressed in white and had a tennis racquet in his hand. He threw the ball with this racquet and the ball flew right onto the side of the house, came into the house, and bumped onto the other side; the ball did not stop at all, but kept on flying around. We were afraid it would hit us; and as we were running out the door the ball hit me on the back and I nearly fell backwards. The man came running and grabbed the ball again with his net and threw it again. The ball went right through another house, so he grabbed the ball again and threw it back to the direction from which he had come running, and the ball went through the roof of another house. The man started to run after it again, and as we watched the ball flying around, I dreamed it turned into a ball of fire [omen of sorcery] with a tail of fire on it. Then I dreamed we were awfully scared, and my old man said, "Let us go away from here; it might come back. Let us go down to the river and stay over there."

So we went out again to the little stable, and I dreamed he hitched up the horse. Only then I thought of our children. They were all up that way from which the ball of fire had come. So I begged my old man to go that way. We did not travel on the road but along the field and when we reached the place of my oldest daughter, Christina, Janet and the rest of the family were there, too. When I told them about this fire they said they had not noticed it. Just as we were getting over our excitement, someone called to us, and we saw it coming again. So we all ran and tried to find a hiding place. The ball was flying around, and this man was running after it. When he caught it, he threw it in another direction. And while we watched him, someone brought the news that this girl who had fought me had escaped from the Mountie just as he was taking her into the jail, and that she was coming back and looking for me [this was portended by the evil ball of fire]. So my daughter Christina said to me, "Mother, run and hide! Run to the well! On the other side is a thick bush. Hide there and we will try and hold her back until the Mounties come!" So I dreamed I ran down to the well and into the thick bush and lay down flat so no one could see me. As I lay there, I heard shouting and yelling. The voices were coming nearer; I dreamed that I got up and looked. Here was the girl coming! She was running straight to the bush where I was hiding. I jumped up and ran from her. The people behind us were yelling at me to try and run fast. But I dreamed I was very tired, so she soon overtook me, jumped me, threw her arms around my neck and started kissing me, at the same time that she was biting my cheeks. I dreamed that she nearly bit a piece out of my cheek. Then I yelled and woke up yelling. So that is the end of it. . . . Such a queer dream it was.

Fear, satisfaction, and anxiety ride these common dreams, as they did Maggie's sacred war vision, and others' visions. The next dream describes marital boredom and a simple wish for romance; it is a secular match for the sacred dream of Hole-in-the-Sky about the two lovely female Supernaturals granting him polygynous rights (mentioned at the end of Chapter 3, above). Maggie's dream related below is not sacred: it lacks the conventional earmarks.

I dreamed I was living in a house and there were a few tents around where some people camped. My husband [a good man, but ailing and incapable of marital relations] was not home. A man lived nearby with whom I dreamed I was in love [in reality she had no lover then]. He used to come to my house and make love to me, and oh! I was in an awful way as I knew my husband would soon be coming home, and I could not bear the thought of my sweetheart leaving me. This man and I sat for hours with his head in my lap, I stroking his hair [conventional gestures between lovers]. I dreamed I was very much in love with him. I hated to see my husband come home. So this man and I planned that I would tell my husband he was a relative of mine and was going to make his home with us. When my husband came home, I told him this. He said it was all right for the man to stay, and oh! I was glad to have my lover there. My husband was always working around outdoors. He was not afraid to leave me and this man alone in the house, and oh! it was great for us to be left alone. I dreamed we carried on like this for quite a while till one time my husband came in, mad, because someone had told him how we were acting. He said, "You told me a lie when you claimed that man was a relative of yours. You are flirting with him, so he can get out of here. I don't want him here!" The man got ready and left. Oh! I dreamed I was sorry, so I started to quarrel and fight [physically] with my man all the time. I even dreamed that I wished he would die, but I did not have the heart to kill him; nor would he let me go away. This man left me his snapshot. I dreamed I would sit for a long time looking at the picture with tears in my eyes. I missed the man very much. So at last I packed my clothes and started off to this man.

Walking along, a car came and picked me up. The driver asked me where I was going, and when I told him, he said I would not have far to walk after he had stopped at his place. But before we got there, he ran off the road. I dreamed I fainted in the accident, and when I came to, I dreamed I was lying on a bed, and when I looked around I saw my husband standing looking at me with tears in his eyes. I tried to lift my left arm, but I could not—it was broken. I dreamed that my husband spoke to me when he knew I was awake. He said, "Where were you going? and what is the reason you left without telling me? You are sinning before God [this idiom, obviously derived from their Christian conversion four years earlier, also had aboriginal significance in beliefs about manito obligations and tabus] and this is your punishment [an idea rooted in aboriginal as well as Christian thought]." I dreamed I felt sorry and was only making a fool of myself. I was ashamed to be unfaithful to my husband, who stood by my side to help me in my pain. Only then I realized I had a good man. And I was leaving him for another. I dreamed that all this came to my mind. He spoke again, "You will get better soon and you are coming home with me. Forget everything." So I started to cry, so hard that I woke up crying.

Appendix 3

BIRCHBARK SCROLLS

AMONG VARIOUS TRIBES of Indians, shell-bead wampum (a word of Algonkian origin) was once used to record trade and perhaps formal agreements. In the 1930's, Ojibwa informants gave me white porcelain imitation wampum that had been discarded completely and its uses forgotten. Among diverse prairie tribes, records of mythic and historic events were painted on buffalo hide, notably on tents; it seems that the records memorialized individual exploits of the hunter constructing the tent, not the lore of an institution like the midéwiwin. The birchbark scrolls that recorded some of the Ojibwa mystic tradition were peculiar to this people. So also were the pictographs they employed.

Birchbark served various purposes and held a unique, cherished place in Ojibwa regard. Until shortly before 1930, it was used almost exclusively to cover the wigwam frame, as it is waterproof, retains the heat of the inside fire, and breaks the wind. It was used like a blanket and called so. Light in weight, it was portable easily. Women rolled it off the wigwam frame into a huge scroll and carried it from camp to camp. Midé scrolls looked like small copies of the "blanket." Birchbark rolls were discarded only when entirely disintegrated by weathering and use; but winds and extreme heat were the only natural influences that could tatter the blanket-bark. It seems impervious to lightning; Ojibwa lore says Nehnehbush marked the birch as his tree, figur-

APPENDIX

ing the bark with its characteristic graceful pattern that reminds Thunders to observe respect. The bark has been used for untold ages as cooking vessels, for it holds water and resists the fire over which it is hung. Pieces or remnants of the young bark's fine inner layers have been used for sheerly decorative purposes, the women biting patterns (floral ones in the 1930's) into them, and swinging them free in the air for light to pick its way through. Maggie Wilson made some for me in a flash, still intact about thirty-five years later. Midé scrolls were regarded against this background of love and utility.

The mnemonic scrolls look dainty and pretty. The outer bark is a light golden tan, nature's short dark lines raised in low relief according to a vague vertical pattern. The inner bark, when freshly picked in spring, is naturally a rich-colored pink; its fleshly consistency is most receptive to the awl scratching mystic figures through it. The figures themselves are charming, small outlines presenting front, back, or profile views, the sure strokes giving an animated air. The forms are humanoid or animal-like, often in the act of walking, talking, singing, or watching intently.

The size of the scroll varies with its intended function, one or more mystic songs being inscribed on small scrolls, while midé rituals and doctrine were inscribed on much larger ones. Individual preferences entered, as some men employed small scrolls for any purpose, and others used large ones for any purpose. Availability of bark determined choices, often.

The particular message on a scroll is generally useless, as explained earlier, unless each figure is labeled or otherwise translated by the knowing owner, usually the scroll's maker. No Rosetta Stone can decipher it, so individual are the meanings, as they were intended to be, for secrecy. In the 1930's, I saw several scrolls in handsome condition at the Museum of the Minnesota State Historical Society; but their communications are as lost to us as if the scrolls never were found, for the owners were dead and no one instructed in their codes could be discovered. William Jones carefully copied figures from scrolls at Bois Fort, Minnesota, but he might have spared himself the task, for they are unexplained, and hence unexplainable.

224

Dr. Jones fared better with other Minnesota scrolls, one from Mille Lacs, one from Leech Lake, and another from Pelican Lake. The first two contain midé details which are essentially the same as those that I obtained from Will Rogers (or Hole-in-the-Sky) in Minnesota and from Mrs. Wilson's stepfather, John Bunyan, at Ontario's Manitou. Jones's third scroll contains directions for a game with migis shells, played by persons seasoned in the midé rite, along lines of the usual Ojibwa gambling games. Jones's informants were two brothers; the one named White-Feather-Flying gave the rules in the account now quoted. Jones wrote, in unpublished notes, that he had discovered

. . . two birchbark scrolls at Pelican Lake, which the owners regarded as games, though not absolutely. The rolls went by the name of the fourth degree of the midewiwin. From one of the men I got an account of the games for the first, second, and third degrees, but did not get the birchbark rolls going with them. My informant told me that the figure would be the same for each of the three as for the fourth degree, but of course, the location of the points and their values would be different. A *migis* or pearl shell is placed wherever a spot is counted, the number of shells used depending on the number of spots on the figure. The point of the game is to place the right migis on its proper spot. Failure to do this means the payment of a forfeit which is put up before the guess is made. Members only of the mide society play, and one has to pay dearly to learn how to place the pearls without mistake. One cannot fail when one has learned how.

For the first degree, one migis is used and four play. One spot is sought for, and that is the heart. For the second degree, eight shells are used and eight play. The spots and their values are:

1 for the left ankle
2 "   " right "
3 "   " left knee
4 "   " right "
5 "   " left wrist
6 "   " right "
7 "   " heart
8 "   " heart

For the third degree, sixteen shells are used, and sixteen play. The spots and the values are:

1 for the sole of the left foot
2 "   "   "   "   " right "

```
 3 for the left hip
 4  "   "  right "
 5  "   "  middle of the left palm
 6  "   "     "    "   "  right "
 7  "   "  upper side of the left elbow
 8  "   "     "    "   "   "  right "
 9  "   "  left shoulder
10  "   "  right   "
11  "   "  left ear
12  "   "  right "
13  "   "  left eye
14  "   "  right "
15  "   "  hollow in the throat just over the collarbone
16  "   "  forehead
```

For the fourth degree, twenty shells are used, and twenty play. The spots and the values are:

```
 1 for the middle between the two balls of the left sole
 2  "   "     "       "       "    "    "    "   "  right "
 3  "   "  knuckle of the left big toe
 4  "   "     "    "   "  right "   "
 5  "   "  second toe of the left foot
 6  "   "     "    "   "   "  right "
 7  "   "  end of the penis
 8  "   "  navel
 9  "   "  pit of the stomach
10  "   "  left nipple
11  "   "  right   "
12  "   "  spot just above pit of stomach but below line on
            chest between nipples
13  "   "  soft part of the left hand between thumb and wrist
14  "   "   "    "   "   "  right "    "    "    "    "
15  "   "  first knuckle of the left little finger
16  "   "    "    "    "   "  right "    "
17  "   "  biceps of the left arm
18  "   "    "    "   "  right "
19  "   "  Adam's apple
20  "   "  crown of the head
```

White-Feather-Flying's brother gave a variant version. It showed small differences in locations of spots and values of the guesses.

Appendix **4**

ROCK PAINTINGS

THE OJIBWA often mentioned to me wonderful "rock paintings" that they had seen in their woodlands, which they considered manito, and not the work of human hands. They regarded the locations as manito-charged and so left tobacco at every passing. Tribesmen did not seek out the rocks nor use them, but felt obliged to mark them as worthy of highest recognition, as we too might recognize a rare object. I never saw these rocks, but William Jones did, at Nett Lake, Minnesota, and copied some figures among his notes. His record states:

These pictures are on stone, and on a small island called Little Manitou Island. The Indians claim that the pictures were already there when they first came to Net[t] Lake. The pictures look as if they were pecked in. Some are partly effaced. The mischief is done by rain, waves and high water. The accumulation of thin crust over the surface of the rocks helps to make some of the figures rather vague. The pictures are mostly on the east and northeast of the island, and near the water. They are in groups, and the figures in the notes [he sketched] are but representative. The Indians claim that the pictures were the work of manitos. So, on passing the island they stop ad leave a little tobacco, not necessarily on the rocks where the pictures are, but somewhere on the island. The tobacco is to give the manitous pleasure.

On the north side of the island is a slippery slant where the rock runs down into deep water. It is said that tiny folk amuse themselves sliding down the slant. The Indians say that the little people were

227

seen on the rocks when their ancestors first came to the island. The pygmies vanished into the water when the Indians saw them. Indians will not camp over night on the island.

The figures Jones sketched are lost to us, for the time, not having been found in Smithsonian Institution Archives as late as 1967; nor did I reproduce his sketches twenty-five years earlier when copying the above excerpt from the manuscript loaned me by Dr. Michelson in Washington. I made verbal descriptions, as follows, however:

Jones's sketched figures are not always easy to identify. Like Ojibwa pictographs, they appear in profiled, rear, or front-view outline.

The first figure seems to represent a large turtle as seen from above: limbs, tail, and head are all spread out. Jones notes that it is seven inches long from head to tail and that its greatest width is four inches.

The second figure appears like a Siamese-twin dog with rather long legs; the heads, in profile, turn in opposite directions.

The third figure is of two humanoid male shapes, seen full face, arms upraised.

The fourth figure is a long-bodied doglike creature, resembling what the Ojibwa call Lion and Water Monster; it is in profile, facing right.

The fifth figure appears like the left profile of a hippopotamus but it might also be a moose or elk; Jones's notes say it is four and a half inches from snout to rump.

The sixth figure, three inches long, is the right profile of some [bullhead?] fish, with only caudal fins indicated.

The next figure seems like another species of fish, left-turned, a foot long from nose to tail, with two sets of fins drawn from the sides, like barbs.

The eighth figure is a headless game animal, perhaps elk, turned left, four inches from neck to tail, three inches from hoof to tail.

The ninth figure has a fox-head, a relatively long body, and a long tail, all in right profile; it is six inches from snout to tail end.

The tenth figure is now weathered headless; it is some large animal, short-legged, facing left.

The eleventh has two figures, one resembling a humanoid male full-face; the other has a tubular body with limblike extensions but the arms continue above the head and join into a circle, and there is a tail extension.

228

The twelfth is another humanoid, full-face, with extensions growing out of the head, and sidewise protruberances in the waist region; it is five inches long from tip of head extension to toe.

The thirteenth is two parallel figures, both full face; the taller has arms spread horizontally, with enormous hands and five fingers, the legs and feet are turned right profile, and a tail or penis droops to the feet; the smaller figure, reaching to below the level of the other's outspread hands, is vaguely humanoid and womanly, its body very full compared with the tubular lines of the other, with fin-like feet and upraised arms.

The fourteenth is two figures drawn full-face but one placed at right angles to the other; the larger is humanoid or froglike, with a long doglike ear at the left side of the head, legs and feet highly frog-like, a very long tail extending from the crotch to form the nearer leg of the small humanoid form placed at right angles to it. The distance from the head of the large figure to the further foot of the smaller is eighteen inches.

The fifteenth is a human figure in full face, with upraised arms.

The sixteenth is a grotesque human figure, with long narrow body, something narrow growing from the crown of the head, an immense four-fingered hand growing out of the thin right arm, and an erect penis.

Appendix **5**

RED LAKE MIDÉWIWIN PUBLIC RITE

THIS ACCOUNT describes the public performance of a midéwiwin at Red Lake's Ponemah village on August 30, 1933, in which Will Rogers, or Hole-in-the-Sky, was a chief shaman and I an observer. It is set down to illustrate actual personal appraisals on the spot, as any knowing observer would voice them.

The rite was scheduled to cure E. S. and her three-year-old daughter. It was a brilliantly sunny, windy day which finally grew very hot. I entered the family's house about 9:30 in the morning and found E. sweeping. Hole-in-the-Sky lodged upstairs and was then being visited by Gehbeh, a chief midé at Ponemah. Hole told me in English that Gehbeh impressed him well. But, I protested quietly, the man was agitating against the two of us, warning people not to tolerate our midé studies; besides, Everwind and his brother-in-law Bios agreed with him. Poor Hole showed alarm.

Now I took Hole for a short drive, to relax him before the arduous ceremonials. Not far from the S. house stood the framework of a small midé lodge on a green, by the road. Hole said rituals had lasted until 2:00 A.M.; yet he had got out of bed at sunrise to hang up the goods for the manitos. Everwind, as chief midé, should have done this but he had returned home to sleep, leaving the chore to Hole, who lived on the premises. I asked Hole why he had not done this before retiring and he objected that this would have risked theft. He fretted that "they have very queer ways of doing the rite here. They omitted the sweat lodge and carried Bear's trip from Cass Lake to Red Lake."

By 11:30 several officers had arrived; they stood around idly in ragged clothes, chattering. Everwind had "invited" (engaged for the regular shaman's fee) five assistant chiefs to conduct this sixth-grade rite. By 1:00 P.M. the ceremonies had not begun, awaiting the Bowman, a man named Jim Cloud. Nor were there more than some scattered onlookers. Hole said that a Cass Lake midéwiwin would have been half finished by this hour.

E.'s grandmother, her mother's mother, asked me to drive her home to pick up her midé sack, besides maple sugar, candy, and cigarettes owing the midé officers. On the way, she said she was of sixth grade, like her deceased husband; she remembered that her son was invited to the dance (midéwiwin). She asked me, worried, if I had proper amounts of food and tobacco for the officers.

I returned to eat and chat with Hole. He said, "I believe J. S. [E.'s father] has lost some respect for his uncle Everwind," partly because of the present delay in starting the affair and perhaps more because J. understood that Hole's version of the rite was completer, truer, than Everwind's; J. saw too that Everwind demanded "too many officers," meaning excessive fees. J. had advised Everwind that he wished to make alterations but the old shaman refused him, saying the manitos had already seen the existing arrangements (and so were expecting these).

Ceremonies began, though with only three of the five assistant chiefs stipulated by Everwind. No one knew or explained why nearly half had dropped out, but "it looked bad." The Bowman, Jim Cloud, was related to old Mrs. Everwind. Gossipers said he was a poor choice because he "always" got drunk and required care. But this day he was not drunk, and Hole thought "he knew his business though he entered at the wrong door of the midé lodge." Steersman was Sam Whitefeather, Mrs. Everwind's brother, who "knew his business." Speeches were very long and enormously repetitive. Because it was the fishing season, there were too few guests and visitors. Did this also explain the officer dropouts?

231

To me Hole complained that the midé lodge was built too short and low; besides it should have been designed as a "nest" since the sixth grade was Sky, meaning that instead of a regular roof, there should have been twigs and boughs placed atop low horizontals. Everwind ought to have given J. S., E.'s father, such directions.

Because Ponemah midéwiwin counted cumulatively through all grades, twenty-nine lesser officers appeared for this sixth grade. The large number appalled Hole, thinking of the fees coming to each one from the patient's family; Cass Lake would require only six such officers, starting the count anew at fifth grade. Among the twenty-nine were Mrs. Everwind, wife of the chief midé, and a wife, daughter, and sister of the three other chief officers. The third grade, handled simultaneously for E.'s small daughter, required ten lesser manitos; Hole approved.

The same individuals officiated at both grades. Officers of the third were sandwiched among those of the sixth; put conversely, the ten needed for third grade were taken from the sixth grade's twenty-nine. To me Hole objected that only the chiefs should be the same, to allow fees to flow more widely through the community and to reduce jealousies.

Each chief officer earned a quilt from each grade. Five were made by E.'s mother and grandmother, worth three dollars apiece, in 1933 a considerable amount. (To illustrate the purchasing power of money then, an excellent full-course dinner in New York City cost 45 cents in a respectable restaurant.) Each lesser officer earned one piece of cotton "print." The head midé customarily told the patient how many items to prepare but did not specify the yardage for each; it was understood there should be enough for real use. For this sixth grade, thirty-four lengths of cloth were paid, each measuring four yards, costing from 12 to 20 cents a yard. Bowman and Steersman got two pieces each, the others got one each. Three quilts and twelve prints were paid to third-grade officers, too. "And all the amounts of food," Hole reminded me, solemnly.

232

When Hole drummed, nobody rose to dance; this left an awkward gap. Perhaps it expressed shyness before a visiting dignitary, or even resentment. Hole advised Everwind that this gap was improper, for manitos require people to dance, to show them respect and to aid the patient.

Hole informed me that Everwind talked too long, even considering that he was the head officer; and that he moved too slowly through the ritual; and that "Bowman talked so low no one could hear him; so did Gehbeh but he sings well." Parents should stay beside their children going through the rite, learning jointly with them. The same was not required of grandparents though they might sit in, if they so wished, as Mrs. S.'s mother did, joining E.'s parents to follow the girl around when she thanked the officers ritually, stroking their heads. Besides, the "old lady" had helped her daughter make the quilts, which were beautiful in design and workmanship.

The fees were not to be used for a night or two after the rituals because of "power" contaminations. Used prematurely, "they prick like nettles." Hole remembered getting seven "prints" at Pine Point and giving all to his daughters in discharge of obligations, such as paying his daughter Kate for minding the house in his absence; he cautioned her and the others about the use tabu.

Most people, entering the lodge after Bowman's first entrance, proffered tobacco and food to the chief and his first and second assistants. Some of this was for the donors' dead kinfolk, some for the Supernaturals, the officers being informed accordingly. Food brought for Supernaturals was termed "cleaning up the lodge," which meant that "you think as well of it as a house when you clean it. The Indian was told never to enter the midé lodge without something in his hand. Now he comes with tobacco and food to feed manitos of this grade, and it is the same as cleaning up the wigwam." The officers, or the substitutes they chose, ate in the lodge center, "to benefit the dead." Food was dished out to others at seats lining the lodge.

The visitors at Ponemah gave their food and tobacco to the

233

chiefs in serial order. Hole found this sequence unnecessary: "the stuff can be given to any chief midé." Everwind received the most. He kept the food package I gave, passing it to his wife; other food contributions were passed to the general supply from which all would feast. When the time came, they ate a great deal of white rice cooked with raisins; this was preferred for cheapness and easy preparation, Hole said.

Bowman held invitation sticks and tobacco in his left hand while opening up the lodge; but instead of using the sticks, he pointed. Hole explained that this deficiency was because Everwind had never got around to the formal invitations and so had to choose available people at hand in the crowd. They did issue proper invitations to the rite of "Sitting by the Sacrifices" (performed in a tent), using trimmed-off feathers for the sixth grade. Hole, who raised these points with me to relieve his keyed-up concern over midéwiwin, had known only about untrimmed feathers until now, each colored wholly red, yellow, blue or white, or uncolored. Red was the color for Bowman, blue for Steersman, white or yellow for any lesser manito (officer). Besides, red and white stripes were possible for Bowman, made by winding a strip diagonally across the stick before dipping it in the red dye. Sticks should be issued, for invitations, even to mere onlookers, "so the head midé knows how many there are." Many people attended rites hoping to "help out at the last minute" as lesser officiants, for which they received some cloth. Nearly every midé member would receive an invitation in the course of the seasons and so get "some goods."

The midé lodge faced east and west. Hole found this orientation correct for first, second, third, and fifth grades but—despite earlier assertions that Earth's lodge always faced east-west—not for fourth, sixth, seventh, and eighth which had to face north and south. So E., entering sixth grade, and her daughter, entering third, ought not to have been together in one "wigwam" (this word was often used synonymously with "lodge" and "tent") as each needed different orientations to their midé structure. (Was

234

Hole in a carping mood and resorting to mystic combat?) The confusion could have been remedied by "talking mystically" about it in the midé lodge, to effect a mystic reversal, but this did not happen. Hole said the bird on the cross should have faced east, greeting people as they entered the lodge, but it was actually turned away west! The lodge had four doors, representing "Bear tracks, where he broke through Earth."

The sixth-grade cross was painted in stripes correctly, Hole said, but the colors were in wrong sequence, red being where the yellow should have been. Coming from another locality, he dared not criticize openly, however. There should have been a post in each of the four corners, six to eight feet tall, each topped with a carved bird, as required for Sky grades. In the southeast, the topping figure should be a tiny owl; in the southwest, it should be a raven; in the northwest, a hoot owl; in the northeast, a nighthawk or whippoorwill. Sometimes the southeast carving was a buzzard and the northeast one a duck hawk, as they are powerful predators.

E.'s face was not painted, Bowman having neglected his duty here. Her small daughter's face was painted in third-grade style, with red and blue strokes above the left eye.

For E.'s grade, a cedar sapling, stripped except for a top brush, was stood west of the cross. Hole had never seen this before and he heard no "mystic talk" about it. Nor was there the necessary "talk" about the other posts and the sweat-lodge stones. He saw two gray stones but not a black one; and these were "talked" over.

Throwing the shells, with singing and dancing, lasted until the drum had made one complete circuit. Every midé member sang a song or gave someone else tobacco to sing for him. The shell-throwing seemed perfunctory, as if the sun's brilliance and heat fatigued people. A man would come along dancing, point his midé "firearm" (sack), and dance a sunwise circle back to his starting point; there he remained "empty" because he had emptied his shell into a person. The latter, now "full," sat down to show

235

his condition. Then immediately he rose, danced, threw his sack at the next "empty" one in the sunwise direction, and continued dancing sunwise until he had returned to his starting point. Most people at this rite, however, did not sit after being "shot" because it was troublesome to rise again. In this dancing round, the sack was not aimed at any particular part of the body.

Each grade required different kinds of "shells," so people sought to trade with Everwind for the right ones. The old man complied with requests for the sixth grade, where "shells" were replaced by birds' claws, but he failed for the third grade which required true midé shells.

The general throwing did not employ actual shells, but their essences. Theory demanded only as many shells as there were manitos or officers, so that in a crowd of fifty there might be only eight shells moving in "spirit." Hole explained that, as one cannot be guided by the *feel* of a shell discharge, the point was to watch one's turn. The number of "spirit" shells was "increased" conceptually this way: those from fourth through eighth grade might shoot four times besides the once allowed ordinarily; that is, "they make four additional spirit shells." These were "made" throughout the dancing, for "use" by the rest of the company.

Hole carried a "shell-digger," an herbal medicine given him twenty-five years before by his cross-cousin (father's sister's son), Sam Garbo. It was to extricate the deadly midé shells that enter defenseless people, such as babies or adults who were not midéwi. He had never used it, though he had seen it used; he carried it for emergency first aid.

Except for Hole, none of the chief officers shot because no one first shot one of them. Were people fearful? It was J. S.'s sister who shot Hole; he commented, "I suppose she wanted to flirt with me." Hole lacked a sack with which to reply, but he used the rattle that accompanies singing.

Hole found this rite dull, lacking the desirable joking and laughter. He said, "They had the wrong kind of people there! Two were drunk. And the others didn't know what to do."

Neglecting to bring a sack to the public rite, one could borrow another's for the duration of shooting allowed him. Steersman should give the patient a sack suitable for his or her grade or should tell her what kind to make. Though E. was being put through the sixth (Sky) grade, she was loaned a weasel skin belonging to first (Earth) grade. But it served the purpose that afternoon.

At each grade, the patient received as many shells as there were officers. Hole had none with him, so he remained indebted to E. and her child.

The ceremony ended at about nine in the evening, having lasted eight hours. Hole said it should have ended at sunset. People grumbled over the delays, suffering from the season's heat.

GLOSSARY

OJIBWA WORDS appear throughout the text of this book in an anglicized orthography that only approximates the correct pronunciation. The glossary below gives a phonetic transcription for each word, using the alphabet of the International Phonetic Association (including the use of small capitals ᴋ and ᴘ to indicate unaspirated sounds). Stress marks show primary stress.

azhassowe [aˈʒɑsˑowe]. The art of tattooing for healing.
baguck [baˑˈgʌk]. A manito in the form of a tiny bird skeleton.
djibai [dˈʒiˑbai]. A ghost or spirit other than manito (q.v.).
Gebegabau [ᴋebegaˑbaʊ]. The name of a Manitou Reserve midé shaman, of the 1930's. The diminutive was **Gehbeh** [ᴋɛbɛ].
ginyu [ᴋiˑnˈɣü]. A manito, probably the arctic owl.
Gitchi gummi [ˈᴋɪtʃˈi ˈᴋʌmi]. Lake Superior.
gitchi webid [ˈᴋɪtʃˈi ˈwebɪt̪] The chief shaman presiding over a midéwiwin rite.
manito [manilt̪o]. A supernatural being.
mashgigiwaboge [maʃᴋiᴋiwʌboˑᴋe]. Herb-brewing for healing.
Medassoguneb [melˈdasˑogŭˈlnĕb]. The name of a Manitou Reserve midé shaman, of the 1930's.
midé [milde]. Used as an adjective or a noun, it means "mystic," "mystically powerful."

239

midéwi [miˈdewi]. Used as "to midéwi" and "to be midéwi," the phrases mean respectively "to conduct the midé rite" and "to undergo the midé rite." Speaking English, the Ojibwa often used the active form to mean the passive.

midéwiwin [miˈdewɪˈwɪn]. Literally, "mystic doings"; connotes the curing society and its rituals.

migis [ˈmi·gɪs]. Tiny shells used in midé curing rites, carrying "mystic power," for good or evil.

Mishi magade wabig [ˈmɪʃi ˈmɑkɑˈde ˈwa·bɪк]. A mythological or supernatural figure, the "great black stone."

monia zibing [mɔnia ˈzibiŋ]. A name meaning "silvery river," also "silver money."

naganid [nɑgɑniṭ]. The Bowman (after canoe terminology) of a midé ceremony. He is the leader of the lesser manitos represented by certain midé officers.

Namepog [nɑˈmeрoк]. An Ojibwa chief at Manitou Reserve, Mrs. Wilson's father-in-law.

nanandawi iwe winini [nɑnɑndɑˈwi ʔiwe wɪˈnɪnɪ]. A "sucking" doctor; i.e., one who sucks out the cause of illness through a bone.

Naugumig [nɑʊʔˈкʌmɪк]. The name of a Manitou Reserve midé shaman, of the 1930's.

Nehnehbush [nɛnɛˈbuʃ]. The trickster hero of Ojibwa mythology.

niganit [ni·gɑ·ˈnit]. The man who takes the lead, as in starting up a mystic song.

pasgigweïge [ˈрɑsкйˈкwe·ige]. A blood-letter, for curing.

patchishgaïge [рɑtʃˈiʃˈкɑʔige], or **patchishga'owe** [рɑtʃˈiʃˈкɑʔowe]. The curer who employs a pointed tool; i.e., a blood-letter, in curing.

Pindigegizig [ˈрindigeˈgiзɪк]. The Ojibwa name of William Rogers, meaning Hole-in-the-Sky.

sahgimah [ˈsɑ·gimɑ·]. The attribute of being "gleaming, attractive."

shigagoweïwe [ʃigɑ·goweˈiwe]. Inducing vomiting, for healing.

240

tcisaki [tʃ'isɑk'i]. The divining doctor, or shaman, using a tent to conceal his ventriloquism and juggling.

Tebwewadang [ţe·bwe·wã·dɑŋ]. The name of an Ojibwa shaman, of the 1930's.

wayan [wɑˡyɑn]. A mystic sack made of animal skin, to contain the migis (q.v.).

wedaged [weˡdɑκeţ]. The Steersman (after canoe terminology) of a midé ceremony. He is the end man for the body of lesser manitos represented by midé officers.

windigo [ˡwi·ndiɡo]. A mystic cannibalistic skeleton of evil power; also, a pathological state of manic depression, paranoia, and possible cannibalism.

BIBLIOGRAPHY

BAILEY, ALFRED GOLDSWORTHY
1937. *The Conflict of European and Eastern Algonkian Cultures, 1504–1700: A Study in Canadian Civilization.* Monographic Series No. 2. Publications of the New Brunswick Museum, St. John, N.B., Canada.

BARNOUW, VICTOR
1950. *Acculturation and Personality among the Wisconsin Chippewa.* Memoirs of the American Anthropological Association, No. 72. Menasha, Wisconsin.

BENEDICT, RUTH FULTON
1923. *The Concept of the Guardian Spirit in North America.* Memoirs of the American Anthropological Association, No. 29. Menasha, Wisconsin.

DENSMORE, FRANCES
1913. *Chippewa Music.* Bureau of American Ethnology Bulletin No. 53. Washington, D.C.

FORTUNE, REO F.
1932. *Omaha Secret Societies.* Columbia University Contributions to Anthropology, Vol. 14. New York: Columbia University Press.

HALLOWELL, A. IRVING
1926. "Bear Ceremonialism in the Northern Hemisphere." *American Anthropologist,* 28:1–175.
1942. *The Role of Conjuring in Saulteaux Society.* Publications of the Philadelphia Anthropological Society, Vol. 2. Philadelphia: University of Pennsylvania Press.

Bibliography

HOFFMAN, WALTER JAMES
    1891. "The Midéwiwin; or, 'Grand Medicine Society' of the Ojibwa." Bureau of American Ethnology, *Seventh Annual Report, 1885–1886*, pp. 145–300. Washington, D.C.
    1896. "The Menomini Indians." Bureau of American Ethnology, *Fourteenth Annual Report, 1892–93*, Pt. 1, pp. 3–328. Washington, D.C.

JONES, WILLIAM
    Field notes left with the late Dr. Truman Michelson, Smithsonian Institution, Washington, D.C.

KROEBER, ALFRED L.
    1944. *Configurations of Culture Growth.* Berkeley: University of California Press.

LANDES, RUTH
    1937a. *Ojibwa Sociology.* Columbia University Contributions to Anthropology, Vol. 29. New York: Columbia University Press.
    1937b. "The Ojibwa of Canada." *In* Margaret Mead, ed., *Cooperation and Competition among Primitive Peoples*, pp. 87–127. New York: McGraw-Hill Book Co. Second ed., Boston: Beacon Press, 1961.
    1938a. *The Ojibwa Woman.* Columbia University Contributions to Anthropology, Vol. 31. New York: Columbia University Press.
    1938b. "The Abnormal among the Ojibwa Indians." *Journal of Abnormal and Social Psychology*, 33(1):14–33.

PARKER, SEYMOUR
    1960. "The Wiitiko Psychosis in the Context of Ojibwa Personality and Culture." *American Anthropologist*, 62(4):603–623.

RADIN, PAUL
    1923. "The Winnebago Tribe." Bureau of American Ethnology, *Thirty-seventh Annual Report, 1915–16*, pp. 33–550. Washington, D.C.
    1926. *Crashing Thunder: The Autobiography of an American Indian.* New York: Appleton-Century-Crofts.

ROGERS, EDWARD S.
    1962. *The Round Lake Ojibwa.* Occasional Paper No. 5, Art and Archaeology Division, Royal Ontario Museum, University of Toronto.
    1966. "Subsistence Areas of the Cree-Ojibwa of the Eastern Subarctic: A Preliminary Study." *Contributions to Anthropology, 1963–64*, Pt. 2, pp. 87–118. Ottawa: National Museum of Canada, Bulletin No. 204.

Bibliography

SKINNER, ALANSON
1911. "Notes on the Eastern Cree and Northern Saulteaux." *Anthropological Papers of the American Museum of Natural History*, Vol. 9, Pt. 1, pp. 1–177. New York.
1913. "Social Life and Ceremonial Bundles of the Menomini Indians." *Anthropological Papers of the American Museum of Natural History*, Vol. 13, Pt. 1, pp. 1–165. New York.
1920. "Medicine Ceremony of the Menomini, Iowa, and Wahpeton Dakota." *Indian Notes and Monographs*, Vol. 4. New York: Museum of the American Indian, Heye Foundation.

INDEX

Index

in death concepts, 194–95, 197, 198, 199
fireball as embodying evil, 220
good and evil manitos, 31
in midé origin tale, 108, 109, 193
in midé ritual, 120–21, 129, 144, 153, 171
in Midé Society, 53
in shamanism, 43–46
in water cult, 31–32
in water-sky opposition, 31

Fees for midéwiwin
  amount of, 52, 53, 56, 57, 74, 79, 232
  display of, 54–55, 74, 126, 144, 145, 146, 152–53, 184, 230
  distribution of, 129–38, 159–60, 172
  monopolizing of, 78–79
  as prerequisite to rites, 56, 57, 74, 76, 79, 81, 116–17
Funerals, midé, 76

Guardian-spirit complex, 8–11, 15, 34

Individualism of Ojibwa, 7, 8, 11, 14, 32, 71
Informants, vii–viii, 16–20

Jones, William, field notes, 170, 182–83, 190–91n, 198–99, 224–26

Life sphere of midéwiwin. *See* Midéwiwin

Magic
  abuse of, 14–15
  availability of, 58
  behavior with, 58, 60
  herbs, 33, 59
  love seduction, 65–66
  obligations and tabus, 38–39
  origins of, 58
  tools, 33, 34, 59
  See also Sorcery; Visions
Manito, 22–30

and Bear visionary, 27–28
and Bird visionary, 29
and blasphemy, 36–37, 51, 89
Characters, mythic, 91, 92, 93
as cosmic force, 7
cult routines, 34–35
evil, associated with water, 31
as guardian spirit, 8–9
indicia of, 30–31
and midéwiwin, 24, 33
and naming, 30
and Nehnehbush, 24–25
obligations to, 26, 28–29, 38–41
and origin of Indian, 24–25, 91
and rock paintings, 227, 228
as shaman, 9, 11, 36
traits of, 10, 22–26
in visions, pursuit of, 8–10, 21–22, 30–31
and war, 29–30
and wealth, 15
and white man, 92
and women, 29
Membership in Midé Society, 76–78
Mementos, midé, 116
Midé Supernaturals, 52, 54, 55–56, 72, 81, 91–95 *passim*, 115, 169
Midéwiwin
  archery rare in, 188, 197
  called Midé Society, 3–4
  and childbirth, 76
  color patterns of, 179–80, 181, 194, 197, 234, 235
  contemporary visions, 44–45, 56, 85, 87, 88, 105, 112
  cures in Life and Ghost spheres, 50, 52, 55
  definition of, 3, 4
  distribution of, 177–78
  doctrine of, 42–43, 44
  dog-Bear symbolism, 136, 145, 146, 148, 156
  and drum, 163–64
  emergency rites, 53, 54–55, 76
  and eschatology, 73, 81
  ethics of, 53, 74–75
  and evil shamans, 43–44, 45, 58

Index

and fees, 87
and humility, 37
implementing of, 33–35
and midé shamans, 43–45, 56
manito patrons of, 26–30, 49
obligations, 38–41
as power, 30, 53
pursuit of, 8–10, 21, 22, 30–31, 207
secrecy about, 9–10, 85, 87, 207, 209, 211
woman's great, 207–12
and women, 46–47
See also Aboriginal culture; Bear

cult; Ethics; Magic; Manito; Midéwiwin; Sorcery; Windigo

Wayan (midé sack), 38, 73, 145–46, 153, 157, 158, 160, 175, 237
Wigwam, midé, 141–42, 184
Windigo
as cannibalism, 13, 39
and cremation, 13–14
and evil, 31
as manito, 7, 13
a pathology, 12–13, $12n$
as retribution, 58